KU-300-271

Preserving the Past

RCHME © Crown Copyright

PRESERVING THE PAST

The Rise of Heritage in Modern Britain

EDITED BY
MICHAEL HUNTER

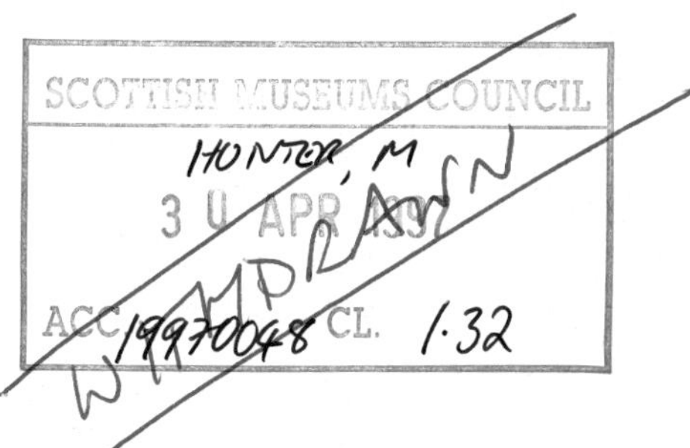

ALAN SUTTON PUBLISHING LIMITED

First published in the United Kingdom in 1996 by
Alan Sutton Publishing Ltd · Phoenix Mill · Far Thrupp · Stroud
Gloucestershire

Copyright © Editor and Contributors, 1996

All rights reserved. No part of this publication may be reproduced, stored in a retrieval system, or transmitted, in any form or by any means, electronic, mechanical, photocopying, recording or otherwise, without the prior permission of the publishers and copyright holders.

British Library Cataloguing in Publication Data

A catalogue record for this book is avilable from the British Library.

ISBN 0-7509-0951-X

Frontispiece; *The Coal Exchange, Lower Thames Street, 1900, with a Great Northern Railway cart in the foreground.*

Typeset in 10/12pt Times.
Typesetting and origination by
Alan Sutton Publishing Limited.
Printed in Great Britain by
Hartnolls, Bodmin.

Contents

Acknowledgements

The contributors to this volume have been highly co-operative, not only in providing their own chapters and helping to see them through the press, but also in reading and commenting on each others' contributions. They have also suggested items for inclusion in the bibliographical essay (though the opinions expressed therein are my own) and have given valuable advice on the book as a whole.

The cost of illustrations has been partially borne by a generous grant from the Marc Fitch Fund. In addition, a contribution has been made by the Research Fund of the Department of Archaeology, University of Southampton. Various expenses associated with the preparation of the book have been borne by the Research Fund of the Department of History, Birkbeck College, University of London.

The 1949 photograph of listing investigators reproduced on page 131 has kindly been provided by Dr John Harvey, together with the details of those who appear in it given in the notes. The owners or copyright holders who have given permission for the use of other illustrative material are acknowledged in the captions to the relevant pictures.

The following have answered queries or helped to trace illustrative material for the book: Stephen Croad and the staff of the National Monuments Record in both London and Swindon; Richard Holder and the staff of the Victorian Society; Ralph Hyde and, through him, Felix Barker; Gerallt Nash of the Museum of Welsh Life, St Fagans; Bernard Nurse, Librarian of the Society of Antiquaries; the Department of National Heritage; and the Prince of Wales's Office.

The following have also crucially contributed in various ways: Peter Burman, Lien Bich Luu, Martha Morris, Ros Tatham and, above all, Robert Thorne. At Alan Sutton Publishing Ltd., Rupert Harding and Sarah Bragginton have been unfailingly helpful. To all referred to here, my heartfelt thanks are due.

Hastings
March 1996

Michael Hunter

1
Introduction: the fitful rise of British preservation

Michael Hunter

'Heritage', and the values, activities and institutions associated with it, have become a commonplace of the last quarter of the twentieth century. Every year, large numbers of visitors are attracted to historic sites ranging from prehistoric antiquities to castles and country houses, many of them held in custodianship by the National Trust and the eponymous English Heritage: indeed, visits to such sites are one of the most popular forms of recreation in this country, numbering 67 million in 1990.[1] In addition, since the 1970s there has been a proliferation of 'heritage centres', ranging from indoor displays such as the Jorvik Centre at York to open-air museums such as Blist's Hill at Ironbridge Gorge and Beamish near Newcastle.

Equally typical is the attention lavished on historic buildings and their settings. Up and down the country, historic town centres, from Bath to York and from Lewes to Whitehaven, have been lovingly restored with period detail. Almost equal attention has been lavished on the rehabilitation of former industrial complexes such as Dean Clough Mills at Halifax or the Albert Dock at Liverpool. Comparable restoration work is in evidence on residential buildings, ranging from mansions to humble artisans' dwellings which are regarded as worthy of protection as part of the ensemble that they comprise. Indeed English Heritage – wearing its hat as a disburser of government funds for such works – offered £27 million in such grants in 1993–4.[2]

Along with this goes an elaborate system of controls, involving the protection both of individual 'listed' buildings and 'scheduled' monuments, and of larger groupings in the form of Conservation Areas comprising town and village centres and residential neighbourhoods. The owners of properties in these categories, or of land on which archaeological remains survive, are significantly restricted in their freeedom of action to alter or demolish these relics of the man-made past of which they are custodians. Any such alteration has to be preceded by consultation with various interested parties, ranging from the local authority to the national amenity societies, and those who ignore such constrictions face severe penalties, as even senior politicans have discovered to their cost.

Although there may be debate as to just how far such control should go (to which we will return later in this introduction), there is no doubt that all this reflects a sense that the relics of the man-made past are important enough to inspire such appreciation and to justify such restriction of property rights in the wider interest. Opinion polls, for instance one commissioned by the Prince of Wales in 1993, show that a high proportion of the population regards buildings with character and history as trademarks of the British way of life, comparable to home ownership and the National Health Service, and considers it important that funds are devoted to maintaining them. Commenting on the poll's findings, the Prince remarked how such buildings were 'at the core of that precious asset we call our national identity'.[3]

Yet none of these phenomena has a very long history. The oldest measures for protecting any relics of the man-made past in this country are only just over a hundred years old; museums and visitor attractions geared to a popular audience are hardly older; and our ancestors in previous centuries would have been amazed by the sheer scale and elaborateness of the machinery concerned with 'heritage' in its many facets that we now have. So dramatic a change requires explanation, yet there is a surprising dearth of literature explaining how the current state of affairs came into being; this book is intended to fill this gap. Not only does it explain how and why the current structures have come into place, and indicate the historical background against which such developments have occurred, but in addition, by going into key episodes in detail, it accounts for some of the anomalies and peculiarities of the current state of affairs.

Certain factors underlying our current approach to the man-made past are so general that they can be glanced at only tangentially in the pages that follow. One is the growth of a mass culture, since this buoys up the demand for historic visitor attractions which is such a notable feature of the current situation. If the first signs of a 'commercialisation of leisure' are to be found in the eighteenth century, this took off in the Victorian period, with a plethora of public museums and other facilities.[4] In addition, the coming of the railways and the conscious introduction of cheap excursion trains opened up access to recreational facilities on an unprecedented scale.[5] The twentieth century has seen an even further extension of access to a range of leisure facilities, of which heritage attractions form part, due largely to the massive increase in car ownership, particularly since the Second World War. As its name suggests, the so-called 'heritage industry' is part of a broader 'leisure industry' which is a characteristic part of the culture in which we live.

The legislative provision for the heritage, which is an equally characteristic part of the current state of affairs, has a context going back over a similar period, in terms of the growing presumption that it was proper for the State to take an active role in governing aspects of the lives of its citizens which had previously been regarded as beyond its remit. Again, from slighter precedents in an earlier age – perhaps particularly concerning national taxation – this became characteristic in the nineteenth century, when an increasingly large range of aspects of people's lives became the subject of such supervision, be it sewerage, building controls or national education.[6] Again, this has peaked in the twentieth century, to the extent that there has been something of a reaction against it. Controls of the kind that now exist concerning historic sites and buildings would be unthinkable outside this context.

But, although we have become so familiar with this juxtapositon that we may take it for granted, it is not self-evident why either mass leisure or State

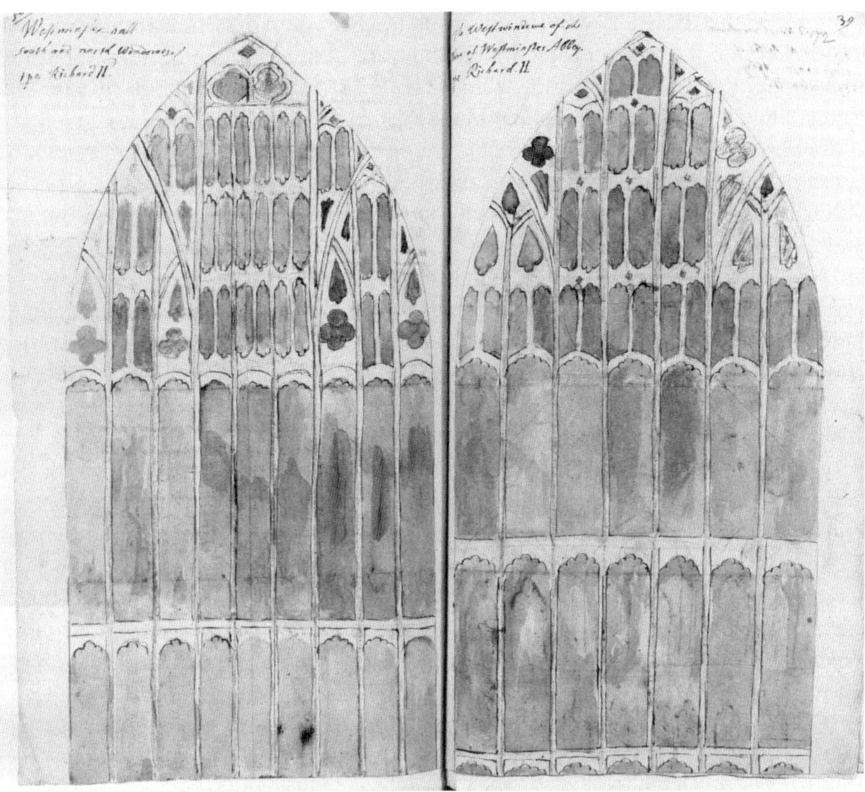

THE BODLEIAN LIBRARY, OXFORD. MS. TOP. GEN. C. 25, FOLS. 171V–172.

John Aubrey's drawings of the tracery of late fourteenth-century windows in Westminster Hall and Westminster Abbey, illustrating his *Chronologia Architectonica* (*c.* 1670), the first attempt at a history of medieval architecture in this country.

intervention should be concerned with the relics of the past, least of all their protection. Hence this is a crucial component of the current state of affairs which needs to be probed further. Some relics of the past have always been so strange and impressive as to attract the curiosity of sporadic tourists: a case in point would be Stonehenge.[7] But for more than a casual interest in historic architecture and archaeological remains, one has to look to a tradition of antiquarianism which started with isolated pioneers in the seventeenth century and became more common in the eighteenth. The first person in this country to take a sustained interest in archaeological and architectural antiquities was John Aubrey (1626–97), best known for his *Brief Lives*, who also wrote the first British book devoted to archaeological remains, and who first attempted a history of medieval architecture.[8] He was followed by William Stukeley (1687–1765), whose topographical writings dwelt on such antiquities to an unprecedented extent, and who built on Aubrey's work in describing the megalithic sites of Stonehenge and Avebury. Their interest was taken up by various successors in the eighteenth century, including Richard Gough, Francis Grose and John Carter, and it was continued into the early nineteenth century, not least in the work of the publisher and topographer, John Britton, whose books set new standards of accuracy in describing and illustrating medieval buildings.[9]

Interestingly, it was from this background that the earliest pleas for systematic preservation emanated. Stukeley wrote feelingly about how the stone circle at Avebury was threatened with 'impending ruin' as a result of the thoughtless and shortsighted destruction going on in his day, but he seems to have been resigned to the fact that the best that he could do was to 'preserve the memory of this most illustrious Work' so that at least this would survive 'when the Country finds an advantage in preserving its poor reliques'.[10] A more sustained preservationist plea was made by another member of this antiquarian tradition, Richard Gough, in a letter to the *Gentleman's Magazine* in 1788. In it, he argued for a higher valuation of such buildings as 'national objects' which formed the proper subject for historical study, whose preservation should be deliberate rather than left to mere chance. He suggested that the Society of Antiquaries, founded in 1707, should take an active role in such matters.[11] Comparable sentiments were voiced in a succession of articles for the same journal by John Carter, in which he complained of the damage done by 'the innovating system of improving (as it is called) our cities and towns'.[12] Then, in the early nineteenth century, it is significant that it was John Britton who (as Timothy Champion notes in Chapter 3) took the opportunity provided by giving evidence to a House of Commons Select Committee in 1841 to suggest that monuments such as historic houses and Roman villas deserved protection.[13] Although prophetic of things to come, such proposals were so isolated that their significance is easily overrated, since virtually nothing was done at this stage to implement them.

In order for the appreciation of antiquities to become more widespread, a change in attitude was needed in a wider segment of the population than among the rarified circles of antiquaries, and this gradually occurred during the nineteenth century. To some extent, it was simply a question of the preoccupations of antiquarian pioneers becoming more widespread: they became popular among a wider segment of the educated establishment through the proliferation of bodies devoted to antiquarian study in Britain, especially in the 1840s.[14] However, underlying this was a broader and more significant cultural shift which led to a heightened appreciation of the relics of the past; this was the ethos which may be encapsulated in the word 'Romanticism'. Initially, in the late eighteenth century, this is seen in the cult of wild nature associated with the appreciation of the picturesque and the sublime, in which old buildings were valued for the harmonious way in which they merged into traditional settings. In addition, one sees the rise of a historical sense which gave emphasis to the particularity of places and their associations, represented particularly by Sir Walter Scott, whose influence was immense. Indeed, quite apart from the impact of his novels, the house that Scott built for himself, Abbotsford in the Lowlands, could in some ways be seen as the original heritage centre, filled as it was with objects, pictures and even fragments of buildings that Scott valued for their historical associations.[15]

In early nineteenth-century England, one finds an increasingly widespread appreciation of historical relics as tangible reminders of the past, seen in such books intended for a mass readership as Charles Knight's *Old England: a Pictorial History of Regal, Ecclesiastical, Baronial, Municipal and Popular Antiquities* (1845), which is full of engravings of old buildings, pictures and objects from every period of the country's history. Indeed, the popularisation of such appeal was seen in the tourist attractions that now came into being, with the Tower of London first opening to the public in 1828 and Hampton Court in 1839: by the 1850s, these were attracting 200,000 and 100,000 visitors per year, respectively.[16]

Ruins as part of the picturesque landscape: vignette from Francis Grose's *Antiquities of Scotland*, vol. 2 (London, 1791).

Associated with this was a developing feeling that these were 'national antiquities', guarantors of national identity: this grew out of an emphasis on the significance and uniqueness of historical change which was associated with nascent nationalism throughout Europe in the nineteenth century.[17] Many of the early measures for preserving antiquities in different European countries explicitly invoke this sentiment, and one symptom of it, as Michael Stratton shows in Chapter 9, was the origin of folk museums dedicated to the preservation of vernacular buildings. Gradually, in this country as elsewhere, such feelings provided a seedbed for seeing such monuments as especially precious, and hence the State as having a role in guarding them, rather than leaving them to private individuals. Having started with the categories of antiquities celebrated in the title of Charles Knight's book, this gradually extended to take in a wider range of ancient remains, prehistoric as well as later. It is thus revealing that, by 1872, no less an author than Charles Dickens in *All the Year Round* could write of the preservation of Stonehenge: 'it should not be left to chance, and a single person, to do that which the State should consider it both its pride and its duty to undertake'.[18]

It would have been surprising if this growing interest in relics of the past had not had some result in terms of attention to ancient buildings, in contrast to the neglect which had typified their treatment in earlier centuries. A pioneer was the architect, James Wyatt, who was called in to assist various Deans and Chapters responsible for cathedral fabrics in the late eighteenth century. In some cases Wyatt concentrated on what were defined at the time as 'necessary repairs', intended to safeguard the fabric from decay and collapse. On the other hand,

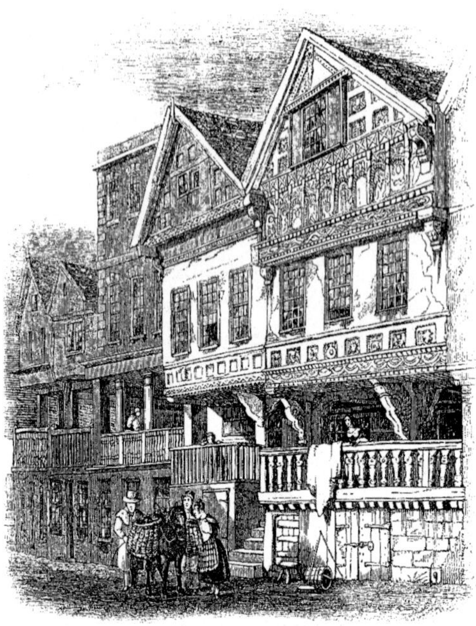

Steel-engraved illustration from Charles Knight's *Old England* (London, 1845), showing 'Old Houses in Chester'.

elsewhere he allowed himself to be persuaded to 'improve' them, tidying away features which he considered detracted from buildings' architectural impact, thus arousing the ire of the antiquarian preservationists of the day. On the other hand, the rarity of such sentiments even among antiquaries at this stage is revealed by the fact that protests from the preservationist clique within the Society of Antiquaries did not prevent Wyatt's election to that body by a massive majority in 1797.[19]

This brings us to the Gothic Revival, the significance of which in the history of preservation is often misunderstood. For this was based on a strong appreciation of medieval architecture, and an urge to reverse the neglect that many ecclesiastical buildings had suffered. On the other hand, it was complicated by an ethical streak associated with the religious revival that lay behind it; this led to a presumption that certain styles – notably Gothic – were preferable to others, and that, even within the Gothic, some phases of development were supreme. This had a tendency to encourage a rather doctrinaire and destructive attitude to restoration. In addition, the ulterior motives associated with church restoration placed a premium on illustrating the vitality of the Anglican Church by smartening up its buildings.

Nevertheless, from the church restoration activity of this period originated what was, in effect, the first comprehensive system for looking after historic buildings in this country. This involved diocesan supervision over such activity, in alliance with the architects who were mainly responsible for restoration work.[20] It was so successful that it formed the basis of a kind of ecclesiastical opt-out from the secular system of preservation that was set up in 1913, on the grounds that the Church was more than capable of looking after its own affairs.

But the destructive nature of certain church restorations stimulated a reaction, and this grew into a parallel and rather different view of how historic monuments were best protected. It was famously voiced by John Ruskin in a passage in his *The Seven Lamps of Architecture* (1849), in which he attacked overdrastic restoration: 'it is again no question of expediency or feeling whether we shall preserve the buildings of past times or not. *We have no right whatever to touch them.* They are not ours. They belong partly to those who built them, and partly to all the generations of mankind who are to follow us.'[21] It is revealing of the milieu in which comparable attitudes had been found earlier that in 1854 it was to the Society of Antiquaries – who had sporadically continued the eighteenth-century tradition of protesting about threats to specific buildings – that Ruskin proposed a scheme for more systematic preservation.[22] As with earlier such appeals, little came of this. But Ruskin's example was explicitly invoked by William Morris in connection with the Society for the Protection of Ancient Buildings (SPAB) that he set up in 1877, the best-known – if not the best understood – landmark in the early history of preservationist activity in this country, which Chris Miele assesses in Chapter 2.

In fact, as Chris Miele points out, there was a significant element of impracticality in the Society's early aims – especially by comparison with the pragmatic programme that architects involved in church restoration had by that time adopted – and the Society's early success can easily be overestimated in retrospect. But, undoubtedly, its ability to arouse public opinion through the media of the day reflected a sense of disquiet about destruction and loss of the country's national heritage which seems to have been growing in the later part of the nineteenth century, and which led to a whole clump of measures which – even if as partial in their success as the early SPAB – nevertheless established a basis for preservationist activity in this country.

Thus we have the early archaeological legislation which Timothy Champion surveys in Chapter 3. More strikingly, we have the initiative of the London County Council both in making a record of buildings in the form of the London Survey and in acquiring the power to protect threatened buildings by taking them into public ownership. In Chapter 4, John Earl surveys these pioneering steps, in some ways the most significant, though little-known, initiative of this era. Lastly, there is the foundation in 1895 of the National Trust. The latter is dealt with only tangentially in this book, partly because it has been studied extensively already, and partly because its initial concern was mainly with the protection of the countryside. Although the Trust did take a rural structure under its care in 1896, the Clergy House at Alfriston in Sussex, and although it continued to acquire occasional properties thereafter, this type of activity only became a priority for the Trust in the 1930s, in circumstances described by Peter Mandler in Chapter 6.

What reasons may be suggested for this early peak of preservationist activity around 1900? One possibility, which has been canvassed particularly by the historian Martin Wiener, is that it reflected a national malaise, a loss of confidence after the heroic optimism of the high Victorian period, involving a retreat to a nostalgic, anti-industrial, rural ethos.[23] But, apart from the extent to which Wiener's thesis depends on an artificial polarisation of pro- and anti-industrial sentiment, there is an alternative explanation of this rise of concern. This is that it reflected an understandable anxiety about the destructive side-

The Tabard Inn, Southwark, 1841 (demolished 1875–6) from Charles Knight's *Old England* (London, 1845).

effects of the rush to improvement of the previous decades, a belief that the national heritage was under greater pressure than ever before, and that unless something were done to protect it it would be irreparably harmed. Thus the pioneering Bill introduced into parliament by Sir John Lubbock in 1873 was inspired by various threats, including that to the great stone circle at Avebury in Wiltshire, which Lubbock had been able to avert by purchasing the threatened land himself.[24] The sense of the need for protection of the open countryside, which led to the foundation of the National Trust in 1895, had a similar basis. The Trust built on the work of the Commons Preservation Society since the 1860s in safeguarding open space from the encroachments of urban sprawl by stressing the need to protect the unspoilt countryside as a national asset, and by taking beauty spots into its ownership.[25]

The preservationist activity of the London County Council was fuelled by a comparable reaction against the inroads into the historic fabric in London made by major metropolitan works from the 1860s onwards, as John Earl indicates in Chapter 4. Indeed, the acute threat to historic buildings which inspired the foundation of the London Survey was illustrated by the long list included in the first volume of the Survey's *Register*, published in 1900, of major buildings destroyed over the previous six years, together with a further list of others under threat. Its editor, C.R. Ashbee, commented on his fellow citizens: 'That they should be so ready to thoughtlessly destroy the noble and beautiful things committed to their charge argues an indifference and a want of trust that it will be difficult at some later time, perhaps even impossible, to explain away'.[26]

It is interesting to note that it was a comparable sense of threat – in this case, from a more determined acquisition policy on the part of better-organised countries such as Germany and the United States – that stimulated concern about the nation's heritage of moveable works of art at this time, leading to the setting up of the National Art Collections Fund in 1903.[27] Similar sentiments were echoed in the Lords' debate on the Bill consolidating and amending the earlier measures for protecting ancient monuments in 1912–13, since, as Champion shows below, the will of the Lords to pass this was galvanised by rumours about the threat to national monuments by million-dollar offers to dismantle them and remove them to America. As Lord Curzon put it concerning Stonehenge: 'under our existing law the owner might sell it to-morrow; he might pull it down to-morrow; he might part with it to an American syndicate to be erected in the Central Park in New York'.[28] Undoubtedly, a sense of crisis impelled people towards taking such preservationist steps as they did at this stage.

On the other hand, although proposals were made, and to some extent implemented, for legislative action on such matters at this time, it is striking how weak most of the legislative provision remained, and how far voluntary initiatives predominated. Lubbock's Bill reappeared in the Commons so many times that it became known as 'the monumentally ancient bill',[29] and the measure along similar lines that was finally passed in 1882 had been partially emasculated, including no element of compulsion in its provisions. Moreover, it is widely agreed that the work of the first commissioner, General Pitt-Rivers, under the powers of the Act was mainly effective in inspiring voluntary co-operation which no legislation had really been needed to achieve.[30] Similarly, the National Trust was a voluntary body – though endowed with the right to hold land 'inalienably' by statute in 1907 – and the National Art Collections Fund was a further voluntary answer to a problem for which State action had been proposed without success. Even the 1913 Act, which built on the precedent of 1882 in ways which Champion indicates in Chapter 3, had little power of enforcement and excluded not only all churches but also all inhabited buildings. For all the anxiety which inspired this flurry of activity, there were powerful constraints on the development of a system of protection such as that with which we are familar today.

This should be a warning against attaching too much significance to the developments of that era. Indeed, it is salutary to remember that the best book on preservation dating from those years – the art historian, Gerard Baldwin Brown's *The Care of Ancient Monuments* (1905), which is cited by various authors in this book – was intended as a monitory tract for the times, chronicling the legislative provision for preservation in other countries by way of illustrating Britain's backwardness from this point of view. Brown was able to point to legislation passed in Denmark in 1807; in Hesse in 1818 and in Prussia and other German States in the following decades; in France in the 1830s; and in Greece in 1834; while in Italy more or less effective measures of an earlier date were supplemented by newly systematic measures in the early nineteenth century. Brown made no secret of his view of the extent to which 'our official machinery, judged by the continental standard, is defective'.[31]

Even the 1913 Act was so bound around by restrictions and had so little power of enforcement that it did little to rectify this situation, as is implied by the parliamentary activity which followed it and which Timothy Champion surveys. Indeed, in 1927 Sir Lionel Earle took the view that 'We certainly have less powers in this matter, I think, than any other country in Europe, with the exception of the Balkan States and Turkey'.[32]

It is therefore hardly surprising that, as the pressures of development in town and countryside intensified in the inter-war period, so did concern about the preservation of archaeological and historic sites. As various authors make clear below, the legislation of the period up to 1913 proved quite inadequate to meet the threats that buildings and sites now faced, and both the erosion of historic features of countryside and the inroads into the urban fabric – especially of London – led to a fresh climax of concern towards the end of the 1930s, and to fresh steps to confront such matters. Thus 1937 saw the inauguration of the Georgian Group to fight threats that it was felt that the SPAB was unequal to, as Gavin Stamp shows in Chapter 5, while the same years also saw the foundation of the National Trust's country-houses scheme. Moreover, although the Second World War may initially have distracted attention from such matters, the experience of the war had the effect of catalysing the vaguer concerns of the 1930s about the need to protect buildings, with the result (as Andrew Saint shows) of spawning the epoch-making provisions for listing that were contained in the Town and Country Planning Acts of 1944 and 1947. The Gowers Report and its recommendations, discussed by Peter Mandler in Chapter 6, reflect a further response to the inadeqacy of existing measures in the context of post-war reconstruction.

Yet these measures were also to prove inadequate, and anxieties rose again as wartime austerity gave way to the development boom of the post-war years. In particular, the damage done to the fabric of towns and cities by comprehensive development, often inspired, paradoxically, by the broader planning provisions of the Town and Country Planning Acts of which the inauguration of listing formed part, led to fresh heart-searching. Sophie Andreae surveys these developments in Chapter 8: the attempts to protect the urban fabric which culminated in the Civic Amenities Act of 1967 and the introduction of Conservation Areas; the toughening of preservationist legislation by successive governments in the late 1960s and early 1970s; and the role both of pressure groups such as SAVE Britain's Heritage and of government bodies in encouraging an approach to conservation that was constructive rather than negatively legalistic. Moreover, the success of SAVE reflected a still broader shift in public consciousness which also helped to raise the profile of 'heritage' matters at the time, and this was a reaction against the destructiveness of the post-war development boom and of the rather intolerant progressivism that had inspired it. Instead, we have seen the growth of a nostalgic celebration of the relics of the past, which is the setting of the proliferation of institutions combining the preservation of historic buildings with their display, which Michael Stratton surveys in Chapter 9.

Hence, as a generalisation, one could say that the current state of affairs has come about largely through a series of key episodes when decisive steps have been taken in response to a sense of crisis in people's awareness of the dangers to cherished buildings and sites, often associated with broader reservations about the ethos inspiring such destructiveness.[33] In this, there is almost a cyclical element, which we may yet see repeat itself. On the other hand, there has also been a cumulative effect, since at each of the stages chronicled above it was possible to build on less effective steps taken earlier. This is particularly true of the rather tortuous development of protective legislation surveyed in Chapter 3, while the country-houses scheme, for instance, used the structure put in place by the foundation of the National Trust and the establishment of the principle of inalienability decades earlier. Even more significant is the way in which, as John Earl shows, the London County Council (LCC) pioneered steps which were to be applied subsequently to the country as a whole – with the LCC setting a precedent in terms of public ownership of historic buildings, and the London Survey inspiring its national equivalent in the form of the Royal Commission on Historical Monuments. Later, the LCC's record in listing buildings provided one of the precedents for the nationwide measures to achieve similar ends, while the Council's expertise in assessing and supervising historic buildings provided a model for similar steps nationally in the aftermath of the Town and Country Planning Acts of the 1940s. Even the pressure groups that Gavin Stamp surveys can, in a sense, be seen as cumulative, with new bodies being founded as the need was perceived to champion buildings neglected by existing ones, with the Georgian Group growing out of the SPAB, the Victorian Society espousing a class of buildings which the Georgians had had little time for, and then yet a further offshoot emerging in the form of the Thirties (now Twentieth Century) Society.

Linked to this is the issue of which buildings or archaeological remains were deemed worthy of preservation, since there has been a striking broadening in the appreciation of such relics. It is thus notable that the original remit of the Royal Commission on Historical Monuments when it was set up in 1908 ended at 1700, thus excluding not only all Victorian but even all Georgian buildings. Clearly, at this stage the presumption was that the really significant buildings were medieval churches, castles and other structures, together with early specimens of vernacular architecture, and culminating with the heroic age of Wren: Lord Curzon's comments in the Lords' debate in 1912, quoted on p. 46 below, suggest just such a conception. Changing taste meant that by the time the original lists under the Town and Country Planning Acts of the 1940s were compiled, these included large numbers of Georgian buildings; but they were very sparing indeed of even the most striking Victorian structures, and a general prejudice against Victorian buildings has only more recently been overcome.

Even clearer is the prejudice enshrined in the procedures for listing instituted in the 1940s, which favoured individual buildings rather than whole groups. This was primarily due to bureaucratic convenience (as Andrew Saint shows), but it also reflected the prevailing trend in architectural history in the inter-war era, which was qualitative in tone, tending to lay emphasis on the work of specific, highly regarded architects, and to undervalue more repetitive work seen as of inferior quality, whatever its historic interest and its attractiveness in forming the built environment. By the same token, industrial buildings tended to be neglected until recently, despite their clear historical significance, while, at the other end of the spectrum, Peter Mandler shows how appreciation of the country house is of more recent growth than is often appreciated. Moreover, in the archaeological sphere, Timothy Champion shows how the early preservationist measures tended to concentrate only on standing monuments, and the rich archaeological record surviving underground has only recently received proper attention.

GRAHAM RICHARDS

Sir John Lubbock, 1st Baron Avebury (1834–1913), one of the pioneers of conservation in this country. In addition to his role in attempting to bring about ancient monuments legislation, Lubbock was a prominent member of the LCC in its formative years.

On the other hand, although such an element of cumulativeness may be real enough, it is equally important to stress the extent to which the developments that have occurred have had an element of contingency, reflecting the circumstances in which they took place, and the personalities of those responsible for them. Chris Miele points out how, for all the extent to which its principles have been enshrined in the subsequent ethos of conservation, the early SPAB was arguably rather obtuse in its refusal to co-operate with the existing system, and might have achieved more had it done so. He also points out the impact of William Morris's personality and views on the Society, and illustrates the element of trial and error that marked its early evolution. Similarly, Peter Mandler rightly stresses the delicacy of James Lees-Milne's negotations with the National Trust's putative clients in the country-houses scheme. He also brings out the significance of other individual personalities in the evolution of policy towards stately homes, perhaps particularly Sir Ernest Gowers, whose committee he credits with a remarkable transformation in public taste. Andrew Saint is able to show the extent to which the specific individuals who advised the wartime government about how preservation might be achieved were responsible for the system of listing taking the form it did – which was somewhat at odds with the expectations of those who had suggested such protection in the first place, the latter having been concerned with historic environments more broadly. And the significance of individual personalities in shaping policy more recently is indicated by Sophie Andreae.

The evolution of policy on such matters has also been conditioned by broader factors, some of which may still be with us. The progress of early legislative measures of this kind was dogged by hostility on the part of those who saw them as an infringement of private property. Lubbock's proposed measure for protecting archaeological remains thus foundered in face of protest – which was reiterated equally strongly in 1882 – about 'the invasion of the rights of property which was to be carried out under the Bill in order to gratify the antiquarian tastes of the few at the public expense'.[34] Even the LCC's scheme for erecting blue plaques ran into difficulties on a similar score, while anxiety about private property remained alive in the 1940s, as Andrew Saint shows, although the experience of interference with such rights in the national interest in wartime conditions had sufficiently weakened such feelings by that time to make feasible a measure involving a degree of constrictiveness that would have been unimaginable half a century before. However, such concerns have recurred since, as seen in the government's preparedness to issue property owners with certificates of immunity from listing, or in the leaflet, 'How to Appeal against Listing', originally issued by the Department of the Environment in 1986, which is highly negative in tone, and does nothing to stress the positive value of living in a listed property.[35]

A further obstacle to the implementation of such measures was an anxiety about the expense that it might incur to the public purse, a consideration voiced in connection with Victorian proposals along such lines, as Tim Champion shows, and the force of which was still felt in connection with the setting up of the National Heritage Memorial Fund in 1980.[36] Moreover, both at the turn of the century and more recently, there have been those who have associated this with a deep-rooted insensitivity towards the man-made heritage on the part of the British public. Certainly, the greatest richness of English culture is literary, and the higher priority given to written sources over material ones is symbolised by the fact that the Royal Commission on Historical Manuscripts, set up in 1869, preceded by nearly a generation even the early, feeble measures to protect antiquities surveyed here. Many of those associated with conservationist measures of the kind dealt with in this book have spoken bitterly about the philistinism of their fellow countrymen. 'Unfortunately, in this country, among some of our legislators at least, the idea also prevails that matters of art are not to be taken too seriously', wrote Sir Robert Witt in connection with the debate over art exports in the early years of the century.[37] The inveterate campaigner Clough Williams-Ellis took the view that 'The generously endowed English seem to have been given a special immunity against visual beauty that only the most violent attacks can break through';[38] and Sir Alfred Clapham, one of those responsible for the system of listing dealt with in Chapter 7, remarked on the 'English indifference' which resulted in 'a certain apathy in regard to the visible illustrations of our history which suffers their passing away without protest and almost without regard'.[39]

More recently, the rise of the 'heritage industry' has inspired a backlash among commentators who have seen our current preoccupation with heritage as unhealthily backward-looking – a kind of escapism obstructing proper solutions to current problems. Thus in *The Heritage Industry* (1987), Robert Hewison writes: 'when museums become one of Britain's new growth industries, they are not signs of vitality, but symbols of national decline'. The message of his and similar books is that such nostalgia is incompatible with a properly forward-looking outlook, and that we should display our cultural vitality by escaping such shackles of the past and investing in the future.[40]

In fact, such prognostics are frequently highly impressionistic. Within a page of complaining of the proliferation of museums in Britain, Hewison himself states: 'the statistic that the number of museums in Britain has doubled since 1960 is not in itself a symptom of decline, for a similar explosion has taken place elsewhere'. But he nevertheless continues doggedly with his argument, as if preservation were morbid in Britain, whatever its corollaries anywhere else. In fact, many European countries, like the United States, have managed to combine progressivism with a more responsible attitude to conservation than ours: there are echoes here of the state of affairs around 1900 and of the arguments of Martin Wiener which are criticised above. A country can easily combine a celebration of the past with confidence in the future, although such a constructively pluralistic interaction of old and new has hitherto proved disappointingly elusive in twentieth-century Britain. Indeed, there is a danger of 'heritage' being blamed for a loss of nerve by contemporary British culture which is really due to quite different factors.

It is also unclear what the critics of 'heritage' want to do about it. The fact is that we have a national heritage, just as we have a national economy and a national environment, and we have a responsibility to manage it in just the same way. It is unhelpful nostalgically to evoke the unthinking destruction of the past, as does Sir Roy Strong in his contribution to this genre, for instance,[41] since there has been a loss of innocence in this regard. Once you have begun to think systematically about preservation, and to worry about what should and should not be preserved, there is no way of going back to the good (or bad) old days. Carefully-considered public decisions have to be made, particularly for people living, like us, in a small overcrowded country in which every aspect of life has to be controlled. It would clearly be wrong to allow random destruction, yet that is what such authors sometimes seem to be advocating. Indeed, the real question for such critics of the current state of affairs is what their alternative is. Satisfying as it may be to launch a broadside against 'heritage', this contributes little to the decisions that need to be made on such issues.

It is also important to stress that Hewison and other critics are prone to impute a false unity to those concerned with 'heritage', implying that such activities either consciously or unconsciously impart a uniform set of values, usually of a conservative kind.[42] In fact, the valuation of the past associated with heritage is less irrevocably linked to particular ideologies than such authors think. Thus Nick Merriman, in a valuable survey of the responses of the public to the relics of the past, has shown how people are much more independent and inventive in their response to the past and its remains than such theories suggest.[43] Similarly, Raphael Samuel has recently reminded us of the extent to which a sense of history has often been radical in its implication.[44]

In fact, there are contrasting ways of approaching relics of the past, and it is right that these should be the subject of debate. It is true that there has been a tendency towards homogenisation in the way in which 'heritage' is presented, seen for instance in the National Trust's penchant for fossilising the kitchen facilities of country houses in the just pre-modern era of *c.* 1900, or in the proclivity to fit out historic town centres with standard cobbling and Victorian-style street lights: such trends are clearly to be avoided. But they are to be eschewed precisely because part of the richness of the past that has come down to us resides in its often surprising variety, which should not be smoothed away. We do not want to perpetrate a sentimentalised version of the past, with its rough edges smoothed off. Moreover, there are unavoidable dilemmas in deciding how the heritage should be treated – dilemmas over the interrelationship of preservationist sentiment and the right of individuals to treat their property as they wish; over the priorities of preservation and display in museums, as Michael Stratton indicates; even over the manner in which historic buildings should be restored. Indeed, a new twist in the latter is provided by the preservation of modern-movement buildings, which may require different terms of reference than those that have prevailed traditionally, concerned less with original fabric than with overall appearance.[45] It would be surprising if there were not room for extensive debate in such matters, and a homogeneous attitude is the last thing that one would expect to characterise the field.

Even within this book, the reader will find divergent attitudes towards the history of the current state of affairs. Some of the contributors present an essentially progressivist view, dwelling even on defeats in a kind of Dunkirk spirit, while some provide a pantheon of heroic pioneers, complete with the dates of birth and death. Elsewhere, on the other hand, greater stress is laid on the broader historical context in which such developments occurred (or failed to occur), emphasising the constraints to change, and the rather gradual shifts in public opinion which have allowed even those developments that have materialised to come about. There is room for both approaches, yet it may be argued that it is precisely the tension between the two that has brought about the current state of affairs, both in terms of

An urban Conservation Area in typical livery of wall-to-wall paving and 'heritage' street-lamps and bollards.

general attitudes, and of the specific institutions and measures that are available to achieve conservationist ends.

Moreover to exploit the current situation to the full we need a comparable combination of idealism with realism about how the tools that we have inherited are best deployed in the context of late-twentieth-century British society. If the current state of the heritage represents the negotiation of diverse, conflicting interests and attitudes, the structures whose origins are described in this book will need to continue to be altered or refined in a compromise with shifting public opinion. It makes for a state of affairs that is highly contingent, yet at the same time notably flexible. Some may aspire to a once-and-for-all philosophy of conservation, yet it is doubtful if any such absolute philosophy will ever prove satisfactory. Instead, we need a pragmatic philosophy, based on an understanding of how the circumstances we are in came about: that is what this volume is intended to achieve.

2
The first conservation militants: William Morris and the Society for the Protection of Ancient Buildings

Chris Miele

Between 1840 and 1875 thousands of medieval churches in England and Wales were restored. The total bill for this work came to more than was spent on new church construction. Even allowing for marked regional variations, the pace of restoration and church building nationwide as measured both in number of projects and cost increased dramatically after 1860.[1] This remarkable achievement had come about through the offices of the Church of England, legal owners of most of the country's medieval churches, and through the financial outlay of loyal churchmen and women. Restoration was one small part of a much larger programme of institutional reform which was intended to fight the steady erosion of the Established Church's traditional privileges and power.[2] New churches, schools and vicarages, old churches restored and redecorated, new diocesan training colleges, new liturgies and church music, these were the tangible expressions of new policies, a more aggressive ministry and an enhanced theology. The change worked on the country's finest medieval remains was dramatic. Buildings that started the century as picturesque accents in the landscape ended it looking upright and four-square, as if centuries of wear and tear had never happened. Far from compromising historic interest, restoration was seen to enhance it. If anything, smart new 'old' work exhibited the marks of medieval style more clearly than withered originals, and so seemed more ancient to those who measured age by the number of characteristic medieval 'features' on display.[3]

This startling architectural transformation was driven by a complex institutional structure of incentives rather than compulsory measures. Starting at the top were bishops who instructed the parochial clergy to restore the churches in their care lavishly as a practical contribution to the struggle against secularism and nonconformity. The message came in the form of regular printed 'charges', and by personal pressure brought to bear through archidiaconal visitations. The faculty system, which had lapsed in many places, was vigorously revived so that the bishop, usually with the advice of a diocesan architect, could encourage the adoption of up-to-date ecclesiological principles. Reinforcing the work of the diocesan hierarchies were the diocesan church-building societies, which made modest grants for 'church extension' from budgets funded mostly by private individuals. Through the application process, works in the diocese were judged by the same criteria. Standards of construction were enforced, as in many cases

CHRIS MIELE

RCHME © CROWN COPYRIGHT

The Church of St Lawrence, Castle Rising, Norfolk, before and after restoration by G. E. Street (from 1860) and his son, Arthur Edmund. Before, from a lithograph from Ladbroke's *Norfolk Churches* (1819); after, from a photograph taken in 1951.

were standards of propriety according to the ecclesiological principles that had been so vigorously enunciated by Augustus Welby Pugin and the Cambridge Camden Society. The result was uniformity of practice. The efforts of the local societies were co-ordinated at the national level by another grant-giving body, the Incorporated Church Building Society, the architectural arm of the powerful Ecclesiastical Commission, itself the creature of the bishops.[4]

Voluntary local history societies, usually featuring the word 'architectural' in their titles, provided another layer of coverage. By bringing together clergy, professional architects and churchmen, these societies bridged the gap between diocesan policy and parochial architectural practice.[5] Anglican architects, for their part, played a leading part in this drive to modernise Britain's medieval churches, specialising in restoration, then writing about its theory and practice. Eventually the Royal Institute of British Architects (RIBA) became involved, publishing 'guidelines' for the care of old churches, promoting debates, and setting up a permanent subcommittee on the subject.[6] Restoration was integrated into the apprenticeship system, with practitioners of the calibre of George Edmund Street arguing that it was perfectly suited to the training of a young architect.[7]

All in all it was an impressive network of influence and control, and by the 1860s it stretched even into the remotest corners of the country. Thus almost a century before the first comprehensive legislation protecting the historic environment, there existed a system for overseeing works on one large and very important class of British monuments. True, it was neither monitored nor funded by the State, as in France, and, equally true, it applied principles which are contrary to late twentieth-century standards, but there it stood to be reckoned with. It is a matter of fact that any party wishing to promote more careful standards of care for medieval churches would have had to engage with this machinery if it were to achieve any success.

Now the truly remarkable thing about the Society for the Protection of Ancient Buildings (SPAB), the most famous preservationist body of the Victorian period, founded by William Morris, was its pointed refusal to come to terms with any of this system's features. Between its founding in March 1877 and the late 1880s, there were a handful of half-hearted attempts to open up a channel of communication with Church authorities. An early suggestion to place a notice in the clerical press was vetoed. Then came a failed attempt to discuss the matter with the Ecclesiastical Commission, and a few years later one brief memorandum to the influential Incorporated Church Building Society. Finally, there was talk of a leaflet, 'Instructions to Churchwardens', to be written by Morris himself. It reached draft form by July 1885, but after that he lost interest and it never saw the light of day.[8] The percentage of clerical members was tiny, especially in comparison with the figures for county archaeological and architectural societies.[9] The SPAB had even fewer contacts with the ruling body of professional architects, the Royal Institute of British Architects, and the number of architect-members was smaller even than the number of clergymen. This catalogue explains why the SPAB achieved so few successes in its first decade. Strongly secular in character (at times positively anti-clerical) and hostile on almost all occasions to professional architects, it was cut off from the very institutions it had to influence. Instead, the Society tried to work round these institutions by putting the case for careful conservation as opposed to restoration to that small segment of the public sometimes called the 'chattering classes', the Anglican oligarchy which provided most of the money for church work.[10] The novelty of the SPAB consists precisely in this, not in any of its intellectual premises, its so-called 'philosophy'. It was the first society to concern itself with architecture that was run by and for outsiders, with no vested interest in what was being done to ancient buildings except an interest in their status as historical monuments and works of art. The many commentators on this early episode in the history of the conservation movement seem to me to have missed this essential point.

For William Morris, there was no great mystery to protection, no complicated set of propositions. It meant doing no more to an ancient building than necessary to keep it in sound condition. Underlying it was the assumption that authentic originals are in all circumstances superior to facsimiles. Of course, this ideal had been around for a long time before the SPAB. The idea that there was anything new about it was largely down to the Society's founder, William Morris himself, who quite deliberately acknowledged only one forerunner, John Ruskin.[11] Contrary to what Morris was willing to admit, there was by 1877 a well-established tradition, albeit a minority view, that restoration compromised the authenticity of ancient buildings. Arguably it was built into the heightened historical and aesthetic sense which was central to the Romantic Movement. Strong preferences along these lines had been expressed by John Carter, Richard Gough and John Milner in their well-publicised opposition to James Wyatt's cathedral restorations of the 1790s. In addition, Carter had written about old buildings in the *Gentleman's Magazine* in a way which shows great respect for the real stuff of medieval building.[12] Outside expert and professional circles an entire literary *genre*, the picturesque travel account, had put a strong case against the modernisation of ancient buildings, if only implicitly through the medium of topographical views. The possibility that notions of authenticity as had been developing among connoisseurs of the fine arts might be applied to the care of old buildings was discussed frankly in the 1840s, particularly in the newly established societies dedicated to archaeology (as opposed to the 'architectural' societies noted above).[13] With a strong base of support coming from that segment of the historical community which was non-sectarian, the 'anti-restoration' lobby gained ground steadily over the next twenty years. By 1860 their views were beginning to find a sympathetic audience among church architects and even within the Anglican Church.[14]

So when Morris founded the SPAB he had a clear choice. He could build on the achievements of the vocal minority already pressing for higher standards of monument care, opening up new channels of communication with interested parties committed to trying something different, or he could turn his back on the lot. By choosing the second he cut the Society's chances for success. The early

RCHME © CROWN COPYRIGHT

The interior of St Mary-at-Hill, City of London. Built by Sir Christopher Wren, 1670–9, and saved through the intervention of the SPAB in 1879. Photograph taken in August 1973.

records of the Society show that by 1883 it could point to at most half a dozen cases where their protests had made a substantial difference, and even in these I am not convinced that the Society won their argument on a level playing field.

In the first months of the Society's existence Morris does not seem to have thought strategically about what he was trying to do. The letter that he sent to *The Athenaeum* in early March 1877 and which led to the formation of the SPAB is passionate and eloquent, but it contains no specific proposals. It is constructed around the claim that clergymen and their architects should have nothing to do with ancient buildings precisely because both groups benefited directly from their restoration. It refers at the start to the plans that George Gilbert Scott had just then formulated for Tewkesbury Abbey, but the reference amounted to nothing. Indeed, as was made clear in subsequent correspondence, Morris actually had no idea what was being proposed and he had no interest in finding out.[15] When the Society was officially constituted a few weeks later nothing was said about Tewkesbury, and no further action came of the now-famous letter that got the whole thing going.[16] The principal outcome of that first meeting – held on the evening of 22 March 1877 at Morris and Co.'s Queen Square premises –

was to charge Morris, George Wardle and Philip Webb with the task of drafting a 'statement of principles' for the new Society. What became the manifesto was ready in draft form by early April.[17] The manifesto's status in the conservation movement today is virtually unmatched, a strange state of affairs when one considers that most of it is in fact taken up with a condemnation of the Gothic Revival. Morris describes the Revival as an evil doctrine whose principal feature was a narrow system of historical knowledge empowering architects to say what was right and wrong with old buildings and then to make the necessary corrections without any regard for what imperfections and peculiarities might show about past life.

All well and good, in theory, but how exactly to change this from the fringes? Morris called for direct action, that is, public protest, but what form should this take? Should the Society be proactive? And if it chose to be purely reactive should it limit its activities to prominent buildings likely to attract the attention of the national press? In the early years of the Society there was a clear preference shown for the latter option. In May 1877, for example, Morris was toying with the idea of a committee to oppose the sale and demolition of Wren's City churches,[18] several of which had already fallen under the Union of Benefices Act of 1860 and its subsequent amendments,[19] but the threat subsided, for a time at any rate. Then he came across some correspondence in the pages of *The Times* between the Revd W. J. Loftie and that staunch supporter of the Revival, Alexander Beresford-Hope. At stake were choir stalls in Canterbury Cathedral then said to be the work of Grinling Gibbons (now attributed to Roger Davis and dated 1680). As the architect in charge of the refurnishing, Scott wanted to remove this work in order to restore the fragmentary remains of the early fourteenth-century stone screen behind. This time Morris made sure of the facts before publishing an open letter to the Dean in *The Times*. It is one of his best-known early efforts on behalf of the Society and concludes with words clearly meant to stir his own party, not win any concession: 'Sir, I think that our ancient historical monuments are national property and ought no longer to be left to the mercy of the many and variable ideas of ecclesiastical propriety that may at any time be prevalent among us.'[20] A memorial was then drafted to the Chapter but the Dean refused to deliver it on the grounds that although the Society could say what it wished in the national press it had no legal right to address the Chapter. The Society threatened to publish the entire correspondence in pamphlet form, adding to it private correspondence on the subject which reflected badly on the Dean, and in the end he capitulated.[21] A compromise was struck. The stalls at the west end of the choir were retained (although not in their original form), and new stalls to Scott's designs were added on the north and south sides. Morris clearly did not see this as a victory, for he did not refer to it in the *Annual Report* for 1879.

In those first few months two other stalwarts used the scandal generated by attacking the Church of England and its architects to put the SPAB's argument to a wider audience. In a long piece published in the spring number of *Macmillan's Magazine*, W. J. Loftie disputed the Anglican claim that church restoration made any difference at all to the spiritual life of a parish; coming from someone who was himself a clergymen it had more authority than anything Morris could say. Although Scott is not named, 'Thorough Restoration' makes its point with churches he had restored, and so Scott responded in the next number with 'Thorough Anti-Restoration'.[22] The rebuttal studiously avoids matters of principle in favour of matters of detail, implying that as an amateur Loftie was not qualified to judge the facts.

This certainly could not be said of the next figure to enter the story, John James Stevenson, who was not only an experienced architect but had spent two years, 1858–60, in Scott's office.[23] The title of the paper he read to RIBA on 28 May 1877, 'Architectural Restoration, Its Theory and Practice', would have sounded benign enough to members, but it turned out to be a frontal assault, listing particular instances of restorations that had gone horribly wrong, every one of them an example taken from the work of Scott or George Edmund Street (who had himself spent two years in Scott's office). Their 'standing and eminence', Stevenson slyly observed, 'are a guarantee that their work is a favourable example of the system'.[24] His particular hobby-horse was the lack of regard consistently shown for post-Reformation furnishings and additions. (Years before Stevenson had nailed his colours to the mast of the Queen Anne Revival.[25]) How was it possible, he wondered, for the history of the Anglican Church to have stopped at the Reformation? And even if one disliked classical architecture as a matter of taste, it was undeniably historic. Echoing Morris's SPAB manifesto, Stevenson begged the Institute to do something to save churches from 'thorough restoration by the architect':

> For it is the knowledge and skill of the architect which destroys the authenticity of the building as a record of the past. He is by profession a clever forger of old documents. He is trained in the tricks of the trade.

The discussion which followed was so heated that it was held over to the next session, the last of the season, when Scott was given a chance to defend himself.[26] What he said on 11 June should reflect well on his reputation, for he accepted many of the charges without rancour, asking only that his critics take note of the fact that in thirty-six years of handling old buildings he had moved from restoration to 'reparation', a claim which, with the benefit of historical hindsight, can be judged true enough. He agreed there was no sense to the bias against post-Reformation work. In fact he did the SPAB one better – for although Stevenson had not spoken on behalf of the Society, Scott and everyone present on 11 June rightly saw him as one of their agents[27] – it ought to declare for the best of eighteenth-century architecture, which, having fewer admirers, was vulnerable. He saw two roles for the new group, first, as a national repository of drawings and photographs of churches about to be restored,[28] and secondly, as a final 'Court of Appeal' to arbitrate difficult disputes. Whatever came of its efforts, Scott argued, he thought it wise for the Society at least to tone down its rhetoric, and in the process admit that the owners of ancient churches had the right to adapt their buildings to a certain extent.

Scott was one of a handful of architects in touch with the church building elites who could actually have helped the Society. In 1864 he had been instrumental in setting up the RIBA's Committee on the Conservation of Ancient Monuments and Remains.[29] He had the respect of the Incorporated Church Building Society and countless local architectural societies, in addition to many influential contacts among the diocesan hierarchy and parochial clergy. More important, though, was the respect he commanded within his own profession. Here was a real chance, and had Morris been minded to take it, the Society might have formed the right institutional links.

From June 1877 Morris and the Society eased off, but the publicity generated in three months of agitation ensured that the architectural papers would keep debate simmering over the summer months. From the beginning *The Architect* sided with the SPAB, giving its claims maximum coverage.[30] A leader of 23 June praised Stevenson for his decision to accuse leading restorers by name, and thereby throw the essential differences between the two positions into high relief.[31] *Building News* and *The Builder* were slower to respond so Morris, true to form, hurled copies of the manifesto into their editorial offices. Only *The Builder* would be drawn. It ridiculed the Society's wish merely 'to stave off decay', rejecting its very premise.

> Such a doctrine is tantamount to the admission that the art we profess is unworthy of our age and of ourselves, that all our study of the past is worthless compared with that of our predecessors, and that really we have no history of our own to record. The result of this 'leave alone' principle would be that in a few years the remains of ancient art would entirely disappear.[32]

That was August. As SPAB supporters returned from the summer holidays, the publicity campaign was renewed. On 20 September George Aitchison read 'The Principles of Restoration' to the Social Science Conference at Aberdeen. In October Sidney Colvin's 'Restoration and Anti-Restoration' appeared in the *Nineteenth Century*.[33] Perhaps they had been urged to speak out by the Society, for at a meeting on 30 August 'names were put forward of people who could lecture' on protection around the country.[34] Two weeks later the W. J. Loftie put the following motion: 'Can nothing be done in the way of agitation just now by writing to *The Times*? This paper would welcome a controversy.' Another call for public speaking tours was made on 11 October.[35]

There was, however, general acceptance that more had to be done than stimulate public debate. If the Society were going to criticise, it had better be able to debate the details of each and every proposal and then suggest how things ought to be done. Canterbury had shown that even the Society could bring pressure to bear, and this was better than nothing. The first opportunity to present itself that autumn was a set of proposals drawn up for Southwell Minster by the architect of the Ecclesiastical Commission, Ewan Christian.[36] The Society at once wrote to the Commission, then to their architect. There was the barest acknowledgement and that was all,[37] and so the Society set about trying to find out what was being planned from other sources. By April 1878 enough information had been collected to prepare a detailed memorandum to the Chapter stating its objections, which boiled down to two points: first, that the post-Reformation choir furnishings, which included an eighteenth-century screen in compo, should be kept; secondly, that the shallow-pitched, largely Georgian nave roof should not be raised to the pitch shown by weather mouldings on the west face of the crossing tower. In a testy answer, Christian admitted that while the details of his new roof would unquestionably be 'conjectural', the overall form was accurate to a degree that was widely deemed to be satisfactory, particularly when dealing with work that was of inferior quality.[38] The Society maintained that although the present work was indeed late, the pitch actually reproduced a late medieval scheme, a conclusion based principally on a mid-seventeenth-century view by the engraver Wenceslaus Hollar. As for the eighteenth-century choir furnishings, these were simply beyond the pale. In so far as Christian was concerned, the matter was now closed. In the summer of 1879, after several failed attempts to reopen the debate, the Society decided to publish selections from their correspondence which were seen to reflect badly on the Church authorities and their architect. Into the resulting fray Street was pulled, for in his report to the Bishop of Lincoln dated 1 June 1876 he was said to have reached very different conclusions from Christian's as to the interest and value of the eighteenth-century remains, as well as to the state of the nave roof. Here, finally, was proof of what Morris had said from the start, that Victorian architecture was in 'an experimental condition' and that therefore the best course of action was to do nothing.[39] Street was livid and claimed his views had been misreported. Letters for and against littered the pages of the architectural journals that autumn.

The Southwell dispute mushroomed because the central issue, the raising of the nave roof pitch, was also at the heart of proposals made for St Albans Abbey.[40] There John Oldrid Scott, who had taken over the project on the death of his father in 1878, had persuaded the principal patron, Lord Grimthorpe, that the roof could be repaired and the nave clerestory righted by hydraulic screw jacks. The *Architect* wrote that 'these works are such that the sternest "anti-restorationists" – except of course the fanatics who prefer ruin to repair – can take no exception at'.[41] The SPAB began to take an interest in these goings-on in April 1878, but by the end of the year the whole business got out of hand. The Society embarrassed itself by misjudging certain portions of the fabric. Street formed a little party opposed to the raising of the roof with A. W. Blomfield and Christian, but the trio refused to ally themselves with the SPAB. Oldrid Scott then lost control of the works to his patron Grimthorpe. By May 1879 there was some very worrying talk of an entirely new west front to go with the proposed steeply pitched roof. Grimthorpe was the designer! Charge and countercharge crossed in the usual way, with the SPAB and Street's group attacking not merely Grimthorpe but each other.[42]

In the meantime the SPAB committee was plotting a more radical solution. In March 1879 it began to consider finding someone in the parish who might be willing to oppose Grimthorpe's faculty in the Court of Arches. On its own the Society had no *locus* to mount such a challenge, but one of its supporters did, John Evans who was a vestryman and a Fellow of the Society of Antiquaries. If he agreed to lodge the petition, the Society would engage counsel and pay costs in the event the decision went against them. Evans eventually agreed, and late in November, when Grimthorpe filed the faculty papers, the Society instructed their solicitor, Tebbs, to go ahead with the cause.[43] In the meantime, Earl Cowper had added his name to Evans's on the Society-backed petition. Did the Society have any reasonable hope of succeeding? There was some legal precedent for getting the Chancellor to rule against one part of a faculty, but these cases had mostly to do with the removal of church monuments against the wishes of the descendants of the original donor.[44] To the best of my knowledge, no architectural or archaeological society had chosen to appeal over a purely architectural matter: however, a variation of this tactic had been used previously, with considerable success, by the Commons Preservation Society (CPS). In the late 1860s the CPS's solicitor, Robert Hunter, hit on the idea that the enclosure of common lands could be opposed through a suit pressed by a commoner on the grounds that one or more rights of common, protected by ancient case-law, were being infringed. The test of this theory came with the proposed enclosure of Epping Forest. In July 1874 the Master of the Rolls decided in favour of the petitioners, the CPS and the City of London (which owned land in the Forest).[45] This triumph for the early landscape conservation movement would not have gone unnoticed by William Morris, whose boyhood homes in Woodford and Walthamstow bordered Epping. Furthermore, two future SPAB supporters, James Bryce and Charles Dilke, had been instrumental in setting up the CPS.

Still, the analogy was not very close. The CPS was the creature of lawyers and politicians, and they naturally thought in terms of legal or statutory relief. The SPAB was run by and for artists and aesthetes. No one on its committee was familiar with the ins and outs of ecclesiastical law. And what exactly was the basis of the petitioner's case? Essentially that Grimthorpe's work compromised the historic integrity of the building. It is hard to see this succeeding, but still Grimthorpe's proposals were so widely disliked that the Society might have expected a precedent to be set. There was no hope of persuading the people who promised to contribute to the work to withdraw their pledges, since by this point Grimthorpe had undertaken to pay for the job out of his own pocket. At the preliminary hearing, conducted by Archdeacon Grant early in February 1880, the Society won a technical point. Grimthorpe had withheld detailed plans for the new west front, realising that public outcry would intensify when he did so.[46] By the time the Chancellor of the Diocese, J. E. P. Robertson, heard the case in mid-April the publicity had subsided somewhat, although whether this made any difference to the outcome is to be doubted. In the event, Robertson decided against the petitioners. An extraordinary meeting was held to decide whether to appeal, but Morris moved that the matter be officially closed. Webb agreed. The Society would not try the ecclesiastical courts again in Morris's lifetime, and in part that decision had been a practical one.[47] The action had landed the Society with a hefty bill, £160 to be precise, more than its funds could bear. A special appeal to wealthy members yielded £45. Tebbs let the balance go until the close of 1881, when Morris managed to persuade him to settle for £75.[48] The Society could at least take comfort in the fact that their efforts had been supported by most segments of the architectural public.

Unquestionably the Society's biggest publicity coup was its campaign against the refacing of the west front of San Marco in Venice. Morris himself started this off with a letter that appeared in the *Daily News* on 1 November 1879.[49] The Society called a special meeting five days later at which public meetings were scheduled later that month at Birmingham, Cambridge and Oxford. (Morris himself delivered an address at the latter.) San Marco had the effect of launching the Society's overseas work, for although the idea had been discussed in the previous spring and summer, nothing was in fact done abroad until this time. By December, more than 1,500 prominent people had signed the Society's official letter of protest to the Italian Ministry of Public Works.[50] Even architects who had gone on record against the Society signed, including Butterfield, Christian and Street. The last went so far as to visit Venice in the company of Stevenson in order to report back to the special 'Saint Mark's Committee' specially established for this purpose as a separately constituted body. By the spring of 1881 word was received that the fixing of new marble to the west front would not go ahead. The Society was quick to claim a success and, since it had been put seriously out of pocket by this campaign (carried on in the same months that the committee was looking at the costs arising from its legal challenge to Grimthorpe), circulated a begging letter to everyone who had lent support. The exercise barely got back what it had cost. Hopes that the campaign would attract more members to the Society also proved wrong. And as for the Society's claim to sucess, this too seems to have been premature. William Bell Scott, who had followed the effects of the campaign from Italy for the Society, felt strongly that the works had been abandoned for financial reasons only. As he saw things, the Society had completely mishandled the whole affair, seriously harming its chance to work on the Continent and especially in Italy, where Morris's presumptive tone had outraged public opinion. What right, newspaper editors in Rome and Venice asked, did the English have to tell Italians what to do with their monuments, and why had there been no protest against works of several years earlier funded by the Austrian government? 'So far as I am aware,' Scott wrote in December 1881, 'the actions taken by the SPAB have not succeeded here in Venice or elsewhere in Italy, in saving any building whose Restoration had been resolved'.[51]

In view of all this, Morris might have been forgiven for abandoning the Society. Four years of hard work had not produced one clear-cut success. Membership had increased initially but it now appeared to be levelling off, and without a significant increase in the number of members the Society's delicate financial situation was unlikely to improve. Morris was gloomy about the Society's prospects in his first annual address, warning members that they might well have to be content with a Society devoted to public education rather than direct action. His address for the following year was no more sanguine. But then, from 1880, there was a marked change. Although the Society's success rate had not suddenly climbed, Morris's reports became confident and businesslike in their delivery. Between the lines it is just possible to make out a glimmer of hope, perhaps a reflection of the general hopefulness which comes across in his writings from about this time. Or perhaps, as I think more likely, something in the way the Society did business reassured him. For what the Society managed to establish by the first months of 1880 was a sustainable programme of day-to-day casework, most of it not particularly glamorous, but slow and steady work to a fixed standard and involving regular meetings, carefully worked-out protocols, a network of reliable correspondents, and, as these methods improved, small gains. What was emerging was an institutional structure, weak in comparison with that infinitely more powerful collection of Anglican and professional interests that Morris had set himself against, but well-defined none the less, and comforting for that. By 1885 the Society had achieved a handful of successes. Suddenly it seemed possible for it to make a greater impact. Morris was at the heart of every one of the changes that led to this new organisational structure.

Its roots can be followed back to the very early days of the Society. At the meeting for 27 September 1877 the committee debated drawing up a national 'schedule of unrestored churches' to be watched over by specially constituted local vigilance committees, thus not only ensuring that the Society could get involved before a definite course of action had been resolved, but also improving the accuracy of the information notified to the committee in Bloomsbury. It was decided to experiment in the capital to see whether the system could work. A trial scheme for compiling a list of all historic buildings in the City of London was initiated, but then soon abandoned for one involving only the churches of Wren and the Wren School, an idea that had been discussed a few months before. The scheme was well in hand by the autumn, and a permanent subcommittee was established, combining staff from the SPAB and another fledgling group, the City Church and Churchyard Protection Society.[52]

Unfortunately, Wren's churches have always constituted a special case, and no protocol developed for the City of London was likely to be relevant in the heart of rural England. So with one eye on St Paul's, the committee turned the other on East Anglia, and asked one of its most active members, Henry Brewer (a successful architectural draughtsman), to record all the unrestored churches in Norfolk. In the process he was to come up with a 'tabular report for obtaining the description of a church' so that the national survey could be carried out by members with no professional knowledge of architecture. The form was soon ready, ordered printed, and distributed (free of charge it would seem) to interested members. (A 'skeleton form' for reporting 'non-ecclesiastical buildings' was being prepared the following spring.[53]) In June 1878 Morris reported that the Society had completed forms for more than 700 churches, 'the greater number [of which] are situated in the counties of Buckinghamshire, Essex, Suffolk, Norfolk, Lincolnshire and Oxfordshire'.[54] (Coventry Patmore offered £10 towards a special fund to publish the schedule.) Brewer's final

[Table 1. Unrestored Churches]

Society for the Protection of Ancient Buildings.

Wm. Morris, Honorary Secretary, 26, Queen Square, W.C.

Information concerning Mells Church
in the Parish of Mells
in the County of Somerset
Deanery or Archdeaconry of Frome

Name and Address of Informant: John W Singer, Frome

Date at which the Building was last seen by Informant: Ten days ago

Name and address of Rector or Vicar: Revd George Horner, Mells Rectory, Frome

General condition of the Building: All in good condition excepting the seats

If any portion of it is in danger of being destroyed: The Seats are about to be removed from the Nave only

Restoration in progress or proposed: Proposed to be soon done

Name of Architect employed: Mr Woodyer

[Table 1. Unrestored Churches]

*Stained Glass: All the Windows are new, and all made in the Village excepting the West Window, and the East Window which is filled with old pieces, from old Windows arranged merely for preservation

* Give as nearly as possible, the date of each Window or fragment, and state whether it is composed of Figures, Armorial Bearings or Ornament.

Sculpture. External. No figures left —

Internal.

Decorative Painting: A long Inscription on south side —

Monuments. (Brasses, Slabs, Stone Coffins)

* Observations.

The Seats in the Nave have doors, and are not in very good state: it is proposed to remove these, leaving the Seats in the Aisles, which have not Doors to them, and are in better state, but these are to be lowered in height a little

* If any remarkable features exist in the Building which are not named in the Table mention them here. The materials used in building, may also be stated; also the Quarry from which stone was taken; and with what the Roof is covered. Or if there are any historical associations connected with the Building state them.

[Table 1. Unrestored Churches]

Society for the Protection of Ancient Buildings.

Name of Church. Mells Church, near Frome Somerset

Parts of Building	Date	Style	Partly or entirely Unrestored	Remarks
Nave	15th Cent	Perpendicular	Wholly Restored	
Aisles of Nave	Do	Do	Do	
Transepts	None			
Aisles or Chapels of same	15 Cen -	Do	Entirely restored	
Choir	Do	Do		
Aisles of Choir				
Lady Chapel	None			
Chancel	15th Cen	Do	Unrestored	
Porches and Parvises	15th	Do	Restored	
Side Chapels				
Central Tower				
ditto (Spire)				
Towers	West Tower 15	Do	partly restored	
(Spires)				
Sacristy or Vestry				
Sancte-bell Turret	15 Cn	Do	Restored partly	
Cloisters or Crypts	None			

* Details of Furniture. (Sedilia, Piscinae, Leper Windows, Squints, Easter Sepulchres, Altars, Reredoses, Stalls, Screens, Fonts, Organs, Pulpits, Reading Desks, Communion Tables, Credences, Galleries, Pews, Lecterns, Faldstools, Aumbries, Bells, Churchyard Crosses, Fireplaces, Chimneys, Lych-gates, Chandeliers, Alms-boxes, Chained Books, Chests, Metal work, Church Plate, Embroidery.)

The Screens have been constructed on the model formed from old pieces found — The Vestry Door has a very interesting old handle formed of Twisted Lizards —

* If possible give date, style and material of each article of Church Furniture described.

SPAB

Tabular reporting form drawn up by Henry Brewer and printed in large numbers early in 1878. This example, for Mells Church, Somerset, was completed on 3 May 1879.

report, which was presented in October 1878,[55] has not survived, so it is impossible to say whether he had actually seen every unrestored church in Norfolk. We know only that the plans for a national survey were abandoned early in 1879, probably because the committee had not been able to set up one local sub-committee to carry it out. In the short term, then, the Society was left with no choice but to be reactive.

Even before Brewer had started this trial survey, events were beginning to overtake the best laid of the Society's plans. In late August 1877 the committee was asked to investigate works proposed for two churches near Duxford in Cambridgeshire. The request had been passed along to the Society from, of all people, G. E. Street.[56] A handful more followed, and Newman Marks was hired on a part-time basis, at a salary of £10 per month, to handle the work generated by these demands, making him the first employee of an architectural amenity society.[57] At the end of September the numbers of these 'cases' had so increased that Brewer proposed 'no new business' be raised until the Society had cleared its backlog. He lost the vote and eight new cases were entered on the agenda.[58] Each letter in required many more out before the Society was ready to make a case, and there were dozens of false alarms. The work was made harder by the fact that the Society did not have even the most basic library of architectural references for some time. The solution to every one of these problems lay in the use of local secretaries, or correspondents.

The first mention of these is in the SPAB agenda paper for 8 November 1877, when a resolution was put to write to Richard Ferguson at Carlisle for 'a view on affiliating with the local archaeological society' through him. In June 1878 Wardle suggested that the members of the executive committee should be *ex officio* 'local secretaries' for their respective districts.[59] Unfortunately, the august names who had agreed to this office saw themselves mostly as lending gravitas. They rarely, if ever, turned up to committee meetings, and they certainly were not willing to travel about the countryside verifying rumours and asking discreet questions. That same month more extended discussions were held about these proposals as part of a new special subcommittee established to consider how 'the work of the Society can be more efficiently carried out'.[60]

Initially the Society decided to tap the network of local informants which had been put in place by the dozens of architectural societies. At the first AGM in June 1878 Morris reported that several approaches had been made. As things developed, though, no official ties were established, and after 1883 the Society completely abandoned this tack.[61] No explanation was recorded, but I think the reason can be inferred from the nature of these societies themselves, for, as already noted, they had strong religious biases which would have put them in favour of church restoration as a matter of principle. The Society did much better with national bodies based in London. By 1879 it was in close contact with representatives of the Society of Antiquaries, whose corresponding secretary for the west of England was Morris's friend, the architect John Henry Middleton, who eventually became, like Ferguson in Carlisle, an SPAB local correspondent. From 1880 the British Archaeological Association was adding its weight to several Society projects, and in the later years of the decade strong support came from the Royal Archaeological Institute's secretary Hellier Gosselin, who visited many sites with the SPAB secretary, attended committee meetings and even pledged RAI funds for the SPAB's campaign against Pearson's work at St Helen's Bishopsgate.[62]

The Society committee, overwhelmed by requests for action from the membership, was left with no choice but to recreate this network using activist members. In July 1878 a preliminary brief was agreed. There would be a minimum of one secretary per county, each of whom would in turn chair a local subcommittee. Their principal duties were to collect information, denounce restorations on behalf of the Society, circulate Society propaganda, and correspond regularly with the London committee.[63] In January 1879 acceptance of local correspondent status was made conditional on their signing a 'code of conduct', which bound them to obtain prior approval for everything written on behalf of the Society and for all exceptional costs.[64] (The Society was prepared to meet travelling expenses but the shire correspondents rarely claimed them.) The newly constituted finance committee reckoned that the Society could afford forty-five correspondents. Twenty-two are noted in the *Second Annual Report*, twenty-six in the next year, thirty-three by 1885 and forty by 1891.

The London committee kept its correspondents on a very short lead, but as trust grew they were given increasing freedom to exercise their own judgment. Interestingly, even the most seasoned local secretaries almost never attended committee meetings in the Society's new permanent offices in Buckingham Street.[65] It was more usual for a regular committee member to travel out to them. Information flowed in two directions more or less equally. Local correspondents reported proposals for restoration to London, but just as often letters from headquarters in the Strand were sent out requesting confirmation of some rumour or further information. The earliest requests were accompanied by one of Brewer's blank reporting forms. From 1881 the stockpile appears to have run out, and after this date the Society took most decisions on the basis of detailed written reports illustrated by photographs whenever possible. By 1885 it had retained the services of a professional photographer in Frome, and it seems likely that there were similar arrangements for other parts of the country. In sensitive or high-profile cases a regular committeeman always went to see for himself in order to brief the committee fully. A few correspondents seem to have been almost incessantly on the move for the Society, investigating as many as ten cases at any one time. It seems to have been the sort of voluntary post that could be developed as the individual wished within certain bounds.

The quality of information available to the principal committee improved markedly in 1880, and the number of cases dealt with in detail climbed. The process was accelerated by the use of the 'Press Information Association', a clippings agency which sent notices of restoration from journals that reported on church architecture, principally *The Builder*, *Building News*, and *The Church Builder*.[66] Eventually the Society took out a special subscription limiting the number of items sent to 200 annually. This was due less to the cost of a full annual subscription (£5 5*s* 0*d* versus £1 1*s* 0*d* for 200 selected items) as it was an attempt to keep the work at manageable levels.[67] By the mid-1880s the Society's caseload had reached saturation point, with something of the order of 250 cases actioned each year. Admittedly, for a 'case' to be counted no more than one letter in and out had to be received. Still, the minute books for the mid-1880s make it clear that easily one-quarter to one-third of cases required in-depth work, an impressive achievement by any standard.

The purpose of this sophisticated information-gathering network was not to engage the promoters of restoration or their architects in extended philosophical debate, although initial letters were usually sent with copies of the manifesto, perhaps along with a sheet bearing Ruskin's famous lines from 'The Lamp of Memory'. The aim was instead to debate every single detail of a proposal and to offer reasonable, affordable alternatives to any course of action that the Society considered harmful to the building's artistic or historic character. In due course this strategy raised fundamental questions about what the Society was trying to do. What was the nature of any practical advice the Society might give? Did the committee wish to operate in the place of an architect if this could be managed? And even if it did not, would it be liable for damages if its advice led to personal injury, damages, delays or cost overruns?

These matters first came up in October 1878 in relation to Higham Gobion Church, where the vicar, on the advice of a local landowner who was also an SPAB member, wrote asking for advice on how to save the crumbling fabric of his church. Henry Brewer surveyed the building and outlined a schedule of repairs which was clearly not meant as a specification ready for tendering. Before signing it 'a long discussion took place as to whether the Society ought to undertake any responsibility in signing and sending reports'. 'It was decided to send reports unsigned so that the Society may not be held responsible for any mistakes that may occur in the carrying out of any suggestions made by the Society. It was agreed to send the report [on Higham Gobion Church] unsigned.'[68]

Unusually, Morris had missed this meeting, but he was present at the next, held on 7 November, where he took issue with this form of words, arguing that unless the Society stood by its advice it would run the risk of appearing frivolous. The following disclaimer was read into the minutes as a possible compromise: 'that the suggestions [of the Society] were worthy of consideration, but that great care must be exercised in carrying them out, but that the Society could not be bound by any results which might follow from carrying out these suggestions'. This was too mealy mouthed for Morris, and he moved an alternative: 'that the Committee be held responsible for all reports approved by the Committee'. Being of a serious nature, the issue was held over for the next meeting to allow all members of the executive committee to consider the case for and against a disclaimer. J. J. Stevenson – who had been present when Brewer's report on Higham Gobion had been signed – wrote in asking for a further postponement. Since he was a professional architect the question of liability would have been in the front of his mind. A parliamentary Select Committee had in the previous year recommended a new law specifying that in cases of personal injury the liability attaching to employers should be extended to professionals who, although not in direct charge of labourers, had been party to the advice that had resulted in their injury. As the law then stood, builders bore the chief burden of liability for workmen's safety. The legislation called for by the Select Committee might extend this to architects and engineers if their specifications could be shown to have been flawed.[69] Some liability might attach to the SPAB by analogy with architects. The committee made up its mind on the matter on 5 December, when Morris's wording was approved. Thereafter, though, the Society's reports never assumed the form of detailed specifications but were intended to function as a 'guidance' document for an architect, who would retain ultimate responsibility for the work.

So the Society would not act as architect, or at least not usually,[70] but it was happy to recommend architects if asked, and after 1885 it did so with increasing frequency. Its preferred architects were unquestionably J. T. Micklethwaite and George Somers Clarke, Jr, neither of whom was ever an SPAB member even though they periodically attended committee meetings and acted as local correspondents. The Society also favoured two West Country architects, George Crickmay, who got the job of repairing St Peter's Shaftesbury through the Society's offices in 1886, and Henry Prothero, who was put in charge of Kiffig Church three years later in a similar way. Other architects, all of them Arts and Crafts sympathisers, agreed to submit their work to the SPAB for approval from time to time: G. F. Bodley,[71] Basil Champneys,[72] C. E. Ponting,[73] E. S. Prior,[74] G. G. Scott, Jr[75] and Frederick Waller.[76] Still more regularly gathered information in the manner of local correspondents: Eustace Balfour, Ernest George, John Honeyman, Temple Moore, J. D. Sedding and Aston Webb.

The only other question of protocol left to be worked out was when, where and how the committee itself did business. From September 1877 to December 1878 it met fortnightly, usually on a Thursday, from five or six in the evening until eight or nine. Early on, at Webb's suggestion, Fridays were tried, to make it easier for members of the press to attend, but Thursdays proved most popular. There was always a long break for the summer, usually from August to early October, but over these months the part-time secretary continued to deal with routine matters. At first, meetings were well attended, with as many as twelve people turning up, but numbers soon dropped to what it is best to describe as the strategic core of the SPAB, usually no more than five or six at any one time, each one a close friend or associate of Morris, Wardle and Webb. As for the venue, until April 1878 this remained Morris and Co.'s Queen Square premises. From May to August operations shifted to the firm's showroom at 449 Oxford Street, but Morris and Wardle were unhappy with these arrangements, and that summer meetings were rotated through other member's homes, first Stevenson's in Bayswater, then J. P. Heseltine's at 196 Queen's Gate. In October it was back to Queen Square before settling in November into permanent offices at 9 Buckingham Street, the Strand, the Society's home for many years.

Each meeting was run from an agenda paper written by and for the secretary:

Newman Marks until autumn 1881, then Thomas Wise and, finally, from January 1883 to 1911, the architect Hugh Thackeray Turner. The regular committeemen usually took turns chairing meetings, although Morris most often occupied this position until 1884. At the beginning of each gathering the minutes from the last were read out and agreed. The high proportion of early casework papers to survive suggests a careful filing system, and there are occasional references in the minutes to small sums spent on an office boy to handle the Society's papers. An ordinary meeting consisted usually in a methodical working through of the agenda, reading correspondence, dictating responses, drafting letters of protest, and so on. All very businesslike and orderly. Complicated cases were another matter, for they ate into precious committee time. So in order to get through increasingly long agendas it was necessary to establish special subcommittees to brief the principal committee. The big early campaigns – Southwell, St Mark's in Venice, St Albans, the City churches – were all handled in this way. Very often the special subcommittees were simply the regulars wearing other hats, but they did have planning meetings (unminuted) in their own, not the committee's, time so the fiction was effective; however, most Society business was actually quite mundane and best handled by the secretary on his own or in conjunction with someone of the inner circle. Still, from time to time important matters did arise which Morris and his associates felt ought to be decided by a more representative body. One way round this problem was to call special meetings, notifying all the members of the 'executive committee' and inviting them to attend – this committee consisted largely of well-known figures from the late Victorian art world who were in fact more like patrons than caseworkers – but this was costly and time-consuming. Morris came up with the idea of dividing the Society's decision-making between two groups, one dealing with the nitty gritty detail of casework and the other with questions of principle. He proposed two committees, a general committee, which took potentially controversial (or expensive) decisions, and a smaller, more select body, the restoration committee, which was the real workhorse of the Society. From January 1879 the two met fortnightly, which meant one meeting each week of alternate committees, and the arrangement appears to have worked well until the winter of 1879, when the numbers at one committee dropped to the same half dozen or so who attended the other the following week. For the next few months a bureaucratic ritual was enacted, with recommendations made by Morris, Wardle, Webb, Stevenson, Brewer, John Hebb, G. P. Boyce or Charles Vinall sitting as the restoration committee being approved by Morris, Wardle, Webb, Stevenson, Brewer, Hebb, Boyce or Vinall sitting as the general committee. That this went on for close to a year can only be explained by Morris's desire to keep the Society democratic and accountable, to prevent it from becoming what, in effect, it was, a Morris–Webb clique. But in January 1881 Morris lost his patience with the whole business, as a campaign he was hoping to run against the widening of Magdalen Bridge in Oxford got tangled up in his own bureaucratic procedures. That an important local landmark could be sacrificed to the needs of modern commerce with the approval of the university establishment – the widening was to accommodate a

REPRODUCED WITH PERMISSION OF THE UNIVERSITY OF YORK LIBRARY

The Church of St Nicholas, New Romney, Kent: saved from restoration in 1881 through SPAB protests. Photograph taken in 1872.

tram line – was to Morris vivid proof of the hypocritical rot at the core of modern Britain. A stern and public rebuke was, he believed, called for, but many of those who were entitled to sit on the general committee but had stopped coming did not see things in such stark terms. Worried of being associated with a scandal, they came back to the Buckingham Street offices in force, or at least in numbers enough to outvote the unreconstructed core. Ultimately the Society was forced to tread a little more carefully than Morris, left to his own devices, would have wished.[77] By the close of the unsuccessful campaign that autumn the two committees were once again being staffed by the same people, and Morris, backed by Wardle and Webb, simply did away with the general committee. The reconstituted committee met from 17 November 1881, and as the decade progressed admission to this inner sanctum became increasingly harder. Even aspirants with impeccable credentials, such as C. R. Ashbee, had a hard time getting an invitation to attend one meeting.

The question remains whether this seemingly efficient structure made any difference at all to the Society's success rate, and it is not an easy one to answer, in part because the survival of early casework correspondence is not complete, and in part because Morris tended to claim more successes than were consistent with the facts. As far as I have been able to determine, before 1883 the Society was justified in claiming only five real successes. The most impressive and unqualified of these arose out of the SPAB campaign against the closure and sale of the City of London churches. Through the influence of members sitting in the Commons and the Lords, a clause was inserted in the Metropolitan and District Railways Bill (City Line and Extensions) of 1879 requiring the retention of Wren's St Mary-at-Hill and its churchyard.[78] In the case of Tisbury Church a destructive restoration was averted through the personal influence of a Society member who was a local landowner, the Hon. Percy Wyndham, MP, who managed to raise just enough discord between the restoration committee and its architect, Ewan Christian, for the project to be delayed several years, by which time a more sensitive scheme was carried out.[79] In 1881 a scheme for the restoration and reordering of New Romney Church in Kent, the work of Sir George Gilbert Scott and his son John Oldrid, was laid aside by the Church authorities when the Society threatened to publish the correspondence.[80] Then there were a number of cases which are hard to classify, cases where the architect was already in sympathy with the Society's views and therefore welcomed the opportunity to debate the finer points of a scheme. One such was George Rackstraw Crickmay, Diocesan Surveyor to the Archdeaconry of Dorset, who appears to have asked the Society to inspect his proposals for the repair of Studland Church and received, with one or two qualifications, Morris's blessing. George Gilbert Scott Jr. received the Society's advice on the best course of action to pursue at Knapton Church in Norfolk 'in a very friendly spirit', at least according to the SPAB *Annual Report* for 1882, though whether Scott was ever directly influenced by the Society is open to question. After 1883 the SPAB's track record is considerably more cheering, to devotees of the Society at any rate: in just two years, 1883 to 1885, the Society had played a role in the conservation of the Charterhouse in London, Llandanwg church near Harlech, the former Water Gate to York House near their new permanent offices in Buckingham Street, the York City churches, Inglesham church, Staple Inn in Holborn, and St Peter's Shaftesbury.

What, then, is to be made of the example set by the Society in its early tumultuous years, and what lessons, if any, does this story hold, either for the conservation movement in general or for the handful of amenity societies which can trace their origins more or less directly back to the SPAB? The answers are not straightforward, largely because the emergence of heritage planning legislation since 1947 has completely altered the conservation environment. Morris's attempt to define conservation as the province of the non-specialist, of the interested member of the public acting in the public's interest, has been recognised in law, so that now the amenity societies have a legal, not just a moral, right to speak. No-one sitting on the SPAB committee during Morris's lifetime entertained any serious hope of the sort of comprehensive statutory relief that is now central to the way conservation works in this country, although from time to time the SPAB did debate the merits of a system of State control as existed in France, with the Society's Liberals, principally James Bryce, putting the case for, and its avowed Conservatives, Leonard Courtney and Percy Wyndham, putting the case against, arguing in the same corner as anti-heritage

Tories do today. Morris was somewhere between, certainly not because he sided with Courtney and Wyndham but rather because he doubted the value of the State. In the socialist utopia he described in *News from Nowhere* (1890–1) old buildings have survived unaltered because public perceptions have changed in response to the death of capitalism; however, at the end of Morris's life, there are definite signs of change. In his last public address (31 January 1896) Morris came out strongly in favour of both the London County Council's first attempts to compile a register of historic buildings and an earlier draft Bill which gave local authorities the power to regulate the size and placement of advertisements.[81] And in the pragmatic world of day-to-day casework, the Society was certainly not averse to using the parliamentary system when the opportunity presented itself, that is, when particular legislation affected the fate of a building (St Mary-at-Hill and the Charterhouse being cases where this was done successfully), or in cases of a building being in the charge of the Office of Works, in theory a body accountable to the public through parliament (the Tower of London, 1882–3, and Westminster Hall, 1884–7, both of which ended badly for the SPAB). As for the one institution the SPAB had the most to do with, the Church of England, it can be argued that Morris's strongly secular line did nothing to ease the tensions that still exist between the conservation lobby and churchmen. The exemptions from heritage planning controls enjoyed by the Church of England until very recently are perhaps the most tangible, and pernicious, sign of this cultural divide. In technical matters, of course, the Society has had a tremendous impact, but this area of its history falls outside the remit of this chapter.

In unpicking the truths of the Society's influence from the fictions, one less well-defined but nevertheless substantial contribution can be identified, this one flowing from Morris's reputation and example. For he and the Society are the nearest things we in the movement have to a foundation myth. They function as twin totems, furnishing an otherwise diverse coalition with a common ancestry and sense of shared purpose. Furthermore, his much-reprinted letter to the *Athenaeum* and the SPAB manifesto, rash and ill-considered though they may have been in their original context, have become literary types. Fragments of them, their tone and feeling as much as any particular phrase, recur in campaigns for building types which Morris explicitly denounced in his own time. What would he think of the Georgian Group fighting to retain speculatively built early nineteenth-century terraced houses, buildings which for him epitomised the degraded state of the modern city, or of English Heritage recommending philanthropic housing from the 1860s and 1870s for statutory listing? And could he ever have imagined that the SPAB itself would argue for the retention of Victorian furnishings in St Helen's Church Bishopsgate, furnishings designed by one of its blackest foes, John Loughborough Pearson? Morris had a feeling for paradox, but I am not sure it was elastic enough to take in these ironies of fate.

3
Protecting the monuments: archaeological legislation from the 1882 Act to *PPG 16*

Timothy Champion

Archaeological monuments were the subject of some of the earliest conservation legislation in the United Kingdom. Yet in subsequent years they have, in general, provoked much less interest and debate than historic buildings; they have certainly generated much less litigation, and much less discussion in accounts of the development of the movement for the preservation of our cultural heritage. Few voluntary organisations, comparable to county naturalists' trusts or period architectural societies, have been founded to act either as owners or managers of such monuments or as pressure groups for their preservation. Even the National Trust, one of the major owners of archaeological sites, has acquired them mostly as part of estates valued for their natural beauty or historic houses rather than for the archaeology itself. Concern for the preservation of archaeological monuments has been primarily a matter of legislation and the development of good management practice among sympathetic owners.

Archaeological monuments attracted such early legislative attention precisely because they were not buildings in current use. As such, they were much less affected by issues concerning the rights of private property; they were also less likely to raise questions of alterations and repairs, and consequent problems of style, taste and cost. The first archaeological monuments to be given legal protection were prehistoric, and were mostly stone structures. Such a perception of the nature of archaeological remains has permeated all subsequent reformulations; as our understanding of the archaeological part of Britain's cultural heritage has developed, and as new threats to its preservation have arisen, so have various attempts been made to find an appropriate legislative response, but some of the key concepts are still rooted in the perceptions of the nineteenth century.

The origins of legislation

The Ancient Monuments Protection Act of 1882 is rightly recognised as a landmark in the history of conservation law.[1] It owed much to the persistent endeavours of Sir John Lubbock, later Lord Avebury, one of the leading archaeologists and anthropologists of the Victorian period, who had introduced a Bill on eight occasions from 1873 to 1880 without success. His proposal would have established a National Monuments Commission, which would have had the power to assume the guardianship of sites named in a schedule, or of any archaeological monument 'of like character'; where the owner of a monument wished to alter or demolish it, the Commission would have had a right of compulsory purchase. The sites in the schedule excluded historic houses in current use, and even ruins such as those of castles and abbeys, since these would have been too contentious; they were limited to prehistoric sites such as megalithic tombs, stone circles and earthworks. Even such a minimal proposal faced stiff opposition in parliament, based on the potential cost to the Treasury, the assertion of the rights of private property, suspicion of the role of archaeologists, reluctance to establish an independent commission with such compulsory powers, and rejection of the prehistoric monuments as of interest in the cultural heritage of the modern nation.

Lubbock had been trying to achieve too much, and the Bill promoted in 1882 by George Shaw Lefevre, which finally succeeded, was an even weaker compromise, permitting the State to take sites into guardianship with the agreement of the owner; in addition to sites specified on the schedule attached to the Act, the Commissioners of Works could also take into guardianship sites 'of like character'. The term 'monument' was not defined, nor were the grounds for the inclusion of specific sites on the schedule; these were left to professional archaeological judgement. Historic buildings and even medieval ruins were excluded, and the sites on the schedule demonstrate the current perception of prehistoric remains: megalithic tombs, stone circles, substantial earthworks. The mechanisms for affording protection to monuments were limited to two: guardianship and the threat of criminal prosecution for damaging a monument.

Although it was a comparatively feeble measure, it did lay the foundation for subsequent legislation, and in particular introduced some of the key features of all later provisions: it included a schedule of monuments selected for preservation, and established the principle of State guardianship and management of important sites. It also conceived of the evidence of the past in terms of 'monuments', envisaged as buildings or structures, which needed protection from demolition, alteration or addition, and these concepts have persisted through all later revisions of the law.

Despite the pre-eminent position given to the 1882 Act, it was not the first attempt to protect monuments or what we would now call archaeological evidence, but had precursors in both spirit and form. The early 1840s were years of acute concern for 'national monuments' and for archaeology in general, shown most clearly in the fashion for founding archaeological societies,[2] both local and national, many of which still survive. The introductory manifesto of the Archaeological Institute, which was founded in 1842 and by 1844 had split into the Archaeological Institute and the British Archaeological Association,[3] was written by its secretary, the archaeologist Albert Way:

> to preserve from demolition or decay works from ancient times which still exist, is an object that should merit the attention of the Government, not merely on account of their interest as specimens of art, but respect for the great Institutions of the country, sacred and secular, and a lively interest in

> their maintenance, must, as it is apprehended, be increased in proportion to the advance of an intelligent appreciation of monuments, which are tangible evidences of the gradual establishment of these Institutions.[4]

In 1845 a proposal was made in parliament for a Museum of National Antiquities and a Commission for the Conservation of National Monuments, but it failed to make any progress.[5] The British Museum was criticised for its failure to pay sufficient attention to British antiquities.[6]

These concerns should be seen in the context of the political disturbances of the 1840s, when there were widespread fears for the survival of the established institutions of royalty, aristocracy and Church, and when archaeology, particularly an archaeology which concentrated on the remains of the medieval period, was a means of reinforcing the values of those traditional institutions. As early as 1841 a Select Committee of the House of Commons had considered the question of national monuments, but the monuments with which they were primarily concerned were the memorials to distinguished people such as those in St Paul's Cathedral.[7] In the course of the evidence given to the committee, especially by the architectural writer and illustrator, John Britton, the idea that remains such as Roman villas and historic houses could also be monuments to the nation was explored. The nation that was to be celebrated was a royal and aristocratic one, but we can see at this time, in the very earliest days of archaeology, how the concept of a monument was being expanded from the memorials of the individual dead to include a wide range of structures.

Britton's evidence to the Select Committee[8] included a proposal for an institution or commission to protect national monuments, particularly historic buildings; he had in mind the model of the arrangements established in France in 1837, about which he was well informed. His proposal was not adopted in the Select Committee's report, but the first legislation soon followed. In 1845 the Portland Vase, one of the finest products of Roman glassmaking skills, was smashed in the British Museum; because of doubts over the legal status of museum objects, the perpetrator was convicted only of smashing the glass case.[9] A law was soon passed to rectify this anomaly. The Protection of Works of Art and Scientific and Literary Collections Act 1845 made it an offence to destroy or damage anything kept for the purposes of art, science or literature, or as an object of curiosity in a museum, or any picture, statue, monument or painted glass in any church or chapel, or any statue or monument exposed in a public place. Similar acts of vandalism to royal statues in London provoked the passing of the Public Statues Act 1854, which made the Commissioners of Works the guardians of public statues in London, as defined in a schedule of statues, and of any further statues they thought fit; it also made it an offence to damage any such statue.

This was precisely the structure of the 1882 Act, which inherited the concepts of schedule and guardianship. However, by 1882 the idea of a monument had developed to include the archaeological remains of the past, and the nation that was to be memorialised was no longer a traditional aristocratic one, but one rooted in progress. Ironically, Lubbock's archaeology, emphasising the evolution of human society, fitted very badly with ideas of preservation; the material culture of modern 'primitive' societies, regarded as the equivalent of Europe's prehistoric antecedents, was displayed in museums to emphasise how different it was from that of modern Europe. Why then should the remains of the distant past be thought worthy of preservation?

The expansion of protection

The eminent archaeologist, General Pitt-Rivers, was appointed as the first Inspector of Ancient Monuments under the 1882 Act, but progress in the acquisition of sites for State guardianship was slow.[10] Pitt-Rivers experienced endless frustrations in persuading owners to consent to guardianship and the Treasury to find money for simple protective measures such as fencing. By the time of his death in 1900, forty-three monuments had been taken into guardianship. No professional replacement was appointed, and the office of Inspector was vacant until 1910.

The Ancient Monuments Protection (Ireland) Act 1892 allowed the Commissioners of Works to assume guardianship, not just of monuments such as those in the 1882 schedule, but of any ancient or medieval structure, erection or monument whose preservation was a matter of public interest by reason of its historic, artistic or traditional interest. Although this opened the way to the guardianship of major medieval sites, the Act was still rooted in the concept of the monument as a single, upstanding structure. It also introduced another provision that has remained through all subsequent legislation: dwelling houses in use were excluded, and remained outside legal protection until the historic building provisions of planning law. The 1892 Act applied only in Ireland, but similar arrangements were made for the rest of the United Kingdom in the Ancient Monuments Protection Act 1900, which also gave county councils powers to act as guardians in a way similar to that of the Commissioners of Works.

O.W.—No. 67.

NOTICE.

Notice is hereby given that, under the provisions of the "Ancient Monuments Protection Act, 1882," the Commissioners of Her Majesty's Works and Public Buildings have been constituted by the Owner the guardians of this Monument, and that any person wilfully injuring or defacing the same will be Prosecuted according to Law.

REGINALD B. BRETT,
Secretary.

H.M. Office of Works, &c.,
12, Whitehall Place,
London.

SALISBURY AND SOUTH WILTSHIRE MUSEUM

Printed notice produced by the Office of Works to display at sites taken into guardianship under the 1882 Act.

The end of the nineteenth century was marked by a growing perception of the destruction of the past and by an increasing realisation of the need for a more soundly based record of the archaeological remains of Britain, if an effective strategy for preservation was to be devised. The Scottish archaeologist, David Murray, made a remarkably prescient plea for the institution of a comprehensive official survey of the antiquities of the United Kingdom as a prelude to a more systematic strategy of preservation.[11]

Some projects were put in hand to begin the process of recording. The Congress of Archaeological Societies[12] was founded in 1888, bringing together more than forty local societies. Its main aims were to co-ordinate research and to preserve ancient monuments and records. Among other initiatives, it distributed in 1894 proposals from the Society of Antiquaries of London for a survey of Britain by counties, and in 1895 it published the report of its subcommittee on a proposed photographic survey of England and Wales. In 1900 the Congress and the Society of Antiquaries of London established an Earthworks Committee, which initiated a programme of survey and recording, and also received reports of damage. The work of this committee was the formal recognition of a new awareness of the nature of the archaeological remains that survived in Britain; as well as the structures recognised in the schedule of the 1882 Act and in the 1900 Act, there still survived a wealth of lesser earthwork monuments, and indeed in places a veritable landscape of archaeological remains. While most investigation up to this time had been excavation, a new form of enquiry was being developed, based on survey of surface features, for which the name 'field archaeology' was invented.[13]

In 1908 three Royal Commissions on Historical Monuments began work in England, Wales and Scotland; their royal warrants included the brief 'to make an inventory of the ancient and historical monuments and constructions connected with or illustrative of the contemporary culture, civilization and condition of life of the people of England [Wales, Scotland] from the earliest times to the year 1700, and to specify those which seem most worthy of preservation'. By 1910 the first reports were being submitted, with inventories of sites and monuments and lists of sites recommended for preservation, both entitled 'schedules', a source of considerable confusion in the ensuing debates.[14]

British archaeologists also began to look abroad, and to compare our legislation unfavourably with that of other countries. In 1905, the art historian Professor Gerard Baldwin Brown published a detailed survey of international practice, with an implicit criticism of Britain.[15] Parliament was stimulated to act, and British ambassadors were required to report on the situation in their various foreign countries.[16] In 1912 there were no fewer than four Bills introduced into parliament to reform the ancient monuments law. A Joint Committee of the Commons and the Lords was set up, and its report[17] formed the basis for a revised Bill in 1913, which in due course became the Ancient Monuments Consolidation and Amendment Act 1913.

The Select Committee's members included Lord Sheffield, brother-in-law of General Pitt-Rivers, and G. F. Browne, the Bishop of Bristol, who had for five years held the Disney Chair of Archaeology in Cambridge and was an expert on the art and architecture of the Anglo-Saxon period. It took evidence from the Secretary of the Office of Works, the Inspector of Ancient Monuments, the secretaries of the three Royal Commissions, and others involved in archaeology and historic buildings. Its deliberations ranged widely, including the destruction of earthworks and the educational value of archaeological monuments; it spent much time considering ecclesiastical exemption, and it heard radical proposals such as the licensing of excavations and the protection of portable antiquities and sites of natural beauty. Many of these suggestions were too extreme for the proponents of legislative reform, who were aware that Lubbock had failed because he had tried to achieve too much in one step, and were destined not to be included in the Bill that made progress in 1913.

The 1913 Act has been unfairly neglected and deserves to be recognised as the measure that formed the basis for the effective modern system of protection. It established Ancient Monuments Boards to give expert advice to the Commissioners of Works, and introduced the system of preservation orders, by which sites in danger of destruction could be given greater protection; an order could be issued by the Commissioners where there was danger to a monument of destruction, damage or removal, and had the effect of preventing work on the site except by permission for a period of eighteen months, after which confirmation was required by a Bill in parliament. The Joint Committee had given some thought to the large number of sites which were not of such outstanding importance as to merit guardianship, and the 1913 Act instructed the Commissioners of Works to issue a list of monuments 'the preservation of which is of national importance'. Owners of such sites were required to give notice of their intention to demolish, remove, alter or add to such monuments; it was also an offence to damage such sites, though curiously the owner was exempt. This is in effect the origin of modern scheduling, for there was no intention that sites on this expanded list, which soon became known as a schedule, were included in order to be considered for guardianship, as was the case with the schedule of the 1882 Act; instead, their inclusion offered them protection through the requirement for notice of works and the threat of prosecution.

Once again, the law was framed in terms of a 'monument', although it also introduced a confusion that has dogged later legislation, since it provided definitions of the two terms 'monument' and 'ancient monument'. A monument was defined as 'any structure or erection', though ecclesiastical buildings in use were excluded. There was some difficulty in accommodating the sites in the 1882 schedule to this definition, since some of them were not obviously structures or erections, and there was also a desire to ensure that the new law reflected the current understanding of the nature of archaeology. As well as arguing for the inclusion of sites of natural beauty, Lord Sheffield was keen to see the Uffington White Horse included, although he considered it neither a structure nor an erection, but an excavation.[18] The Act therefore defined ancient monuments as those sites on the 1882 schedule and 'any other monuments or things which, in the opinion of the Commissioners of Works, are of a like character'. This phrasing caused some comment, not only because of the most unparliamentary term 'things', but also because of the interpretation of 'like character'. The Marquis of Salisbury enquired if the White Horse was 'like' anything on the 1882 schedule, and was assured by Lord Beauchamp that there were tumuli on the schedule, and they were earthworks, and the White Horse was an earthwork.[19] Similarly, in the Commons debate, it was asserted that Scottish carved stones, though not structures, were 'of like character', and could therefore be protected by scheduling.[20]

The much wider scope of the 1913 Act, and its more stringent powers, indicate a significantly different climate of opinion from 1882. The debate in the House of Lords brought out a few defences of private property, but as an interesting sign of the declining fortunes of the landed aristocracy, this was argued not so much on the grounds of the absolute right of the owner, but more because of the possible loss of sale value if the estate were subject to the restrictions of scheduling. For the most part, however, the debate was characterised by a recognition of the need to reform the law in favour of public interest. This is typified by the ringing words of Lord Curzon:

> The whole attitude of this country and of the civilized world in general has changed towards archaeology in recent years. We regard the national monuments to which this Bill refers as part of the heritage and history of the nation. They are part of the heritage of the nation, because every citizen feels an interest in them although he may not own them; and they are part of the history of the nation because they are documents just as valuable in reading the records of the past as is any manuscript or parchment deed to which you can refer. . . . I believe they [the owners] do generally recognise that they stand with regard to these monuments not merely in the position of private owners of property, but that they are owners of that which is, in a sense – a broad sense, I admit – a national possession, for which they are trustees to the nation at large.[21]

The almost total unanimity in parliament, and the support for restrictions on the rights of the private owner, could not have made a stronger contrast with Lubbock's tribulations. To quote Curzon in 1912 again:

> It is almost incredible, if one looks back at the Parliamentary history of that time, to find how much opposition was excited by that mild and inoffensive measure.[22]

What had happened since 1882 to bring about this dramatic change?

Archaeology itself had made great progress. The problem of survey had been addressed, and the true extent and nature of the archaeological record was beginning to be appreciated. The various archaeological survey projects, and in particular those of the three Royal Commissions, were starting to show positive results.

This work had helped to provide evidence for the true rate of damage to and loss of archaeological sites. The English Royal Commission's first surveys, of Hertfordshire and South Buckinghamshire, showed that less than 20 per cent of all monuments were in poor condition, but 50 per cent of all earthworks.[23] Albany Major, the secretary of the Earthworks Committee, giving evidence to the 1912 Joint Committee, provided details of the known cases of destruction in one year:

> Perhaps I might give the committee a list of some cases of the destruction of earthworks which have been reported to my Committee last year, and roughly the causes. There were three cases reported of damage by quarrying; three cases of earthworks being injured or destroyed in making golf links; and three cases of earthworks being built upon, or of threatened building; one case of damage by excursionists and picnic parties; one case of damage from farming operations; one case due to the improvement of a garden; one of unauthorised digging; one of digging for gravel; one of planting trees; two of chalk digging; one of tipping rubbish into the fosse of the earthworks; and one of digging sand.[24]

Spectacular threats also raised public awareness. In 1911, Tattershall Castle, Lincolnshire, a most important late medieval brick structure, had been acquired by an American syndicate who had removed some of the fireplaces and were widely believed to be about to demolish the whole building and ship it to America. Lord Curzon saved the situation by buying the castle and then rescuing the fireplaces, but the affair received wide public attention.[25] Similar stories also surrounded Stonehenge; the owner was believed to have demanded a high price from the State, otherwise he would sell it to America.[26]

In part, the change was also due to the work of energetic individuals. As well as Lord Curzon, much credit should be given to Charles Peers, who had been appointed Inspector of Ancient Monuments in 1910, filling a post left vacant since the death of Pitt-Rivers in 1900. Peers was a man of remarkable ability, who established the Inspectorate on a professional footing and secured it the necessary staff and expertise. He also realised that he would need increased legal powers and his annual reports made this case.

But perhaps the most important factor was a reorientation of ideas about the nation, and especially about the English nation. From the 1880s, there had been an increasing disenchantment with the supposed benefits of empire and industrial development, which came to be seen as a digression from the true nature of England as a tranquil, prosperous, rural, communal country; modern developments such as industrialisation were essentially foreign.[27] America in particular was regarded as the source of such evils, and the threat of the physical export of part of England's past would have had a special piquancy. This rural myth of England was portrayed in literature and painting, and sparked a revival of interest in folk song and dance, as well as an attempt to record the rural past before it finally disappeared. The concept of national heritage of monuments was now once more very different; to quote Lord Curzon again:

RCHME © CROWN COPYRIGHT

Tattershall Castle, Lincolnshire, photographed in 1857, showing its state before it was bought and restored by Lord Curzon.

> The last speaker raised the question of what a national monument is. I take it that the national monuments to which reference is made in this Bill are structural monuments which may be, on the one hand, old stone circles and remains, and on the other may be fabrics – and by fabrics I mean castles, the castellated structures that recall to us the traditions of the feudal times; the mansion houses, or great houses inhabited in many cases by the nobility; the manor houses which reproduce so much of the traditions and life of bygone times; and then descending the scale, the smaller buildings, whether they be bridges, market crosses, cottages, or even barns, which carry on their face the precious story of the past.[28]

The passing of the 1913 Act was not the end of the matter, however. In 1914 the six MPs who had formed the House of Commons side of the 1912 Joint Select Committee, dissatisfied with the extent to which the ideas discussed in the committee had been implemented in the Act, introduced another Bill 'in order to give greater security to all monuments of unquestioned national importance'.[29] It proposed that the Commissioners of Works should be given the power to schedule any monument, defined as 'any moveable or immoveable monument, in the widest sense of the word, whose preservation is desirable in the interests of the public on account of its importance in the history of the country, the history of civilisation, or the history of architecture or art, or on account of its aesthetic value', including 'any earthwork, excavation, structure or erection, as well as any natural object or site, any prehistoric or historic work of craftsmanship or art, made or apparently made or excavated in the United Kingdom, the preservation of which is a matter of public interest by reason of the historical, architectural, traditional, artistic, or archaeological interest attaching thereto'. Since this would greatly extend the scope of the Commissioners' powers, and the consequent burden of work imposed on them, the Bill proposed to facilitate their task by immediately scheduling all important monuments built before 1600 in certain classes, including cathedrals, monasteries, parish churches, chapels, other ecclesiastical buildings, castles, gates and bridges, city or town walls, guildhalls, civic halls, other buildings of national, historical or important local interest, whether ruinous or not, vessels (e.g. HMS *Victory*), sites of natural beauty or interest, sites for excavations, earthworks, prehistoric and historic monuments or other stones or other monuments (flint and other implements not necessarily included), and in addition all gold and silver plate or other precious or historic articles made before 1800 and belonging to corporate bodies. The Bill also proposed stronger powers in respect of scheduled sites or objects: permission would have been required for any export, or if anyone wished to injure, destroy, alter structurally or add to or part with possession of a monument (interiors of dwelling houses were to be exempt); local authorities would have been able to condemn any plans for new buildings or alterations that would 'blemish the historic or picturesque amenities'.

These proposals accurately reflected the concerns of the Select Committee, but such a drastic extension of the powers of the State, in excess of what has been achieved by all later laws put together, was clearly too much for parliament. In any case, by 1914 there were also other more pressing concerns and the Bill failed to make any progress.

The inter-war years

Both the myth and the reality of England as a rural nation were further threatened in the decades between the two World Wars, as roads, petrol stations, advertisements, electricity pylons and suburban sprawl eroded the tranquillity of the countryside.[30] The loss of the countryside and rural traditions was a theme that ran through much writing in the 1930s.[31] Public concern for the rural landscape culminated in the foundation of the Council for the Preservation of Rural England in 1926.

Archaeology also made significant advances. The development of aerial photography, pioneered in particular by O. G. S. Crawford,[32] revealed the extent of the evidence for human occupation in the past; much of the early work was concentrated on the uplands, especially the chalk downs of Wessex, and reinforced the idea of prehistoric settlement being largely confined to the hilltops. Crawford was appointed as Archaeology Officer to the Ordnance Survey in 1920, and began the systematic mapping of archaeological remains at a level of detail not hitherto attempted by the Royal Commissions.

Protection from the threats of modernisation was limited; planning laws were in their infancy, and local authorities were reluctant to implement even the restricted powers given to them by permissive legislation, such as the Advertisement Regulation Acts 1907 and 1925 and the Petroleum (Consolidation) Act 1923, which allowed them to make by-laws to control advertising and the construction of petrol stations, where these had a damaging impact on the amenities and aspect of historic sites and monuments.[33] The writer, Henry Williamson, visiting Stonehenge, lamented the spirit of materialism that allowed the proliferation on Salisbury Plain of advertisements for motor tyres, oblivious to the irony that he was travelling on his much loved Brooklands Road Special Norton motor cycle.[34] Crawford, who founded and edited the periodical *Antiquity*, wrote in an editorial in 1929:

> Conservation, not excavation, is the need of the day; conservation, not only of purely archaeological features, but of the amenities which give them more than half their charm. Who cares for Oldbury and St George's Hill now that they are infested with villas? . . .
>
> In most instances, nothing short of the purchase of the land is of the slightest use, though in others an intelligent application of the Town Planning Act may suffice. The need is really urgent; for with the approaching electrification of Southern England, the coniferous activities of the Woods and Forests Department and of private planters, the demands of the services, for land for aeroplanes and manoeuvres, the spread of bungaloid eruptions and the threat of arterial roads and ribbon development – with all these terrors imminent it is unlikely any open country or downland will be left in southern England in a hundred years time.[35]

The progress of scheduling was rapid after the First World War, and between 1923 and 1931 nearly 3,000 entries were added to the new schedule of monuments whose preservation was a matter of national importance. Nevertheless, a series of highly publicised incidents exposed the limitations of even these expanded powers.[36] The landscape around Stonehenge had been given over to military activity during the war, in particular to a military airfield, and large and visually intrusive buildings now marred the setting of the stones. Instead of being demolished when no longer required for military purposes, as expected, these buildings were returned to the former landowner in lieu of restoration, and became a pig farm. In 1927 there was a scare that the land would be sold for housing, and that the Stonehenge landscape would be forever blighted by suburbia. There were no powers to prevent the impact of such a development on the monument, but the public outcry prompted the Treasury into secret negotiations, in excess of any legal authority, to acquire

SALISBURY AND SOUTH WILTSHIRE MUSEUM

Stonehenge from the east in the 1920s, showing the hangars of the First World War airfield in the background, custodians' cottages in the centre and a café on the right, all removed after the National Trust acquired the land in 1929. Taken from a cutting from an unknown magazine.

options to purchase land around Stonehenge. With the options secured, a public appeal eventually allowed the land to be acquired for the National Trust, to be held safe from development. The process of removing the modern clutter from the Stonehenge landscape began with the demolition of the airfield buildings.

A similar threat to the setting of an equally important monument materialised in the form of quarrying next to Hadrian's Wall. The reality of this threat had already been reported to the 1912 Joint Select Committee, but the 1913 Act had not included any powers over large areas of landscape. The quarry-owner purchased options to exploit a very extensive area of whinstone, highly valued for road building, which would have intruded right up to the foot of the wall, and would have included the construction of a tower sixty feet high. Negotiations secured a voluntary agreement to limit the extent of the quarry, and lack of capital eventually halted the work, but the inadequacy of the existing powers had been exposed.

In the 1920s a wireless station had been proposed for the site of the neolithic causewayed enclosure at Windmill Hill, Wiltshire above the great henge site at Avebury. This was eventually forestalled in 1924, when Alexander Keiller, the marmalade millionaire, purchased the site, but there were continuing threats of development at the site of Avebury itself.

These cases, and in particular that of Hadrian's Wall, were the stimulus to yet another attempt to bring the legal powers of protection in line with contemporary understanding of the nature of the archaeological evidence and the extent of the threats to it. The Ancient Monuments Act 1931 simplified the procedures for making and confirming preservation orders, but, more importantly, it tried to address the problem of protecting large areas of archaeological importance and the setting of monuments, rather than just the individual monuments. It introduced the concept of a 'preservation scheme' which would operate within a 'controlled area'. The extent of such controls was considerable: there were powers to prohibit or restrict any building or other works, and alterations which would materially affect the external appearance of existing buildings; the position, height, size, design, materials, colour and screening of any building could be prescribed in detail; tree felling, quarrying or excavation could be prohibited. Penalties for transgression were severe, up to £20 per day, in addition to costs of restoration. Compensation was payable to those materially affected by such a designation.

The concept of preservation schemes was well intentioned, but in practice they proved very difficult to implement. The complexities of multiple ownerships and the potential costs of compensation made them an administrative nightmare. A scheme was proposed for Hadrian's Wall itself, but it did not come into force until 1943, and even then was limited to only the central section of the wall. It was the only such scheme ever to be confirmed. Another was begun for Avebury, but Keiller again stepped in to purchase much of the land, and the region's safety was secured for the time being by a combination of enlightened private ownership and a planning scheme prepared under the then new planning laws.[37]

By the outbreak of the Second World War there was a much greater appreciation of the nature and extent of the archaeological record of Britain, and of the rate at which attrition was occurring. Development was regarded as the main threat, and it was increasingly obvious that the too easily ignored system of prior notice and the complicated procedures for preservation orders were not adequate for the preservation of individual monuments; between 1913 and 1967 only twenty such orders were made.[38] In the case of archaeological landscapes, the concept of a 'controlled area' had been found ineffective. The response to destruction arising from development was found more and more in rescue excavation, and this was accentuated during the course of the war. There was an urgent need to take land for military construction purposes, especially airfields, but even in time of war the archaeology was not forgotten; emergency excavations had occasionally been undertaken in advance of development projects, but the first large-scale systematic programme of rescue was initiated on defence sites.[39]

Post-war redevelopment

The legacy of the war included not only the loss of many historic buildings, but a further threat to the archaeological remains of the historic towns that had sustained bomb damage and were now undergoing redevelopment. In Canterbury the rescue archaeology began even before the end of the war,[40] while in London the excavation of the Roman Temple of Mithras caught the public imagination and vividly demonstrated once more the archaeological potential of such urban areas.[41] The scale of the threat increased with the economic prosperity of the 1950s and 1960s, and the wave of urban redevelopment projects which so drastically altered the centres of many historic towns. An organised archaeological response was mounted in some cities, such as Winchester, Southampton and Oxford, but in many others there was little that could be done.[42]

There were also renewed development pressures outside the historic towns. The construction of motorways presented the first major linear threats to the countryside since the railway mania of the nineteenth century. Gravel-digging grew to unprecedented levels, and vast areas of the countryside were lost to new towns. The archaeological observations made in the course of these operations, and the continued application of survey techniques and in particular of aerial photography, showed more clearly than ever the extent of the archaeological evidence of Britain; much of it was not upstanding ruins, as envisaged by nineteenth-century perceptions, but huge areas of remains surviving as low earthworks or even as subsurface features. A survey of the extent of the archaeological evidence for human occupation of the river gravels was aptly titled *A Matter of Time*.[43] It showed clearly how much was now surviving only below ground, and thus undermined for ever the assumption that prehistoric people had lived on the uplands; the monuments had survived there only because of the lower levels of destruction from Roman and medieval ploughing. It also showed how fast this evidence was being lost.

This appreciation of the destructive force of earlier agriculture was matched by a growing awareness of the damage caused by modern farming and forestry. The rise of mechanisation and such practices as deep ploughing and drainage, coupled with the economic incentives offered by protective post-war agricultural policies and tax structures, even before Britain's entry into the European Common Market and the effects of the Common Agricultural Policy, turned agriculture into as serious a threat to rural archaeology as urban development was to the towns. The farmer was no longer the natural friend and protector of the rural environment.

Under these pressures the inadequacy of the existing legislation was cruelly exposed. The economic and social demands for urban renewal and new housing were powerful forces which easily outweighed the archaeological interests; only a small percentage of the now known archaeology was protected by inclusion in the schedule, preservation orders were too cumbersome and issued only with the greatest reluctance, and the prior notice arrangements were easily ignored. Prosecutions were few, and fines trivial. The Town and Country Planning Act of 1947 had created an entirely new environment for the control of development, but archaeological considerations were given little or no weight in the preparation of strategic plans or in specific development control decisions. In the countryside, matters were worse; agriculture and forestry fell outside the definition of development and were subject to no effective control at all.

The Historic Buildings and Ancient Monuments Act 1953 was mainly

CAMBRIDGE UNIVERSITY COLLECTION OF AIR PHOTOGRAPHS: COPYRIGHT RESERVED

Air photograph of cropmark sites at Mucking, Essex, including Middle Bronze Age field systems, a circular Late Bronze Age enclosure, Anglo-Saxon burials and settlements and other features; much of this area was subsequently excavated in advance of gravel quarrying.

concerned with provisions for historic buildings, but it also repealed the preservation order arrangements of 1913 and 1931, and introduced a revised system of 'interim preservation notices', 'preservation orders' and 'guardianship orders'. It also removed the anomaly by which owners could not be prosecuted for damaging scheduled sites.

The pressures of destruction came to a head in the late 1960s and early 1970s. The government initiated a consideration of rural archaeology and the Walsh Committee made its report on the management of field monuments in 1969.[44] The committee had gathered extensive evidence and the report documented in detail the destruction caused by agriculture: of 640 monuments in Wiltshire, 250 had been severely damaged or totally destroyed, and another 150 had suffered lesser damage. The report made a number of important recommendations, including the grading of monuments for levels of importance, the appointment of

Field Monument Wardens to conduct regular inspections, and the compilation of detailed local records of monuments for the information of planning authorities. When the Field Monuments Act 1972 was passed into law it contained only one of these proposals, although others, such as the wardens and the county sites and monuments records, were subsequently implemented; the Act introduced a system of 'acknowledgement payments' to landowners with scheduled monuments on their land. The payments were little more than token, but marked a significant change in the approach to preservation, with a new recognition of the importance of raising awareness among owners and the public, and of instituting good management for scheduled sites. But the destruction of unscheduled sites continued apace, and the only solution was the expensive one of emergency excavation.

The 1970s saw the continued destruction of important sites in urban development projects, a process documented by the Council for British Archaeology in 1972 in their publication, *The Erosion of History*.[45] In 1972–3 there was a series of spectacular cases and the by now increasingly well-organised archaeological pressure groups had realised the power of publicity.[46] In 1972 the important site of Baynard's Castle in the southwestern corner of the medieval city of London was destroyed with limited excavation and a blaze of publicity in the national press. More embarrassing still was the construction in 1973 of a new underground car park for the House of Commons, which resulted in the unrecorded destruction of a large part of the Palace of Westminster, contrary to the policy of archaeological investigation which the government was trying to promote. The response to such drastic losses of important remains was to make available increased finance for rescue excavation, and archaeological activity in the 1970s was characterised above all else by large-scale rescue excavations. The additional resources allocated to archaeology would never be sufficient to meet the needs of all development projects, and the massive excavations undertaken in some towns soon posed the problem of post-excavation analysis and publication, which presented still further financial demands.

Attention was also given to the need for reform of the law, and there was a considerable measure of agreement in parliament for new proposals which eventually became law as the Ancient Monuments and Archaeological Areas Act 1979, on the last afternoon of the expiring Labour government. The Bill had received lengthy debate in the Lords, preceded by extensive consultation. The debates were marked by the enthusiastic support of all parties and firm agreement that something needed to be done to counter the destructive effects of redevelopment. The Act contained two major innovations. The protection afforded to sites included in the schedule was increased by the scrapping of the system of preservation orders and prior notice, and the institution of a system of consent similar to that in force for listed buildings protected under planning law, but decided at national rather than local level.

Part II of the 1979 Act was an attempt to deal with the problem of the historic towns, where the archaeologically significant layers could be very extensive and the severe restrictions imposed by scheduling would be incompatible with the need for urban renewal. Instead, the Act introduced the idea of an 'archaeological area'; where such an area was designated, developers would be required to give notice of their intentions and to allow access for archaeologists. While this overcame one problem, the reluctance of some developers and contractors to allow any access for archaeological observation or recording, it still suffered from the weakness of the prior notice arrangements which the Act had abolished for scheduled sites: it made no provision for what should, rather than what could, happen in the interim period, and in particular it made no provision for the resources needed to carry out recording, let alone full excavation and publication. In the end, only five archaeological areas were designated, an indication that few towns thought that the system offered any serious solution to the problem.

Part III of the Act responded to yet another new threat to archaeological sites that had emerged in the 1970s, and made it illegal for anyone to use a metal detector on a scheduled site without consent.

Despite the enhancement of the consequences of scheduling by the introduction of the need for scheduled monument consent, the major flaws of such an approach to protection still existed. In the first place, the schedule is a selective list of sites of national importance, and only a small percentage of the known sites of Britain can be protected in this way. It is of course impossible, as well as politically unacceptable, to try to preserve everything of archaeological interest, however slight, and some system of compromise and balance of interests is therefore required. However, scheduling is a very severe restriction on the rights of the owner, and reliance solely on such a schedule as the only means of protection will inevitably tip the balance too far in favour of development and against preservation, since much will remain outside its powers.

Secondly, the protection was offered to archaeology in terms of 'monuments', an idea inherited directly from the 1882 Act; however, both in the historic towns and in the countryside there had been a growing realisation that such a characterisation of the archaeological record as comprising discrete sites was far removed from reality. Scheduling could do little for the problem of either historic towns or rural landscapes. The concept of a 'monument', still defined in the 1979 Act as a 'building, structure or work' but with the addition of 'a cave or excavation', was proving to be an increasingly irrelevant way of characterising the nature of the archaeological evidence as it was understood by modern research. In the debates on the Act, Lord Avebury, the grandson of the nineteenth-century archaeologist, attempted to widen the scope of protection to include 'any area of archaeological importance', specifying in particular wet sites with palaeoenvironmental data, flint scatters, and ridge and furrow ploughing as types of site that fall outside the definition of 'work', but this was firmly rejected by the government as setting virtually no limit at all to the possibility of scheduling.[47]

Thirdly, scheduling was not well adapted to the processes of development control; a scheduled site could be given appropriate consideration in the determination of a planning application, but if, as often happened, the true nature

FULGONI PHOTOGRAPHY, LONDON

Dame Peggy Ashcroft at the site of the Rose Theatre excavations, May 1989, in a demonstration by the acting profession to save the remains of the theatre.

of the archaeological remains in a particular development site only became known after permission had been given, scheduling the site would require the payment of compensation, and hence such a step would only rarely be taken.

The idea that scheduling, though valuable in some cases, was not the only, and not necessarily the most appropriate, way of protecting archaeological sites began to gain acceptance in the 1980s, and some planning authorities began to give greater weight to archaeological evidence in the discussions that took place before the determination of planning applications rather than afterwards. This critically important change in practice culminated in the issuing in England and Wales of *Planning Policy Guidance Note 16, Archaeology and Planning* (*PPG 16*), in November 1990, followed shortly afterwards by similar documents in Scotland, *National Planning Policy Guideline: Archaeology and Planning*, and an accompanying planning advice note. By then, the need for a change of practice had been highlighted by yet another spectacular case which achieved wide publicity in the press. In 1989, redevelopment of an office block in Southwark revealed the foundations of the early seventeenth-century Rose Theatre, where Shakespeare's plays had been performed. The remains, though structurally rather unimpressive, had an enormous appeal for the acting profession and for the public in general, as an emotive reminder of a key part of our cultural heritage.[48] The costs of scheduling the site and preventing the development would have been impossibly high, and in the end the remains were, by agreement between the developer and English Heritage, partly excavated and then reburied under the building. The Rose Theatre demonstrated in the clearest possible way what had already been appreciated by some archaeologists, that the best strategy for protection of archaeology from development required good knowledge of the likely nature and importance of the remains before any decisions were taken. The accompanying publicity also demonstrated the need for political action.

PPG 16 and its Scottish equivalent represent the most important innovation in archaeological protection since 1913. They embody a switch from reliance on specifically archaeological protection laws, to the use of the planning laws to give proper consideration to the value of the archaeological remains when weighed against the merits of development. They assert that archaeological remains (a much more general term than the restrictive 'monument' as used in the 1979 Act) are a material consideration in the planning process, and that, where it is a question of archaeological remains of national importance, whether specifically scheduled or not, there should be a presumption in favour of their physical preservation *in situ*. In order to allow proper consideration of the merits of the archaeological remains, the developer may be required to present adequate evidence of the nature of the archaeology, and that in turn may necessitate the prior assessment of the archaeological potential of the development site by competent archaeologists.

The adoption of the principles of *PPG 16*, and familiarity with its requirements, have produced a major change in the nature of archaeological activity. Large-scale rescue excavations are progressively becoming a thing of the past, as sites with important archaeological remains are protected from development; where there are remains of less importance or scale, excavation may still be an appropriate solution to allow the development to continue. The critical importance of good prior knowledge has led to the development of better techniques for cost-effective assessment of the archaeological potential of a site.

Thus, in just over a century, the legal protection of monuments has developed from a permissive measure for assuming guardianship to a complicated structure involving both special ancient monuments legislation and the incorporation of archaeological remains into the planning system. It has responded to changing threats and the growing perception of the nature and extent of the archaeological evidence, but is still rooted in its nineteenth-century origins.

4
London government: a record of custodianship

John Earl

The sheer extent and density of the built fabric of the capital city and the pressures for change combined to make London, first, a pioneer in the field of conservation, and thereafter a test bed for each stage of development. The record cannot be represented as being entirely free of disappointment and defeat, but for ninety years London consistently set the pace and provided an example and an inspiration for others to follow.[1]

Professor Gerard Baldwin Brown wrote in 1905 that there could be no action to preserve monuments 'unless there be in the mind of the people a certain force of intelligent belief' in the need for it. But public opinion, he said, 'is in its very nature an unorganised force, acting spasmodically upon stimulus provided by some striking event or by the initiative of individuals who can magnetise their fellows'. He concluded from this that 'what is needed is some permanent agency representing the public mind at its best and always kept in working order'.[2]

In London the role of 'permanent agency representing the public mind at its best' was filled from 1889 to 1986 by its democratically elected governing body, first by the London County Council (LCC) then, from 1965, by the Greater London Council (GLC). For most of that time the two councils attempted to lead rather than simply follow public opinion and they achieved national recognition for their expertise and vision. Since 1986 London has had no such leadership, no unifying elected authority and no unified voice on conservation or any other matter of metropolitan concern.

The prerequisites for successful action to conserve are the same for a city or a region as they are for an individual historic building, namely:

1. A detailed knowledge of what exists, requiring investigation of its history, architectural and structural characteristics and condition, and
2. access to the specialised skills needed to deal with necessary works of sensitive repair and replacement and (where relevant) adaptation for modern practical needs.

In the case of public authorities charged with the protection of whole populations of buildings, it is necessary to add:

3. The ability and the will to use the available statutory controls and sanctions for the benefit of the public.

The third of these is commonly seen as the sole contribution to be made by local government bodies, but however firm may be their resolve in exercising control, their moral authority is open to challenge if they have little or nothing to show in the way of achievement in the other two areas.

London's governing bodies acquired notable skill and experience in all these fields. The pioneering work of the LCC before 1900 was followed by fifty years of development and refinement. By the mid-1950s an administrative apparatus had evolved in which the various professions involved in recording, research, inventorisation, physical care and statutory control of historic buildings worked in daily contact, each activity informing and enriching the others.

This was the culmination of a long evolutionary process. The London County Council of 1889 had to make a standing start. There was no established model to follow and next to nothing in the way of general legislation for the protection of historic buildings; the Ancient Monuments Protection Act of 1882 was an extremely limited measure, of little relevance in this context.[3] But the Council was, almost from the beginning, committed to protecting London's architectural inheritance. Before the end of the century, it had begun to take historic buildings into direct custodianship and was promoting architectural historical research, not for its own sake, 'as a paper record',[4] but with the preservation of buildings specifically in view.

Public works and public unease

Before looking more closely at the LCC's first attempts to preserve the visible evidence of London's past, it will be useful to glance back at what had been happening in the preceding forty or fifty years.

Preservation movements commonly make progress following the shock of some single traumatic act of destruction (the Abbey of Cluny, the Euston Arch, New York's Pennsylvania Station) or from popular reaction to a surfeit of change. Through the first half of the nineteenth century London was changing, as it had in the past, largely and rapidly by addition. New cuts through the old fabric occurred from time to time (Regent Street, 1813–35; King William Street, 1829–35; and Trafalgar Square, 1830–40) but the pace of renewal was far from overwhelming until the mid-1860s when the road system of the metropolis underwent radical reconstruction.

Intelligent plans for providing London with a comprehensive network of new thoroughfares had been published by John Gwynn as early as 1766[5] but, save for the Crown lands, there was no readily available administrative and financial apparatus to turn such ambitious plans into reality. It was not until the creation of the Metropolitan Board of Works in 1855, followed by the London County Council in 1889, that the rate of restructuring accelerated and many of Gwynn's proposals, or closely similar ones, were put into effect. Interestingly, Gwynn was one of the first architect planners – the modern term seems wholly appropriate – to make a plea for the preservation of a building (Henry VII's Chapel) intact and unaltered, in terms that modern conservators might be happy to adopt as their own.[6]

Between 1855 and 1888 the Metropolitan Board of Works (MBW) changed the face of London. Among more than fifty major engineering works, it created Clerkenwell Road, Northumberland Avenue, Charing Cross Road, Shaftesbury Avenue, Southwark Street, the western extension of Commercial Road and the Victoria, Albert and Chelsea Embankments. During the same period the City Corporation was responsible for the new Smithfield Market and its approaches, Holborn Viaduct, Queen Victoria Street and the City end of the Thames Embankment. It is difficult today to imagine London without these principal structural elements, but there is no doubt that in some places the new cuts destroyed great tracts of old fabric which would now be highly valued.

Concerns were voiced in parliament and the press in the 1870s over the loss of landmarks like Northumberland House and Temple Bar, but a more general reaction against the ruthless progress of the road engineers was slow to manifest itself. The emergence of a Society for Photographing Relics of Old London in 1875 was a sign of growing concern about the rate of loss (not only in the path of road works), but the recording work the Society did and the representations it made in its twelve years of existence lacked the backing of a well-organised, broad movement.[7] Those who wished to see historically important buildings preserved, other than for the protection of vested interests, spoke out from time to time but they had yet to find a unified voice.

In this connection, it is interesting to read the words of Percy Edwards, clerk of the Improvements Committee, in an early LCC publication:

> It has been said that street improvements do not always confer benefits upon the community and in support of this it has been alleged that too frequently the line for a new street has been laid irrespective of any buildings of historic interest or old public gardens which have stood in the way. But this charge cannot with justice be made against either the Metropolitan Board or the London County Council.[8]

Percy Edwards's defence must, of course, be read in the light of contemporary ideas of what constituted a building of historic interest. A report of 1866 on street improvements in the City had noted that the widening of London Bridge 'could only be carried out to the utter destruction of one of the finest bridges in Europe' (an interesting assessment, in the light of what was to happen in the 1960s) but went on to remark that 'the chief obstacles (to improvement) were the churches . . . Where they were allowed to remain . . . the thoroughfares have been thoroughly spoiled'.[9]

In 1866 it was possible to dismiss Wren's churches as impediments to free traffic movement. Thirty years later, Edwards felt that he had to offer some sort of explanation – hardly an apology –for the demolition of Northumberland House by the MBW. He noted that it was 'the last relic of the palatial residences of the nobility which formerly skirted the banks of the river' but said 'there was little to recommend its preservation [since] it could not boast of

JOHN EARL

York Water Gate (Balthasar Gerbier, 1626). The first building acquired specifically for preservation by the LCC in 1893. Restored 1961.

any great antiquity, its existence dating from the reign of James I'. Eighteenth-century and later remodelling was dismissed as modern and unworthy. Part of the Glass Drawing Room by Robert Adam was later reassembled in the Victoria and Albert Museum but Edwards thought that few would regret the old building having given way in 1874 to 'a necessary and handsome public thoroughfare'.[10]

A shift in the climate of opinion was discernible before this 'handsome thoroughfare' was lined with new buildings. The Society for the Protection of Ancient Buildings (SPAB) had emerged in 1877 as the first organised body campaigning for building conservation in a modern sense. Its manifesto plea for the protection of 'buildings of all kinds and styles'[11] suggests today an all-embracing policy which was not intended and would, indeed, have been impossible to comprehend at the time but, from the beginning, the society took an interest in the lesser as well as the greater. One of its early forays was against the MBW. It concerned a pocket monument, the York Water Gate, which had been left isolated, well away from the river, by the building of the Victoria Embankment – and which just happened to be visible from the Society's offices in Buckingham Street.

The Water Gate, executed by Nicholas Stone, probably from designs by Balthasar Gerbier, was erected in 1626 as the river entrance to York House. The house had been demolished in the 1670s and, by the time the embankment was created, the ownership of the gate was in doubt. The MBW had a mind to take it down and re-erect it. The first thought was that it should ornament the embankment wall, but this idea gave way to a proposal to raise it up to the new general ground level and make it serve as a gateway to the gardens being laid out over the reclaimed foreshore.

William Morris, the first Secretary of the SPAB, wrote to the MBW in 1879, expressing deep regret at this 'unnecessary, mischievous and damaging' proposal which 'in the opinion of this Society is worse than useless'. It would be desirable, he said, 'if the Gate passed into the possession of your honourable Board'. He urged the Board to leave it where it had always been, build a retaining wall around it and carry out essential repairs without 'restoration' (a highly emotionally charged word at that time).[12]

The Board gave way in the face of this pressure and left the Water Gate in a hollow in the Victoria Embankment gardens. But the unelected MBW was essentially an agency of change, narrowly focused on the tasks before it. It was ill designed to act as the kind of protector the SPAB was looking for, and, having done the bare minimum of works to keep the building in existence (to that extent, but with quite different intent, complying with the Society's exhortations to avoid unnecessary interference) it saw no reason why it should become the owner and permanent custodian of the monument. That had to await the arrival of an elected and altogether more flexible body.

First steps: the LCC and the Survey Committee

In 1889 a county of 117 square miles was created to give the people of London their first unified and directly elected authority. It did not enjoy an immediately favourable press, but the need for it was urgent and its early achievements were obvious to all but the most politically prejudiced.

The new LCC had two immediate advantages in what were to prove, from the viewpoint of preservation, pioneering years. One of its most prominent members was Sir John Lubbock (Lord Avebury), who was behind the Ancient Monuments Act that was steered through parliament in 1882. He was chairman of the LCC from 1890 to 1892. Among the officials, G. Laurence Gomme (1853–1916), a respected antiquary, was the statistical officer. He later became clerk to the Council.

Two key decisions were taken in the first decade of the Council's existence. In January 1896 Lubbock proposed and the Council resolved that the General Purposes Committee should be charged with recommending action in the case of the threatened destruction of a historic building.[13] The following year the Parliamentary Committee was instructed to insert a clause into a Council Bill, to enable the Council to purchase buildings or places of historic interest.

The immediate effect of the first decision was that the General Purposes Committee identified the need for an inventory or register of historic buildings to enable it to fulfil its duties effectively, since 'frequently it was only realised that a building was of historic interest when that building was in danger of being removed'.[14] The committee reported to Council in February 1897 that it had

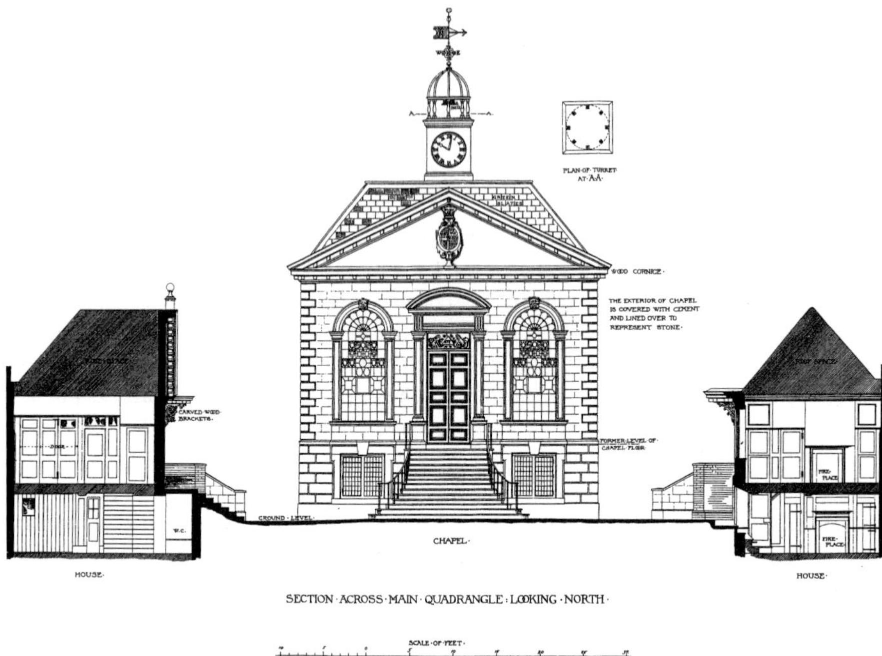

Trinity Almshouses, Mile End Road (William Ogbourne, 1695). Measured drawing by Ernest Godman for the first *Survey of London* monograph, 1896.

appointed a subcommittee to deal with the matter and in December a conference took place at the County Hall (then in Spring Gardens) to determine the best procedure. It was attended by representatives from the National Trust, the Society of Antiquaries, the Society of Arts, the London Topographical Society, the Royal Institute of British Architects, the Surveyors' Institution and a number of other learned bodies.

The voluntary Committee for the Survey of the Memorials of Greater London, which had been formed in 1894, came well to the fore at the conference as the only body which had actually embarked on the compilation of a register. Its chairman C. R. Ashbee (1863–1942) had led the victorious campaign to prevent the demolition of Trinity Almshouses, Stepney, in 1896. The committee's monograph on the Almshouses, their first publication, had been a rushed job, designed to mobilise opinion. It was scantily researched – in fact, hardly researched at all – but superbly produced by the Essex House Guild of Handicraft, and illustrated with measured drawings and lithographic plates. It immediately set a new standard for architectural recording and presentation.[15]

When the General Purposes Committee reported back to the Council it recommended that the Survey Committee should be asked to continue its work (up to that time limited to the East End and neighbouring out-county areas) and that similar registers should be compiled for the rest of London. The Survey Committee, for its part, offered 'to hand over the results of its labours so far as they related to London' if the Council would print the register. In July 1897 the Council voted money for this purpose.[16]

The Survey Committee was optimistic. Ashbee wrote: 'I believe . . . that if a time limit of ten years were set and a sum of say £10,000 placed at the Committee's disposal . . . the London County Council could have on its shelves at the close of this period a complete historical survey of London . . .'.[17]

The first of the regular series of parish volumes of the *Survey of London* was published by the Council in 1900 and the second in 1909, establishing a partnership with the Survey Committee which was to continue for more than fifty years. From 1910, the Council and the Survey Committee carried out the research and made the measured record drawings for alternate volumes, all of them being printed and published by the Council.

Both the range and the purpose of the *Survey* were to change over the years in ways that Ashbee could never have foreseen, but its early works provided exemplars for action on a national scale. By the time the Royal Commissions on Historical Monuments started on their own painfully slow recording work, the first *Survey of London* parish volumes and a series of eight monographs had already been published.

The *Survey* was a remarkable enterprise but time was to show that the 'paper record' could never, in itself, constitute an effective preservation tool. The rate of destruction in London at the turn of the century was unprecedented. In the introduction to volume 1 of the *Survey* (1900) C. R. Ashbee recorded the loss 'during the last six years' of most of Adam Street, the Adelphi, the Haymarket Colonnades, Bromley Palace (recorded in the volume; it had been demolished by the London School Board), Clement's Inn, Emanuel Hospital, the Cock Tavern in Fleet Street, Coopers' Almshouses, Skinners' Almshouses and many other buildings of note. On rare occasions, some external authority could be persuaded by the force of public argument to use its own powers to block destruction (the Charity Commissioners in the case of Trinity Almshouses, 1896) or an owner might be prevailed upon to have second thoughts (as happened with Eastbury Manor, 1917) or to give way to the extent that something could be salvaged from the wreckage (Crosby Hall, 1908) but those cases were exceptional.

The 1896 direction to the General Purposes Committee, that it should report to the Council recommending action when an historic building was threatened with destruction promised, in fact, more than it could readily deliver. The only real option in most cases was acquisition by agreement (and here the Council's record was to prove exceptional) or acceptance that the most that could be done was to make a record before demolition took place. Even this required the owner's co-operation.

Two noteworthy cases – a threat to Christ's Hospital in 1901 and a proposal in 1919 to demolish nineteen City churches – highlighted the fact that there was, as yet, no general power of intervention to prevent such acts of destruction, and this remained true long after the First World War. Christ's Hospital was demolished in 1902. Most of the threatened churches survived (some of them to be destroyed later in the Blitz) but the Council's sole weapon in that case had to be public opinion, informed by the publication of an excellent illustrated report by the Clerk and the Architect (actually the work of W. W. Braines and C. J. T. Dadd of those departments).[18]

An activity equally backed by scholarly research, but which might have been expected to have more immediate popular appeal, commenced in 1901 when it was resolved that 'the work of indicating houses of historical interest . . . be undertaken by the Council'. The Royal Society of Arts had, since 1867, been fixing commemorative Minton tablets to identify the homes of famous people, and a few of these can still be seen, but its work had been slow and inconsistent. Only thirty-six tablets were fixed in thirty-three years. Over a period of sixty-five years the LCC erected 331, most of the later ones in the form of the familiar (and now widely copied) 'blue plaques'. The LCC's work was continued by the GLC and, since 1986, has been taken up by English Heritage.

It is an interesting reflection on the contemporary climate of what Baldwin Brown called 'intelligent belief' (or, rather, in this case, the lack of it) that such a seemingly non-controversial activity should run into opposition. The original motion proposing the scheme was carried by only two votes. Objections also came later from a number of householders who, when asked to allow inspections in connection with the compilation of the register or the erection of a tablet refused, protesting that the rates should not be used for such purposes.[19]

An example of an LCC blue plaque, as reproduced in the LCC's *Indication of Houses of Historical Interest in London*, vol. 1, 2nd edn (London: J. M. Dent for the LCC, 1915), p. 37.

Preservation by acquisition

In 1893, four years before the County Hall conference, the LCC became the first local authority to obtain a specific statutory power to preserve a monument (it was the York Water Gate) by acquisition. Even earlier than this, the Council had come into the possession of buildings which would now be considered to be of special architectural or historic interest, but at first this occurred almost casually. The immediate intention of, for example, the relevant sections of the London County Council (General Powers) Act 1890 was the preservation of open land at Waterlow Park, Brockwell Park and the old pleasure gardens at North Woolwich. The importance of preserving public open space for the enjoyment of Londoners was then more readily accepted than the need to preserve historic buildings. Lauderdale House, included in Sir Sydney Waterlow's gift, was recognised as a fairly remarkable survival, but Brockwell Hall (by D. R. Roper, 1813) would not in 1890 have excited notice in its own right.

The York Water Gate acquisition was, in much the same way, embedded in a measure mainly concerned with other matters (the London Open Spaces Act 1893) but the intention of preserving a building by taking it into custodianship was, on this occasion, spelt out clearly. The Gate, described in the preamble to the Act as 'an object of public interest . . . in danger of . . . falling into decay', was vested in the LCC to preserve and maintain it 'in its present position', bringing to a conclusion the earlier unfinished business between Morris and the Metropolitan Board of Works.

The Council's Improvements Act in the following year brought into ownership Lincoln's Inn Fields (as a public open space) and Highgate Archway, but in neither case were precious buildings seen to be at issue. The Archway was, in fact, acquired to clear the way for Alexander Binnie's (now listed) replacement viaduct, a John Nash structure of 1812 being, as yet, well outside the range of buildings which could even be discussed as candidates for preservation.

The important milestone was the LCC General Powers Act of 1898. This gave the Council power 'to purchase by agreement buildings and places of historical or architectural interest or works of art or to undertake or contribute towards the cost of preserving, maintaining and managing any such buildings and places'. Gomme commented: 'It is pleasing . . . to record that the London County Council has set an excellent example of public influence in the preservation of historic buildings by obtaining parliamentary sanction to spend money for this purpose. By this means it is to be hoped that what little still exists will be allowed to remain and . . . that the economics of preservation may be carefully considered before destruction is decided upon'.[20]

The new power, although unlikely to be used frequently, was a vitally important addition to the Council's armoury. The first building acquired in this way was No. 17 Fleet Street, known as Prince Henry's Room,[21] purchased for £20,000 in 1900. (Its subsequent restoration is considered later in this chapter.) Other important early acquisitions included Marble Hill House (1902 and, at that time, outside the LCC area)[22] and the Geffrye Almshouses (1908).[23] In both cases the Council was under pressure to save open land from development, but the buildings were retained and treated with sensitivity. Soon after the acquisition of Marble Hill there was a public outcry about the demolition of the fifteenth-century Crosby Hall in the City. The purchase of a prime site in the centre of the banking area was too costly to contemplate, but the owners agreed to store the materials and the Hall was re-erected in 1908 in

GREATER LONDON RECORD OFFICE

Royal Watermen's Asylum, Penge (George Porter, 1841). They were saved from redevelopment by the GLC's purchase for housing purposes in 1970 and adapted and restored by the Historic Buildings Division.

Chelsea (by Walter Godfrey, as part of a hostel).[24]

Acquisition for preservation continued into the postwar years with bomb-damaged buildings like Trinity Almshouses, Stepney (the great survivor from Ashbee's pioneering campaign) and the tower of St John of Wapping. By 1975, ten years after the creation of the Greater London Council, the number of listed and unlisted buildings of special architectural or historical interest in direct ownership, inherited from the Metropolitan Board of Works or the LCC or acquired by the GLC itself, stood at just under 1,000.[25] Some had come into ownership in the course of projected public works involving major land transactions, for example Lindsey House (creation of Kingsway, 1900–5) and the Lyceum Theatre (proposed new approach to Waterloo Bridge, 1939). Others had been acquired in postwar years, to meet housing or educational needs, especially in the 1960s and '70s for housing rehabilitation projects. Others again, like a number of early Fire Brigade stations, housing developments and Board Schools, had been built by the LCC itself or by the London School Board. As late as the 1960s and '70s endangered buildings, like Wilton's Music Hall and the Royal Watermen's Asylum, Penge[26] were still being acquired.

The LCC's historic buildings officers

A separate cadre of officers dealing exclusively with the Council's research and architectural work on historic buildings did not emerge until well into the twentieth century but, from the beginning, the expertise of individual officers in the Clerk's and Architect's Departments could be called on when required. Gomme's department, for example, had a historian of distinction in W. W. Braines, who is credited in some of the first Council publications. Braines researched the LCC volumes of the *Survey of London* up to volume 16 (1935) and in 1921 he wrote a slim but authoritative pamphlet on *The Site of the Globe*

Playhouse, Southwark. The accuracy of his work on the location of the Globe (a matter much disputed at the time) has been demonstrated recently by archaeological excavation.[27]

It is more difficult to identify Architect's Department officers, owing to a convention that all drawings had to be signed by or for the Architect to the Council himself and only initialled, if so much, by the executant. However, the fact that the Department included architects like Reginald Minton Taylor, Charles Canning Winmill and their young colleagues, devoted to the values of the Arts and Crafts movement, some of them early members of the Society for the Protection of Ancient Buildings (Winmill was a committee member from 1898), meant that any work to old buildings was likely to be in sensitive hands.[28]

In 1901 with a new and massive wave of reconstruction gathering momentum, the increasing weight of the Council's historic buildings responsibilities led to the creation of a Historical Records and Buildings Committee, to deal with matters arising from the 1898 Act and the Ancient Monuments Act of 1900. It took over the Council's library and records and the then new commemorative plaque project. It was also responsible for all historical publications.

A small but significant advance occurred as a result of the laying out of Kingsway. The line for the new highway cut across Great Queen Street, 'the first regular street in London' and threatened to shave off the west side of Lincoln's Inn Fields. The need for such a link between the Strand and Holborn had exercised minds long before the existence of the Metropolitan Board of Works. The Board itself having failed to win parliamentary sanction for the enormously costly project, it had been taken up by the LCC. In 1896 the Improvements Committee presented a number of alternative schemes to Council, one of which (incorporating suggestions from the Royal Institute of British Architects (RIBA) but not at the time recommended as the best option) closely resembled the Kingsway as it was eventually built.[29] Even then, only slow progress could be made, and the new road was not actually opened until 1905.

The 1896 report was concerned entirely with the effectiveness and cost of the various ways in which traffic needs might be met and, as a subtext, the desirability of clearing away old and insanitary property. The effects on views of St Mary le Strand and St Clement Danes were noted, but only in passing.[30] By the time the proposal was in its final planning stages, however, the LCC was publicly committed to a protective attitude toward historic buildings.

In the course of debate and inter-departmental argument it was pointed out that the Council had announced that work was in progress on a *Survey of London* volume for Lincoln's Inn Fields and it would be placed in an invidious position if a footnote had to be added to say that 'the Council had decided that Lindsey House should be destroyed to make room for a building of greater commercial value'.[31] In the event, preservation of all the buildings on the west side of the Fields was decided upon and Gomme was able in his preface to the volume, published in 1912, to rehearse the Council's record and policies without fear of challenge.[32]

JOHN EARL

No. 17 Fleet Street (Prince Henry's Room), a tavern of 1611 incorporating the Inner Temple Gateway. The current appearance results from the first major restoration carried out by the LCC, completed in 1905–6.

The beginnings of what was to become the Historic Buildings Section (and, later, the GLC's Historic Buildings Division) are traceable to this test of resolve. A full-time officer was appointed to the Architect's Department to make and keep architectural records, record archaeological finds and be the point of contact with the voluntary *Survey of London* committee. The Historic Records Section, as it became, had at first no fixed establishment. Officers with the required skills were seconded to it as the need arose (mainly for the preparation of measured drawings for *Survey of London* volumes and other historical publications) and then moved back to their former offices when the work was done.

At about this same time another part of the Architect's Department was carrying out the Council's first major work to a historic building. No. 17 Fleet Street, called Prince Henry's Room, had been acquired in 1900 under the Act of 1898 to ensure its preservation, as we have seen. It was an early seventeenth-century timber-framed building with a front much altered in the early nineteenth century. A fine panelled room on the first floor had an old plaster ceiling incorporating the badge of the Prince of Wales. A traditional association with Henry, son of James I, was without foundation, but the building (originally the Prince's Arms tavern) was a rare and interesting survivor in its own right.

With the City Corporation contributing to the cost, the Council set back the ground floor to the City's road improvement line and carried out a scholarly restoration of the jettied timber front, rebuilding the Georgian rear parts (described then as 'uninteresting') in charming Arts and Crafts manner, reminiscent of the work of the Council's housing architects on the new estates in Westminster and Shoreditch. A number of detailed rendered drawings of this restoration project – each one an outstanding example of draughtsmen's work of the period – still exist.[33]

The further development of the work of the Historic Records Committee and its successors and the evolution of the Historic Records Section into what would now be called a multidisciplinary conservation office, were largely bound up with events immediately preceding and following the Second World War. Its fifty years of experience gave the LCC a flying start when statutory controls were at last introduced over a wide range of historic buildings.

The Historic Records Section and listing

Effective statutory controls (not very effective at first) over historic buildings in private ownership have existed, so far as local authorities are concerned, only since 1944. The Ancient Monuments Act of 1900 had given local authorities the power to acquire monuments by agreement, but London was already well ahead of the field in this respect. The Town and Country Planning Act 1932 gave county, county borough and county district councils the power to make building preservation orders in respect of buildings of special architectural or historic interest, but only within areas for which planning schemes had come into effect. Such orders, which prevented demolition only, needed ministerial approval. There was no national inventory of historic buildings to guide local authorities and the power was, consequently, sparingly used.

Even when the hesitant 1932 Act power became available, it could not be employed to preserve ecclesiastical buildings, and it was never likely to be used to extend the boundaries of preservation without the support of a strong body of public opinion. When the heart of the Adam Brothers' Adelphi was threatened with demolition in 1936, there was no general perception of the qualities of Georgian architecture (the Georgian Group was formed the following year) and distinguished architectural historians such as H. S. Goodhart-Rendel were prepared to countenance its destruction. A building preservation order could have been made, but a scholarly report by the Architect (i.e. by Historic Records Section) was followed by a decision to take no action.

The Council was, nevertheless concerned that the slow progress of the *Survey of London* made it an unsuitable tool for considering urgent building preservation order action. An accelerated scheme of inventorisation was clearly necessary, and in February 1938 it was reported that 'classified lists of buildings of architectural, artistic and historic interest are being prepared'. These lists were to pay particular attention to buildings constructed before 1830 and were to classify them in grades.

The architect in charge of the Historic Records Section at the time was William Dathy Quirke (1878–1955),[34] whose drawings appear in some of the earliest LCC *Survey* volumes. The listing process was speeded up during the Second World War and was combined, whenever possible, with photographs, sketches and measured drawings to ensure that buildings of interest did not disappear without record. Despite the fact that the Section in the war years was reduced to Quirke and one assistant, a salvage system was also started to rescue architectural features from bomb-damaged buildings, partly for their intrinsic value as records but also (with what must have seemed at the time to be extraordinary optimism) with a view to seeing them reused in restoration works.

The Council's reputation in historic buildings matters was well established by the end of the war and it was consulted over the ways in which the 1932 provisions needed to be amended before incorporation in the 1944 and 1947 Planning Acts. The initial LCC lists, sketchy as they were, were also of crucial importance in influencing the Ministry of Town and Country Planning's postwar decision to ask the Council to prepare the first drafts of the statutory lists for London. This task, carried out in consultation with the Ministry and the National Buildings Record was completed over a period of about ten years. The first of the provisional lists (for the Metropolitan Boroughs of Bethnal Green, Bermondsey and Kensington) were officially certified in 1949 and the last (for Westminster) in 1958.[35]

The control powers introduced by the 1947 Act became available at a time of low building activity but, by the early 1950s, it was clear that if the Council was to carry out its responsibilities effectively the Historic Records Section would need to be strengthened and given a broader brief.

J. H. 'Joe' Farrar (1887–1958) whose initials are found on *Survey of London* drawings from the 1920s, was in charge of the Historic Records Section from 1944 to 1952. He was a graduate of the Royal College of Art, neither an architect nor a historian, but a knowledgeable and thoroughly practical man, admired by those who knew him as a shrewd judge and a tough fighter for historic buildings. The Section he led was fated to be almost invisible at a time when it was laying the foundations for the coming forty years of building conservation activity, but under his leadership it grew to seven or eight architects, surveyors and draughtsmen, with an administrator (F. R. Buggey) who also had a keen knowledge of architectural history.

Most of the work of producing the draft statutory lists was done in Farrar's time by an architect, H. M. A. Armitage (1896–*c.* 1993). Armitage was an accomplished draughtsman, who had worked in the Depression years on the production of strip elevational records of important London streets, a project that had made use of teams of unemployed architects. All town planning observations, reports and recommendations to the Council on historic buildings matters were written by Farrar or a single member of his staff, Kenneth S. Mills. Their work created models for a generation of later statutory controllers, but scope for decisive action was, at that time, sadly limited.

Recording, care and control in one office

Farrar's successor, W. A. Eden (1906–1975), an architect and academic, was the first leader of the newly formed Historic Buildings Section which was to assume responsibility for all the Council's preservation, recording and control activities. The substitution of 'buildings' for 'records' in the title marked an important change of emphasis. The new Section took over the staff and functions of the Historic Records Section and also became responsible for the care of all the historic buildings then in Council ownership which, by this time, included Kenwood House, the council having become administrative trustee of the Iveagh Bequest in 1949.

At the same time, the *Survey of London* moved into a new phase. In 1953, the ageing voluntary committee gave notice that it could no longer continue its work and the LCC decided to carry on alone, appointing a general editor, Dr Francis Sheppard, the following year. By then, the original idea of creating by way of the *Survey* a comprehensive register of historic buildings in London had been overtaken by the compilation of the national statutory lists. The past alternation of Council and Survey Committee volumes had also led to inconsistencies of coverage, with the Council volumes tending toward documentary history in which the measured drawings illustrated the text, while the committee volumes leaned heavily on the drawn record.

The first parish volume produced under the new regime was for the southern half of St Mary Lambeth. It set new standards of extended coverage and richer illustration than had hitherto been attempted. It also stated and exemplified a new policy, that of concentrating on areas where changes were occurring and '[taking] serious note of nineteenth century buildings to which many students of the history of architecture have paid increasing attention in recent years'.[36] The *Survey*'s professional team remained divided, as it always had been, with the Historic Buildings Section within the Architect's Department responsible for providing measured drawings, directing photographic recording and writing architectural descriptions as a service to Sheppard and his historians in the Clerk's Department.

Under Eden the Historic Buildings Section steadily enlarged until it had six or seven architects, surveyors and technicians working on the care and restoration of buildings, an archaeologist, an architect dealing with planning matters (in particular, notices of intended demolition or alteration of listed buildings), an architectural historian (Walter Ison) and three or four highly skilled draughtsmen, headed by Frank A. Evans (1910–91) providing drawings for the *Survey*.

Major works carried out in ensuing years on Council-owned historic buildings included the restoration of Ranger's House, Trinity Almshouses and its chapel, Marble Hill, Lauderdale House, the York Water Gate, the parts of Holland House which survived wartime bombing, the tower of St John of Wapping and the Brixton windmill, where wind-driven machinery was reinstated. Occasionally the Section provided designs in connection with works by other departments. When, for example, Roehampton Lane was widened in the early 1960s, the Section designed and built a pair of new gate lodges in completion of Archer's unexecuted intention at Roehampton House.[37] At about the same time, Mount Clare was restored as part of the development of the Roehampton Estate.

Preservation by intervention

Statutory control work was becoming daily more important. Armed with the still imperfect but vital statutory lists, backed up by the Section's accumulated knowledge of London's fabric, the building preservation order powers were used to the full. The Council rarely flinched from a preservation battle recommended by its Historic Buildings Subcommittee on the advice of Historic Buildings Section.

The process frequently led to hard-fought public inquiries at which expert witnesses from the Historic Buildings Section, serviced by its team of historians, architects, building surveyors and *Survey* draughtsmen, distinguished themselves by the quality of their evidence. Eden decided that the Section must be strengthened to deal with the demands of statutory control work and recruited Ashley Barker (who was to succeed Eden in 1969 as GLC Surveyor of Historic Buildings) to specialise in this field. A series of landmark cases followed in which the Council regularly created precedents by working for the preservation of buildings whose merits were not at the time widely recognised.[38]

A particularly significant early contest, in which the Council's expert witness was Eden himself, concerned a building preservation order made in 1958, covering almost the whole of Westbourne Terrace. An order to protect a group of buildings extending for a quarter of a mile on either side of a broad highway was enough in itself to make it an unusual event. The fact that none of the buildings had ever been included or considered for inclusion in the statutory list, that they were all in the then unadmired early Victorian stucco Italianate manner, in the heart of the blighted area known as 'Rachmanland' (after Peter Rachman, a notorious property owner) and mostly in deplorable condition, made it an extraordinarily daring act of faith. Confirmation of the order changed perceptions of the value of such buildings and, by degrees, transformed the economic fortunes of a whole quarter of London which had seemed destined for total clearance.

JOHN EARL

National Provincial Bank, Bishopsgate (John Gibson, 1865). One of more than 600 buildings successfully protected by the LCC under the pre-1968 legislation.

Another key case was that of the National Provincial Bank, Bishopsgate (John Gibson, 1865). The public inquiry went on for three full weeks. In the climate of the time (1964) it was by no means certain that such a building, even though listed, could be saved from destruction. The successful outcome of this case occurred within two years of the totally unnecessary destruction of two of the greatest monuments of the Victorian age, the Coal Exchange and the Euston Arch. (Eden had taken a leading part in the unsuccessful deputation to the Prime Minister to argue the case for Euston.)

The council made its first postwar building preservation order (BPO) in 1951. By the time the BPO system came to an end in 1968, ministerial confirmation had been given to about two in three of all LCC and GLC orders, giving protection to well over 600 buildings – a large proportion of all the confirmed BPOs in Britain and a remarkable score, given the postwar climate of belief in clear-fell redevelopment as a cure for all ills.

Statutory control work grew rapidly during the property boom of the 1960s and '70s and, as is invariably the case, the existence of a body of expertise prompted new demands. In 1965 the new Greater London Council inherited the old Section and expanded it to carry the additional burden of covering 600 square miles of territory. It was henceforth styled the Historic Buildings Division.

The GLC Historic Buildings Division

The regard in which the Division was held was apparent in the unique powers of direction given to the Greater London Council in 1965, which were extended when listed building consent controls were introduced in 1968:

> Since the Greater London Council already has a Historic Buildings Division of recognised standing, whose services are available to that Council in dealing with consent for alterations to listed buildings, the Minister has decided to exempt them from the duty to notify applications [to him] relating to proposed alterations; and he hereby so directs . . . Where an application for listed building consent is made to a London borough they must notify the Greater London Council of the application . . .[which Council] may authorise [them] to grant or refuse the application or direct them how they are to determine it.[39]

The integration in one local authority office of expertise in recording, physical care and statutory control of historic buildings was maintained and developed from 1965 to 1986. The concerns of the Historic Buildings Division now extended from the commercial and government centres of the City of London and Westminster, through the great residential estates and old inner suburbs to isolated rural buildings and recently captured dormitory villages on the outer fringes of Greater London.

The last twenty years of conservation activity were even more varied and intense than the previous sixty, encompassing – to take only representative examples – the problems of the silk-weavers' houses in Spitalfields, the restoration and revival of Covent Garden central market, the public inquiry into the future of Liverpool Street Station, the defence of Danson House and its stables, the preservation of Orpington Priory outbuildings and the establishment of a stained glass repository for London.

GREATER LONDON RECORD OFFICE

Orpington Priory, a fine group of timber-framed outbuildings saved from destruction by GLC action.

The Division's knowledge base was reinforced with special studies of particular topics and building types, including timber-framed buildings, almshouses and theatres. Its contribution to the *Greater London Development Plan*, incorporated into the GLDP Report of Studies (1968), analysed as well as might be attempted in such a document the historic structure of urban, suburban and village London and set down markers which have helped to shape conservation policies until the present time. Most of the historic areas defined by the report were later designated as Conservation Areas under the Civic Amenities Act 1967.

Revisions to the statutory lists for Greater London were again drafted by the Division as a service to the Department of the Environment and, in later years, a computerised sites and monuments record, combining information on listed buildings, unlisted buildings of interest, scheduled monuments and archaeological sites and finds, was created in co-operation with the Museum of London.

An odd but significant fact about the long-combined lives of the Historic Records Section, Historic Buildings Section and Historic Buildings Division is that although, from 1952, their officers reported to a subcommittee which, under various names, itself reported to a Planning Committee, the officers were never attached to a Planning Department. This proved to be an advantage on many occasions. If the historic buildings specialists had been controlled by chief officers concerned with major planning and transport schemes (the normal situation today for local government conservation officers) their reports would undoubtedly have been edited to suit departmental policy. The fact that they were able to deliver independent expert advice was a frequent cause of inter-departmental and inter-committee friction but, in a curious way, such interventions seemed to be accepted as a necessary check even by those most inconvenienced. The presence on the LCC and GLC Historic Buildings Committee (to give it its final name) of co-opted advisory members of the distinction of Sir John Summerson, Sir John Betjeman, Sir Paul Reilly and Sir Hugh Casson undoubtedly reinforced the authority and independence of the officers.

Abolition

Just before the GLC was abolished in 1986, the Division had more than sixty professional officers in a variety of disciplines, plus administrative and clerical staff, working together in a single, tightly integrated unit. Its reputation was such that a government undertaking was given that it would not be broken up and it was, in the event, transferred lock, stock and barrel to become the London regional office of English Heritage. Inevitably, the long-standing administrative split between the two wings of the *Survey of London* staff was made final and complete, with the *Survey* being taken over by the Royal Commission on Historical Monuments, rather than English Heritage. A further, particularly regrettable and not widely publicised consequence of the dissolution of the Council, was that many active records not already earmarked for the Greater London Record Office (GLRO) and not within the Division's control, but of importance to historians, were divided and scattered with indecent haste to the thirty-three boroughs.

The way in which the democratic governance of London was terminated can fuel angry debate years after the event, but the end of the LCC/GLC tradition of care for historic buildings may be regretted for completely practical reasons. The need for a national body of expertise like English Heritage, free from direct political control, is not to be contested. It has resources beyond the dreams of any local authority, making the Historic Buildings Division, even in its prime, seem puny. The forces at the disposal of the high command are, undeniably, impressive. The foot soldiers in the Borough Councils – the lonely, under-graded and not infrequently overridden conservation officers – are valiant. But there is now nothing in between.

When English Heritage in December 1992 decided to shed some of the special powers of direction it had inherited in London the problem was brought sharply into focus. The high command, concerned with strategic matters, saw the London tradition as an oddity, an office unlike any other within the organisation, with an irritating tendency to fuss over what were represented as minor architectural details. It was, of course, precisely its comprehensive knowledge of, and care over, detail which had sustained the authority of the Historic Buildings Division and its predecessors for half a century, but the official view was that such unimportant matters should be delegated to a lower level of command if, indeed, they called for any attention at all.

The yawning gap between English Heritage and the next level of care and expertise cannot be bridged by the present expedient of providing the odd salaried post to London Borough Councils which, as everywhere else in the country, vary widely in competence and commitment. The best, as always, will do well, with or without handouts. The worst will not even try. London not only deserves but *has had* much better than this. The LCC/GLC tradition, with all its faults, was fashioned by and was constantly adapting to the special conservation needs of the city region. During the campaigns which preceded the abolition of London's government it was said that 'the Council's [historic buildings] team is unique in Britain. It serves "the Unique City". The fact that after the last twenty five years of intensive redevelopment London still has a recognisable character is due more to its work than to any other single factor'.[40]

London, in fact, provided an example to be followed rather than a freak to be eliminated.

5
The art of keeping one jump ahead: conservation societies in the twentieth century

Gavin Stamp

'These differences of opinion, and the formation of numerous societies, committees and commissions etc. to give them expression, are characteristics of our time; they harass the unfortunate artist and hamper the production of the work . . .', complained Sir Giles Scott in 1947.[1] The occasion was the rejection of his design for the rebuilding of Coventry Cathedral by, among others, the Royal Fine Art Commission, but Scott's words have a contemporary ring, echoing the exasperation of so many modern architects today who are frustrated by the opposition of amenity societies acting within the statutory planning system.

Scott clearly felt that interfering societies and committees were proliferating – as they certainly have done since – but the formation of societies, clubs and other fellowships because of shared interests or to achieve particular aims is a deep-rooted aspect of English life. Only in the twentieth century, however, have so many such societies been concerned with architecture and its preservation. This is a reflection of the fragmentation of the universal architectural culture which last existed in the eighteenth century, for today laymen and the architectural profession have different aims and different expectations. At a simple level, there is a long-standing conflict between the self-interested desire for change by the architect and the sentimental affection for what exists felt by the interested amateur – between optimism and pessimism perhaps.

This conflict has been exacerbated by the utopian idealism of the twentieth century which has so often proved to be megalomaniac and totalitarian in its aims. Opponents of conservation argue, correctly, that change is inevitable, that previous generations were happy to replace old buildings with new for practical reasons and did not fear modernity. All this is true, but it is important to appreciate that such change in the past was usually slow and piecemeal while in the twentieth century the sheer scale of redevelopment is without precedent. The intention of the Modern Movement to rebuild from scratch, to create a new world, unleashed a process of comprehensive redevelopment which was really a form of terror. This both discredited the architecture and provoked resistance.

What, therefore, has long been conspicuous about societies concerned with the preservation of historic buildings is that a majority of the membership – and of the active leadership – consists of non-architects. Architects have always been involved – there are always some with a broader and more civilised vision than is generally characteristic of the modern profession – but the leading lights have usually been interested amateurs (and often journalists). Indeed, in the cases of the three principal societies founded this century – the Georgian Group, the Victorian Society and the Thirties Society (now the Twentieth Century Society) – many of the founders have been architectural historians, a novel species whose advent reflects the fragmentation of architectural culture and the divorce between modern architectural practice and tradition. A predominantly non-architectural membership – writers and painters – also characterised the Society for the Protection of Ancient Buildings (SPAB) at its foundation (although the Society could not have functioned without the expertise of skilled architects). Indeed, this opposition between interested laymen and the profession may be traced back to the eighteenth century and the assault on Wyatt's cathedral restorations by antiquarians and others.

And, in every case, the task of the new societies was to educate, that is, to persuade the general public as well as the architectural profession to look beyond fashion and to appreciate the merits of a type of architecture of comparatively recent date which was conventionally regarded as worthless. Architecture is as much subject to cycles of fashion as any other activity, and to a remarkable extent the history of conservation has been the art of keeping one step ahead of public opinion. Although founded by Morris to protect medieval structures from restoration, the SPAB was soon pleading for the classical churches by Wren which the Gothic Revival had dismissed as 'pagan' and worthless; the Georgian Group arose to challenge the conventional, official view that architecture stopped in 1700; the Victorian Society to counter the mindless prejudice that Victorian architecture was self-evidently ridiculous; the Thirties Society was founded – initially – to defend interwar buildings outside the approved canon of the Modern Movement.

'Architecture shares with art, literature, poetry, rhetoric that dead reaction of smug superiority which comes after the lapse of forty to sixty years', Sir Josiah Stamp informed the Royal Institute of British Architects (RIBA) in 1933 while discussing the problem of St Pancras Station. 'The pre-Raphaelites we can put in dark corners or obscure places; Tennyson we can relegate to girls' schools, Froude can be superseded; Carlyle can be ignored, the rhetoric of Gladstone can be turned into a museum piece; but the architecture of that day we have to live with and use. We can either keep it for a revival of appreciation, with a dead economic loss for the site that it occupies and the use to which it is put, or we can pull it down and impose on the site something that can be equally condemned in its turn in sixty years' time'.[2]

As Chairman of the London Midland and Scottish Railway, my great-uncle had the responsibility for two apparently obsolete London termini – Euston and St Pancras – and he was well aware that no architect had a good word to say for the Victorian Gothic of St Pancras. Stamp did, not because he was avant-garde but, as he confessed, because, 'I am the last remaining man, with the mid-Victorian spirit, who is sufficiently philistine and bourgeois and altogether out of the running, to be an unashamed admirer of the Albert Memorial'. As such, he could try to be objective; yet even he, with his sense of the cyclical nature of fashion, could surely never have imagined that it would be Gothic St Pancras that would survive and the Greek Revival at Euston which would perish.

For the past century, conservation societies and their supporters have been pulling conventional taste forwards, dragging whole periods of architecture out of the darkness of unfashionability into the light of a renewed appreciation – with the interval between initial creation and revival of respectability getting shorter and shorter. This struggle has mainly taken place since the First World War. In the late nineteenth century, despite a slow attrition of City churches by the Bishop of London, the architecture of Wren and the English Baroque had come back into fashion, to be regarded by some as the essence of Englishness in the Edwardian decade. Indeed, these years can be seen as complacent – the complacency summed up by the Archbishop of Canterbury's insistence that the Church did not need to be coerced into looking after its ancient buildings. A bill to protect London squares was rejected by the House of Lords as it did not sufficiently recognise the interests of landlords. Similarly, the Ancient Monuments Protection Acts of 1882 and 1900 – so strenuously opposed by Lord Salisbury – only allowed the protection of monuments with the consent of the owner. However, the Ancient Monuments Consolidation and Amendment Act of 1913, despite excluding ecclesiastical property, did succeed in establishing legal means for ensuring protection.

That the 1913 Act had some teeth was a consequence of the controversy over Tattershall Castle in Lincolnshire in 1911. After its owner removed its fireplaces and threatened to sell them – and perhaps the whole building – to America, it was saved and eventually left to the National Trust by Lord Curzon, the former Viceroy of India who had done so much to preserve historic buildings in the subcontinent. The Trust itself had been founded in 1895 – by non-architects – and would eventually develop into the largest organisation in England interested in historic buildings. This lay interest in architecture owed much to the magazine *Country Life*, founded by Edward Hudson in 1897.[3]

The comparative complacency of the Edwardian years was shattered immediately after the First World War, and the next two decades witnessed a major assault on the seventeenth-century and, especially, the eighteenth-century buildings of London. This was inaugurated by the Bishop of London who, in 1919, announced the closure and sale of the sites of nineteen City of London churches, by Wren, Hawksmoor and others. To quote Robert Byron's great polemic, *How We Celebrate the Coronation* (of which more later), 'Dr Winnington-Ingram's proposal, however, was too much even for a nation of shopkeepers. Thanks to the efforts of the London Society, opinion for once grew articulate, and the scheme was quashed by parliament in 1926 on a petition from the Corporation of London. As a result, people began to realise how precariously situated were the central monuments of our national architecture'.[4]

The London Society was one of the first environmental amenity societies and it interested itself in the planning of London and such matters as the rebuilding of Charing Cross Bridge. Founded in 1912, it grew out of the Town Planning

Conference held by the Royal Institute of British Architects two years before and was an expression of the growing interest in town planning and civic design, particularly among professionals. The first meeting was held in the Chinese Room of the Holborn Restaurant on 17 January 1912, and an inaugural public meeting took place in the Galleries of the Royal Society of British Artists on 9 February. At this, a resolution was passed on 'the need for united effort . . . to advance the practical improvement and artistic development of London'. The first president was the Earl of Plymouth and in the early days the new Society was dominated by architects and planners: Sir Aston Webb (the real founder), Raymond Unwin, Stanley Adshead, Thomas Mawson, Edwin Lutyens and H. V. Lanchester. There were also sculptors and painters as well as the Labour MP, John Burns. Another important member was the architectural illustrator Raffles Davison who, in May 1912, lectured to the Society on 'London as it is and as it might be'. The first secretary and then honorary secretary (until 1940) was the architect Percy Lovell (1877–1950), former secretary of the London Survey Committee. It was Lovell who confronted conservation issues after the First World War.[5]

Another important battle fought by the Society in the 1920s was to preserve London's squares. The inutility of the London Squares Act of 1906 was soon demonstrated by the sale and the building over of the gardens of Mornington Crescent and the south side of Euston Square – Endsleigh Gardens – and by the threat to move the Covent Garden market to the combined site of Mecklenburgh and Brunswick Squares and the Foundling Hospital – a scheme promoted by the Beecham Estates and Pills Company in 1927.[6] No protection was achieved and, although no more gardens were lost, the rebuilding of some of London's finest squares continued. The Georgian Group fought hard (in vain) for both Brunswick and Mecklenburgh squares shortly before the Second World War, and the foreign visitors who so admired the austere elegance of Georgian London were astonished to learn that even Bedford Square was threatened with partial demolition – by the British Museum.[7]

The London Society and its allies simply could not resist the commercial pressures which, in the space of a few years, swept away most of the finest Georgian buildings in the capital. The principal victims were the aristocratic mansions, or 'Private Palaces' as Beresford Chancellor called them in his eponymous book published in 1908. 'What . . . are we to suppose will be the fate of some of those which to-day would seem to be armed so as to defy Time? Some we know are held on leasehold tenure, and when their time has run, may be ruthlessly demolished; others stand proudly in the midst of ever-changing building development; will they be, in their turn, attacked, and if so – what then?'[8]

Chancellor was right to be pessimistic. Devonshire House in Piccadilly, by Kent, came down in 1924; Vulliamy's Dorchester House in 1929; in 1934 Lansdowne House by Robert Adam was hopelessly mutilated; Chesterfield House designed by Isaac Ware came down the following year and in 1938 Norfolk House by Brettingham was sold and demolished. This was not all. In the

RCHME © CROWN COPYRIGHT

Devonshire House, Piccadilly (William Kent, 1733) being demolished in 1924.

early 1920s the replacement of Nash's stuccoed facades in Regent Street by larger and more pompous structures in Portland stone was completed – with only the architect Trystan Edwards protesting – and most of Soane's unique banking halls in the Bank of England were lost during Sir Herbert Baker's arrogant enlargement of that remarkable building. The Foundling Hospital, threatened since 1926, was demolished despite it being a most suitable new home for London University. Most of the Adelphi, that uniquely coherent speculation by the Adam Brothers, was destroyed in 1936.[9] The demolition of old Waterloo Bridge, the sublime Doric structure by Rennie, was commenced in 1934 by the London County Council – in deliberate defiance of the wishes of parliament. What those who would protect such masterpieces were up against is well shown by Harold P. Clunn, the pedantic, modern-minded compiler of *The Face of London*; despite the fact that the great Canova had pronounced it 'the noblest bridge in the world, worth a visit from the remotest corners of the earth', Clunn maintained that 'Waterloo Bridge has no claim, on historical grounds, to be retained' and that those who would do so were 'short-sighted fanatics . . . the existing plan of repairing the old bridge is . . . an indefensible and wanton piece of extravagance'.[10]

In 1933, it was revealed that Nash's Carlton House Terrace was to be rebuilt by the Crown Commissioners to a design by Sir Reginald Blomfield (who had defended Waterloo Bridge). Despite the spirit of progress abroad in the land, this was going too far. J. M. Richards organised a campaign against this vandalism in the architectural press, which attracted influential support,[11] and Carlton House Terrace was saved (for the moment) – possibly owing to the personal intervention of Queen Mary, that assiduous collector of Georgian furniture. From this campaign the Georgian Group emerged, for in the absence of any protection for any building erected after 1700 and the apparent indifference of the SPAB to the fate of Georgian buildings, a new society to fight for them was clearly needed.

The actual founder of the Georgian Group was Douglas Goldring (1887–1960), novelist, poet, travel-writer and journalist, who had waged a campaign against the destruction of the Adelphi in the pages of the *New Statesman*. A Londoner, Goldring was exasperated by the failure of the SPAB to defend the little shops in front of St Ethelburga's, Bishopsgate, 'on the ground that they had been rebuilt not much more than a century ago and were therefore not "old"',[12] and he floated the idea of a new society. In 1936 Goldring was introduced to Lord Derwent (1899–1949), who was preparing a motion to the House of Lords that the Royal Commission on Historical Monuments should extend its work and prepare a list of buildings of the period 1700–1830. Derwent – a cosmopolitan, grand and urbane figure, with a Roumanian wife, who alternated between his Yorshire seat and Paris – was an unlikely founder of a new preservation society, but he was an effective catalyst.

Even Goldring, among several others, was worried that too many societies duplicated and dissipated effort and so confused the public. Lord Esher (1881–1963), the chairman of the SPAB, therefore proposed to Derwent that an active 'Georgian Group' be created within the senior society.

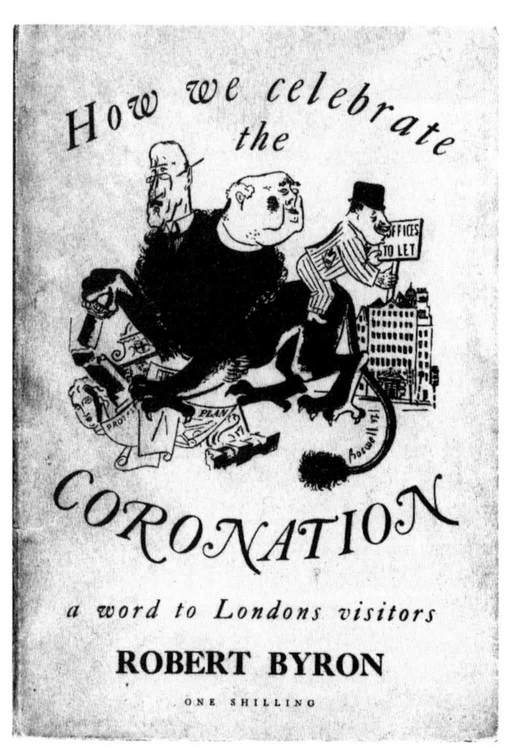

The cover of Robert Byron's *How We Celebrate the Coronation* (1937), a visual evocation of the passage of text quoted here.

Although younger enthusiasts like James Lees-Milne (b. 1908) then felt that, 'the S.P.A.B. was too Arts and Crafts and totally uninterested in, if not hostile to Georgian architecture', this was achieved.[13] The Georgian Group offically came into existence at the committee meeting of the SPAB on 2 April 1937, with Lord Derwent as chairman and Douglas Goldring as secretary. A letter was published in *The Times* seven weeks later announcing that the new society 'will concern itself primarily with buildings erected from 1714 onwards. The word "Georgian" has been adapted for convenience, only good Victorian buildings will come equally within the scope of its activities' – a qualification made with *classical* nineteenth-century buildings like the Euston Arch in mind.[14]

The delay in launching the Society was to avoid the excitement surrounding the coronation of George VI on 12 May. With this in mind, the May number of the *Architectural Review* carried a long article by Robert Byron entitled 'How We Celebrate the Coronation' which was subsequently published as a pamphlet. It was strong stuff. After a survey of threatened buildings, Byron concluded that:

> The Church; the Civil Service; the Judicial Committee of the Privy Council; the hereditary landlords; the political parties; the London County Council; the local councils; the great business firms; the motorists; the heads of the national Museum – all are indicted, some with more cause than others, because of some more decency might have been hoped for, but all on the same charge. These, in the year of the coronation, 1937, are responsible for the ruin of London, for our humiliation before visitors, and for destroying without hope of recompense many of the nation's most treasured possessions; and they will answer for it by the censure of posterity . . . The attitude of the Englishman to art is extremely conventional. Painting he knows is an art, because he is told so. He is not told that architecture is an art; on the contrary, thanks to the brutish ignorance of Church, Government and speculators, he is strongly encouraged to believe that it is not. Some pieces of architecture, he is allowed to believe, are worth preserving; but if they are, it is not by any means on account of their value as works of art. The value of architecture in England, according to official and ecclesiastical standards, varies in proportion to 1, its antiquity, 2, its quaintness, and 3, its holiness. By these standards, a bit of the old Roman wall is of more importance than Nash's Regent Street, and one ruined pointed arch than all Wren's churches put together.[15]

It was such attitudes – still prevalent today – that the Georgian Group set out to challenge. The first committee meeting was held at the offices of the SPAB in Buckingham Street on 4 June and a second on 28 June in an apartment belonging to the Baroness d'Erlanger in the new Stratton House, Piccadilly. There was a strong contingent of historians, academics and aesthetes among the early committee members – John Summerson, John Betjeman, James Lees-Milne, Margaret Jourdain, H. Clifford Smith, Tancred Borenius and Christopher Hussey (editor of *Country Life*), among others. But there were also architects, notably Albert Richardson, Gerald Wellesley, Trystan Edwards and Frederick Etchells. Some of these, of course, were known as upholders of the classical tradition but Etchells was the translator of Le Corbusier into English and several younger architects saw a parallel between the austere elegance of Georgian architecture and the simplicity demanded by the Modern Movement; there was then a significant overlap of membership between the Georgian Group and the radical MARS (Modern Architectural Research) Group, founded in 1933.[16]

From the outset, the Georgian Group was smart. Early members included the likes of Evelyn Waugh, Sir Kenneth Clark, Osbert and Sacheverell Sitwell, Edward Sackville-West, Brian Guinness and Oliver Messel (who designed the Group's first two balls – one in Mecklenburgh Square and the second at Osterley). The Group was also rather grand, numbering thirty-five peers of the realm among its members by 1939 and no fewer than eleven on the committee (one member was the dowager Marchioness of Norfolk, furious that her son had been persuaded to sell his private palace in St James's Square for redevelopment by Rudolph Palumbo). There was, indeed, a marked social distinction between the Georgian Group and its parent body, which exarcerbated existing tension with the SPAB.

But none of this affected the vigour and pugnacity of the early Georgian Group. Indeed, offence was caused by its assertiveness and self-promotion. Mrs Philip Trotter, who had founded the Londoners' League in 1936, 'to defend and foster the beauties and virtues of London home-life, architectural, horticultural and sociological', was annoyed to be upstaged by the Group. In particular, Goldring took up one of her own causes, the destruction of Portland Town: an area of small stuccoed houses to the north-west of Regent's Park. (Mrs Trotter lived nearby in 'The Mutilated House', Maida Vale – so-called as the other half of the semi-detached pair had been replaced by Rudolph Palumbo by a block of flats.) She was 'scandalised and disgusted' by Byron's pamphlet and its 'irrelevant unbalanced anti-clericalism'.[17]

The real vigour of the Group, indeed, came from Byron who, as Deputy Chairman, effectively ran it during the crucial months from the withdrawal of the cantankerous Goldring early in 1938 until May 1939. Robert Byron (1905–41), travel-writer, architectural critic and a master of eloquent invective, was passionate about the cause. After his death – a victim of the *Scharnhorst* while on his way to Persia – his mother wrote in reply to a letter of condolence from Albert Richardson that, 'I always felt he was more interested in his work for you than anything else in his life'.[18] Byron's publicity campaigns and his delight in 'using the bludgeon' in print alarmed the staid and cautious SPAB, which vainly attempted to censor them. 'The Group does not claim that its methods are better or worse than those of the other amenity bodies. But it does claim for them the virtue of novelty. It is this novelty which has enabled the Group to arouse public opinion that was previously latent and through which, therefore, its existence has been mainly justified'.[19]

On 4 January 1938, the BBC broadcast a wireless debate entitled 'Farewell

Brunswick Square' between Byron and John Summerson (1904–93) on the one hand and W. Craven-Ellis, MP, and W. Stanley Edgson, an estate agent, on the other. It was for this novel public forum that Byron wrote his most eloquent defence of eighteenth-century London:

> The Georgian style commemorates a great period, when English taste and English political ideas had suddenly become the admiration of Europe. And it corresponds, almost to the point of dinginess, with our national character. Its reserve and dislike of outward show, its reliance on the virtue and dignity of proportions only, and its rare bursts of exquisite detail, all express as no other style has ever done that indifference to self-advertisement, that quiet assumption of our own worth, and that sudden vein of lyric affection, which have given us our part in civilisation.[20]

What the Georgian Group was up against was exemplified by the smug MP, who argued that, although he was 'strongly in favour of preserving properties possessing real historical interest . . . civilisation today is suffering many disadvantages because our forefathers have not paid sufficient attention to demolition of properties which have passed their useful life', while the problems of traffic congestion 'necessitate the entire rebuilding of our cities . . .'. The estate agent, of course, argued that sentiment should not prevail against higher site values and that 'the Georgian houses of London's streets and squares . . . are obsolete'. After the broadcast, Byron wrote to Summerson that, 'I thought Edgson had a pleasant and companionable way with him. As for Ellis – I can only wonder he isn't in prison'.[21]

With such commercial pressures, and the belief – articulated by Craven-Ellis – that town planning and slum clearance would relieve unemployment, the Group had much to do. The fate of Norfolk House and, incredibly, of Wren's church of All Hallows', Lombard Street, was already settled when the Group came into existence, but there were plenty of other causes to fight.[22] But not all members of the Group were willing to march as far in advance of conventional taste as Betjeman or Byron: the latter considered that Munster Square with its modest stuccoed houses – threatened with redevelopment by the Crown Commissioners – was 'a perfect and unspoiled example of Nash's quieter manner', but Lord Gerald Wellesley, the architect who later became the 'Iron Duchess' of Wellington, dismissed it as 'of very little value', and Munster Square disappeared during the Second World War.[23]

During the war, the Georgian Group would play a leading role in establishing the listed building system, but what, in retrospect, is sad is how many of the Group's early victories turned out to be Pyrrhic. There was the case of the facade of James Wyatt's Pantheon in Oxford Street which was to be replaced by a new store for Marks and Spencer, whom the Group persuaded to pay for its re-erection elsewhere. Edward James expressed enthusiasm for rebuilding it as part of a new house at Monkton, but in the event nothing happened and the stones were eventually lost.[24] Then there was the dignified terrace of plain houses in

Abingdon Street which made an effective foil to Barry and Pugin's Victoria Tower. These were threatened with redevelopment by the Ecclesiastical Commissioners while the stone-fronted houses around the corner in Old Palace Yard were to be gratuitously demolished to make way for a large Gothic memorial to the late king designed by Sir Giles Scott and proposed by a committee dominated by the Archbishop of Canterbury. 'It means nothing to them that their choice is opposed by the whole artistic opinion of the country, or that it will link not only their names but also that of King George V with an act of indefensible vandalism', protested Byron.[25]

The memorial design was criticised by the Royal Fine Art Commission, among others, and the Georgian Group generated much publicity about the whole business. Anne, Countess of Rosse, Wilhelmina Cresswell (now Lady Harrod) and Nancy Mitford threatened to chain themselves to the railings of Abingdon Street in protest and the Group took an office in No. 27 to collect signatures for a petition against the proposals. This was signed by, among others, Sir Kenneth Clark, Mrs Anthony Eden, Duncan Grant, Lord Shaftesbury, Sacheverell Sitwell and the Duchess of Westminster. After only two days, the Memorial Committee announced that it would proceed no further with the scheme. Today, John Vardy's stone-fronted houses still stand next to a more modest memorial to George V by Scott and William Reid-Dick, but the houses in Abingdon Street have gone. Wartime bomb damage enabled the government to clear them away and now there is but an open space, affording a prospect of the overrestored and quite uninteresting Jewel Tower, on which Members of Parliament may posture in front of television cameras. What Betjeman called 'Antiquarian Prejudice' had triumphed.

Perhaps the saddest case was that of the Euston 'Arch'. The confused collection of buildings at Euston was threatened with destruction by the proposals for a grand new American-style Euston Station designed by Percy Thomas and unveiled in 1937 to mark the centenary of the London and Birmingham Railway. The Georgian Group accepted that Philip Hardwick's Great Hall had to go but believed that the great Doric propylaeum could be saved. In May 1938 Albert Richardson and Lord Gerald Wellesley went to see the directors of the London, Midland and Scottish Railway (LMS) and their architects, and persuaded them that the Arch could be re-erected further south on the Euston Road. This probably would have happened had not the outbreak of war in 1939 put an end to the plans for a new station.[26] So, twenty years later, the battle for the Euston Arch had to be fought a second time – and lost.

Between the wars, while Georgian buildings fell like ninepins, the architectural legacy of the Victorians remained largely intact. This was certainly not because they were admired; on the contrary, Victorian architecture was considered self-evidently hideous when not a joke, particularly by the ostensibly educated. As Kenneth Clark recalled in 1949, 'in Oxford it was universally believed that Ruskin had built Keble, and that it was the ugliest building in the world. Undergraduates and young dons used to break off on their afternoon walks in order to have a good laugh at the quadrangle'.[27] And in 1950, when

Nikolaus Pevsner gave his inaugural lecture as Slade Professor in Cambridge, he chose as his subject Sir Matthew Digby Wyatt, 'an interesting man but an indifferent architect. When I tried to analyse his mixed style just as I would have tried to distinguish in Gibbs's work between elements of Wren and elements of Carlo Fontana, the undergraduates found it a huge joke and laughed so much that I had to step off the platform and say: "This is not funny"'.[28]

'In this context', Mark Girouard has written, 'it is remarkable how relatively few good Victorian buildings were demolished. They survived for reasons of economics rather than of taste. Victorian buildings were relatively new, superbly solid, still in mint condition and mostly used for the purposes for which they had been built. In the years following the slump all this weighed the odds in favour of their survival'.[29] And while many indifferent commercial buildings were destroyed in the Second World War, few first-class buildings were lost and of these most were churches which, once damaged, the ecclesiastical authorities afterwards declined to restore: for instance, Butterfield's St Alban's, Holborn; Pearson's St John's, Red Lion Square; and Gilbert Scott junior's St Agnes', Kennington. Among secular buildings, only Norman Shaw's New Zealand Chambers in London and Waterhouse's Assize Courts in Manchester were serious losses.

But in the 1950s the situation changed. Not only were many Victorian country houses, ravaged by Allied occupation, now threatened with destruction but, in a climate of comprehensive redevelopment and utopian planning, allied with the professional triumph of the Modern Movement, major Victorian public buildings began to be proposed for removal. A start was made with the demolition of Gilbert Scott's Preston Town Hall, damaged in a fire in 1947. In 1955 that eclectic symbol of Empire, the Imperial Institute in South Kensington, was to be replaced by functional new buildings for Imperial College of the University of London. John Betjeman fought this vigorously and, with the help of the Royal Fine Art Commission and others, at least managed to save Collcutt's fine campanile.

It is difficult now, perhaps, fully to understand the influence in favour of Victorian architecture exercised by Sir John Betjeman (1906–84). As John Summerson put it, in his de-mythologising address to the Victorian Society in 1968, 'His story . . . is a mystery of our times and it may be that, as in some other things, we are too close to it to understand. Betjeman has not written even one book about Victorian architecture nor ever to my knowledge promoted any general claims for its qualities. Yet his name has become an illuminant and a sanction; through him, kindliness toward Victorian architecture is permitted to thousands whose habits of mind would drive them in a quite other direction', although this, perhaps, was to underestimate the effect of Betjeman's journalism and broadcasts, many of which, on nineteenth-century themes, were gathered in his book *First and Last Loves*.[30]

Betjeman's profound sympathy with the efforts of Victorian architects began, however, with finding it amusing. In the patronising climate of the 1930s, Betjeman, Osbert Lancaster and others of their generation could be avant-garde by finding humour in the dark, remote world of their parents and grandparents before the First World War and in rediscovering aged survivors of the past like Voysey and Comper.[31] The other attitude characteristic of the 1930s was to single out strands in the nineteenth century which seemed to anticipate the revelation of modernism. This was greatly encouraged by the publication of *Pioneers of the Modern Movement* in 1936 by the young German *émigré*, Nikolaus Pevsner (1902–84). In this, exclusive emphasis was given to the engineering tradition, represented by the Crystal Palace and King's Cross Station, on the one hand, and the world of William Morris on the other. Such attitudes prevailed right through the 1950s.

The only historian (who was also an architect) who demonstrated a deep and tolerant understanding of the architectural aspirations of the Victorian Age was H. S. Goodhart-Rendel (1887–1959) – 'the father of us all' as Kenneth Clark described him. In 1958, following the launch of the Victorian Society, Rendel lectured to the London Society on 'Victorian Conservanda' and, in introducing him, Betjeman noted how, 'while the rest of us were still looking at Georgian, he has for years been going ahead and looking at Victorian buildings, sifting the good from the bad and making notes about them for us which we have all copied and found invaluable'. Goodhart-Rendel began his lecture by stating that terrible truth which lies behind the growth of conservation societies this century, but which most of us involved in this field dare not articulate for fear of providing a hostage to a confident and articulate enemy who believes he has the spirit of the age on his side. 'Conservanda – meaning things we ought to keep, or, as school-grammar books would say, "things meet to be preserved". Nowadays, we feel a much greater obligation not to throw things away than people used to feel, because we are much less confident than they used to be of being able to replace them with things of equal value' (a cultural pessimism which, today, needs intelligently to be reinforced by the environmental argument that we no longer have the resources or materials available to our more prodigal ancestors). 'Victorians did not feel at all like that.'[32]

Rendel concluded by arguing that 'the scandal of the destruction of the Imperial Institute has put a wide public on the alert against repeated toleration of vandalism of that kind. The Victorian Society, at any rate, is, and I am sure will remain, alert in such respects, and probably already commands more sympathisers than did the Georgian Group at the beginning of its activities'. This may seem surprising, but the ground had long been laid for the appreciation of the best Victorian classical buildings – Albert Richardson had written about them sympathetically since before the First World War and in his chapter in G. M. Young's collection on *Early Victorian England* published back in 1934, and few now disputed the eminence of Barry and Cockerell. The buildings that needed friends and which commanded no sympathy from members of the Georgian Group were Gothic, or 'Queen Anne' eclectic. So Waterhouse's Eaton Hall could be demolished in 1961, and even the destruction of the Oxford Museum could seriously be contemplated by Oxford University during the same year. Hence the necessity for a new society.

The Victorian Society emerged from two meetings held at 18 Stafford Terrace in London – the house owned by the Countess of Rosse, Oliver Messel's sister, which is now the museum called Linley Sambourne House. The first meeting was held on 5 November 1957, the second on 25 February 1958.[33] Perhaps it is significant how many of those present on one or both occasions had been involved with the foundation of the Georgian Group two decades earlier – Lord and Lady Rosse, Christopher Hussey, John Betjeman, James Lees-Milne, Ralph Dutton – while the first chairman, the 3rd Viscount Esher, had been the chairman of the SPAB who acted as midwife to the birth of the Group. There was a sprinkling of architects, some modernist, such as Sir Hugh Casson and Robert Furneaux Jordan, and some more traditional, such as Goodhart-Rendel and Ian Grant; and there were historians: Peter Ferriday, Mark Girouard and Nikolaus Pevsner. The last, who was performing a crucial role in encouraging the serious appreciation of Victorian buildings through his volumes of the *Buildings of England*, would replace Lord Esher as chairman in 1963.

The new society had to fight two great battles almost immediately. Both were lost, but the resulting demolitions both strengthened the Victorian Society's position and helped to change public opinion. The first, of course, was round two of the fight for the Euston Arch. In the 1950s the Great Hall at Euston had been restored and a history of the station was commissioned from John Summerson by the Curator of Historical Relics of the British Transport Commission. This was

THE VICTORIAN SOCIETY

'The Man who tried to look at a Medieval Building on a Victorian Society Outing', cartoon by P. E. Clarke and T. A. Greaves, illustrating a group of Victorian Society members outside the then threatened Oxford Museum (from *The Victorian Society Report,* 1961–2).

RCHME © CROWN COPYRIGHT

The Euston 'Arch'.

printed in 1959 but never published because, that same year, the Commission decided to rebuild the station and demolish both Hall and Arch. The rest of the story is well known. Because neither the British Transport Commission, nor the London County Council nor the Ministry of Works nor the Treasury was prepared to foot the bill for re-erecting the Arch nearer the Euston Road (the solution accepted by the LMS in 1938), permission was given in July 1961 for demolition. This decision was made without benefit of public inquiry, and the sum needed to save the Arch (£190,000) was, as the Victorian Society later noted, 'rather less than the Treasury ungrudgingly paid out about the same time for the purchase of two indifferent Renoirs, which no one was threatening to destroy'.[34]

A last-ditch campaign was waged by the Society, supported by the Georgian Group and the SPAB, and on 24 October 1961, a deputation led by Sir Charles Wheeler, President of the Royal Academy, and consisting of John Summerson, Nikolaus Pevsner, Sir Hugh Casson, John Betjeman, the (then) Earl of Euston and J. M. Richards, went to see the Prime Minister, Harold Macmillan, to ask for a stay of execution. Richards later recalled that, 'Macmillan listened – or I suppose he listened; he sat without moving with his eyes apparently closed. He asked no questions; in fact he said nothing except that he would consider the matter. A statement was issued later to the effect that the Government had decided not to intervene'.[35] Even the plea that the stones of the Arch be numbered and kept for future re-erection was ignored. Such cynical indifference disgusted even the demolition contractor, Frank Valori, who in 1962 presented the Society with a model of the great Doric propylaeum he had just destroyed; this was later stolen.

The Euston Arch battle was significant as both modern architects and conservation-minded historians were firmly united against an unashamedly philistine British establishment. After the event, the *Architectural Review* published 'The Euston Murder' written by the editor, J. M. Richards, which was later reprinted in the valedictory book on Euston by Peter and Alison Smithson, the 'New Brutalist' architects. Richards was particularly disgusted as he had been prevented from intervening as the architectural correspondent of *The Times* and was then further humiliated when a leading article was published, 'Not Worth Saving', written by the editor, Sir William Haley, himself, advocating the demolition of the Arch on dubious or mendacious grounds.[36]

The case of James Bunning's Coal Exchange was similar. This remarkable building, with its circular cast-iron domed rotunda, was threatened in 1958 when the City Corporation decided to widen Lower Thames Street and redevelop the site. In 1960 the Victorian Society submitted three schemes to the Ministry of Housing and Local Government, showing how the road could be widened without destroying the building, and demolition was deferred. But in 1962 the Minister of Housing released the Corporation from its undertaking to defer demolition and a majority at the Court of Common Council voted for destruction. The site remained empty for many years. In its depressing annual report for 1961–2, the Victorian Society concluded that, 'We believe that even our lost battles are not altogether fruitless, for on each occasion, successful or not, we recruit more and more disciples to the cause of protecting the best Victorian and Edwardian architecture. Soon we hope thereby to turn the forces of public opinion so much in our favour that no one will dare to allow such needless destruction'.[37]

The truth of this was shown by the unlikely survival of Euston Station's neighbour at St Pancras. In 1966 British Railways announced that it intended to combine both St Pancras and King's Cross stations in one new terminus. But public opinion, led by the Victorian Society with Betjeman as vice-chairman, fought back and in 1967 both the stupendous train shed at St Pancras and Gilbert Scott's Midland Grand Hotel were listed at Grade I – the old prejudice in favour of engineering at the expense of Victorian architecture had at last been defeated. Similarly, the Victorian Society's Annual for 1972–3 could announce the reprieve of Whitehall, 'representing, for us, a triumphant grand finale to nearly ten years of hard work'.[38] For in 1963, the demolition of Scott's Foreign Office had been approved as part of Sir Leslie Martin's megalomaniacal scheme to rebuild the whole of Whitehall for the convenience of civil servants; New Scotland Yard and other government buildings had also been threatened.

By the 1970s the Victorian Society was well established and influential with government. What might be described as the 'Victoriana' tendency among some of the founder members had been overwhelmed by a new seriousness, particularly with Pevsner as chairman – John Betjeman complained (surely without justification) in a letter to Summerson in 1968 that 'I have been so denigrated by . . . the Professor-Doktor as a lightweight wax fruit merchant, I will not carry the necessary guns'.[39] Indeed, the Professor-Doktor-Chairman once instructed committee members not to use the term 'Victoriana'. By the end of the 1960s, through the Society's vigorous educational programme of conferences and visits to buildings, a younger generation of historians, such as Nicholas Taylor, Anthony Symondson and Peter Howell, were now looking beyond the Victorians to the Edwardians.

Adventurous tours by Roderick Gradidge even looked at Lutyens both before and after the First World War, but the Society was primarily concerned with Victorian and Edwardian architecture, while the statutory list of historic buildings had ended its scope at 1914. By the 1970s, however, buildings of later date were beginning to be threatened – particularly cinemas of the 1920s and 1930s. Again the feeling arose that a new society was needed: to defend inter-war buildings. The result was the Thirties Society. But the motivation behind this was complicated by the architectural politics of the period. There had always been stylistic preferences among conservationists, of course – within the Victorian Society there was tension (inseparable from snobbery) between the admirers of classical buildings and country houses and those keen on Gothic and churches – but the conflict between traditional styles and the Modern Movement which dominated British architecture in the 1930s was still a very live issue.

And the Modern Movement was officially approved. In 1970 the official terminal date for historic architecture was advanced to 1939 when the Ministry of Housing and Local Government began to list inter-war buildings. This was, in part, a response to the needless and commercially stupid destruction in 1969 of the entrance canopy and hall of the Strand Palace Hotel designed by Oliver Bernard. The selection, however, reflected the prejudices of, in particular, Pevsner, who sat on the subcommittee of the Historic Buildings Council chaired by Lord Holford and who had prepared his own list of fifty inter-war buildings worthy of preservation.[40] As successive volumes of the *Buildings of England* revealed, the chairman of the Victorian Society only allowed merit in buildings after 1914 which acceded to the perceived *zeitgeist* of modernity. So the selected elect of modern masterpieces consisted of famous buildings by Lubetkin, Goldfinger, Connell and Ward, Maxwell Fry, Owen Williams and the like. The only candidates that could be considered as representing a slightly less narrow approach were Norwich City Hall and Goodhart-Rendel's Hay's Wharf offices. As Summerson had written in 1959, 'It seems natural, writing about the past thirty years of English architecture, to write as if the only things worth bothering about were the local initiation, progress and achievements of the "modern movement". Historically, this is evidently lop-sided; but, also historically, it would be extremely difficult to write about the architecture of the period as if it could all be evaluated in much the same way. It cannot be. In architecture, as in painting and sculpture, there has been a deep and wide gulf between the moderns and those who are vaguely and misleadingly described as traditionalists'.[41]

And so, at first, it was the partisan historiography which vaunted the Modern Movement which prevailed. It was this attitude which informed the Arts Council's 'Thirties' exhibition at the Hayward Gallery in 1979 – to which the special number of *Architectural Design* published that year was a deliberate antidote.[42] For by this significant date the moral rightness of the Modern Movement was being seriously questioned, and the publication of *Morality and Architecture* by the historian David Watkin in 1977 put the modern architectural establishment on the defensive. The Lutyens Exhibition at the Hayward in 1981 both redressed the historical balance and gave a boost to the Post-Modern reaction. Criticism – and praise – of this show was strictly on party lines, with particularly humourless venom displayed by the relentlessly modernist critic Reyner Banham against 'King Lut's Navy . . . The National Trust Navy, those roving bands of mansion-fanciers and peerage buffs who go around invading stately homes . . . for fun and profit in the guise of historical scholarship'.[43] In retrospect it can be seen that the belated (and richly deserved) award of the RIBA Gold Medal to Berthold Lubetkin in 1982 was part of a desperate counterattack.

Controversy over the value of 'traditional' British architecture of the 1920s and 1930s first came to a serious issue over the building in the City designed by Edwin Cooper in 1925 for Lloyd's of London together with the Royal Mail. This austere classical pile, strongly influenced by American Beaux-Arts classicism, was threatened with total demolition apart from the exhedra-entrance in Leadenhall Street to make way for the project by Richard Rogers (backed by the RIBA) for a new Lloyd's. Of course, Cooper's building was unlisted and it was clear that there was general uncertainty over evaluating its architectural importance. The rhetoric of Rogers prevailed and the Portland stone building with its grand interior spaces was taken away in 1980; 'the retention of fragments of the original in the new Lloyd's will not compensate for the loss of what has claims to be Cooper's most sustained creative effort in the Classical style', lamented Alan Powers, the future honorary secretary of the Twentieth Century Society.[44] Indeed, by the 1980s, the alliance between modern architects and conservationists which fought for the Euston Arch was quite dead, as was illustrated when the battle lines were drawn for the (first) public inquiry held in 1984 over Peter Palumbo's obsessive wish to replace nine listed Victorian buildings by a posthumous tower by Mies van der Rohe.[45]

A further ingredient in the cocktail of the Thirties Society was the enthusiasm for Art Deco. The revival of Art Nouveau in the 1960s – particularly associated in Britain with interest in Aubrey Beardsley and Charles Rennie Mackintosh – was succeeded by that of the next non-historical but decidedly decorative style. Bevis Hillier published his pioneering survey of *Art Deco in the 1920s and 1930s* in 1968 and cult interest in the phenomenon was further encouraged by enthusiasm for Hollywood movies, as well as by the demise of the high street cinema. Much of this interest was centred on Brighton where, partly owing to Martin Battersby, the Brighton Museum had a fine collection of interwar decorative arts, forming the base of the Decorative Arts Society 1890–1940, founded in 1975.

Bevis Hillier (b. 1940), author and journalist, was a prime mover in the foundation of the Thirties Society and became its first chairman. He was approached by Marcus Binney, the chairman of the new and radical conservation body, SAVE Britain's Heritage (of which more below). Also involved were Clive Aslet (b. 1955), later editor of *Country Life*, who became the first honorary secretary and was particularly exercised by the threat to Edwin Cooper's Lloyd's; and the journalist and future editor of *The Times*, Simon Jenkins (b. 1943), in whose house in Regent's Park Road the initial meetings took place.

Other important early supporters were Jeffery Daniels, of the Geffrye Museum, and the antique dealer Michael Pick. The preponderance of journalists and the absence of architects is conspicuous; indeed, one of the few practising architects involved was the unorthodox Roderick Gradidge (b. 1929) with his bold enthusiasm for despised Neo-Tudor.[46]

The principal problem with the new society was finding a suitable name. Bevis Hillier later recalled that, 'This caused a lot of difficulty. "The Art Deco Society" would not include important neo-classical buildings. "The Inter-War Society" sounded too militaristic. The compromise we arrived at, "The Thirties Society", was not a very happy one (like most compromises) but it had the virtue of being snappy, and before long we were making it clear that the brief we wanted was to protect and preserve the best architecture between say 1914 and 1940 – without crossing wires with the Victorian Society, who had spread their tentacles forward just as we were stretching back ours'.[47] Hillier was also active in acquiring patrons. These included: as president, Sir Osbert Lancaster, the cartoonist and inspired pre-war cataloguer and namer of architectural styles such as 'Stockbrokers' Tudor' and 'Pseudish', as well as Sir John Betjeman, Lady Diana Cooper and Peter Fleetwood-Hesketh (1905–85), an early secretary of the Victorian Society who was an architect turned preservationist. But it must be said that the Thirties Society was consciously distant from the well-established 'Vixoc', which was perceived as too establishment and snobbish (the inevitable fate of all conservation societies as they age, as the Georgian Group had long demonstrated), while the Victorian Society regarded the upstart body with suspicion and envy.[48]

The inaugural meeting was held on 13 December 1979, in the Park Lane Hotel in Piccadilly. This was perhaps unfortunate as the use of this fine Art Deco setting, soon followed by a meeting in Norman Hartnell's salon, gave the Thirties Society an impression of frivolity and led to accusations of dilettantism and lack of seriousness. The magazine *Building Design*, indeed, began a campaign of ridicule of the 'Thirties girls' which the nascent society had to live down.[49] The problem with the Art Deco aficionados was, in fact, analagous to that suffered by the Victorian Society with 'Victoriana'. But the essential seriousness of the Thirties Society's purpose was soon demonstrated by the affair of the Firestone Factory.

Designed by Wallis, Gilbert & Partners and built in 1928–9, the Firestone Factory was the best of several decorative modernistic industrial buildings along the Great West Road which expressed the optimism and Americanisation of the period. In the summer of 1979 the Firestone Tyre Company decided to cease production and sell the site of the factory to a subsidiary of Trafalgar House Ltd. Both the Thirties Society and SAVE Britain's Heritage then requested the Department of the Environment to 'spot-list' the building. On Friday 22 August, the Department revealed to a demolition company approached by the purchaser that the listing of the Firestone Factory would be approved the following week. The consequence was that, although the sale had not been completed, Trafalgar House ordered the smashing of the ornamental centre of the building over the following bank holiday weekend. By the time the civil servants were back at their desks, the Firestone Factory was lost.

MARCUS BINNEY

The Firestone Factory before and after demolition begun over the August bank holiday weekend, 1980.

In the first issue of the Society's journal, Simon Jenkins wrote that, 'The Thirties Society could have asked for a less tragic launching pad than the destruction . . . of Wallis Gilbert's Firestone Factory . . . But it could hardly have wished for a wider coverage – nor for a swifter response from the Environment Secretary, Michael Heseltine, in promptly listing a further 12 inter-war buildings and drawing up criteria for further spotlisting . . . Of the importance of the Firestone even the most cynical observers had little doubt. I can recall few buildings of the past decade whose destruction has produced more spontaneous outrage from laymen . . .'.[50] This was to the new society what the Euston Arch was to the Victorian Society, and this shabby pre-emptive strike had a similar effect on both public and official opinion. The Secretary of State eventually listed some 150 interwar buildings, including the Hoover Factory, also by Wallis, Gilbert & Partners and Battersea Power Station, as well as monumental classic town halls by Edwin Cooper, Vincent Harris and Berry Webber. The argument that there was more to the twentieth century than the Modern Movement had at last been won.

But there were plenty more battles to fight. The Thirties Society was soon embroiled with London Transport in trying to prevent the best Underground stations being gratuitously mutilated, and with the newly privatised British Telecom to mitigate the proposed cull of every 'traditional' red telephone box in Britain (designed by Sir Giles Scott). Also, in 1986, in alliance with SAVE Britain's Heritage, the society launched a campaign to save Monkton, the house by Lutyens in Sussex transformed by Edward James, the great patron of the Surrealists, as the trustees of the Edward James Foundation at West Dean were, inexplicably, set upon dispersing its extraordinary contents following their founder's death in 1984. This battle was lost, denying the nation the chance of enjoying a uniquely enjoyable twentieth-century creation of immense historical and artistic significance.[51]

In these campaigns, the Thirties Society published reports that were closely modelled on those published by SAVE Britain's Heritage. SAVE had been founded in 1975 as a novel ginger group. Following the 'Destruction of the Country House' exhibition organised by John Harris and Marcus Binney, a meeting was held at the RIBA late in 1974 and a working committee established the following year. This consisted of Colin Amery, Peter Burman, Timothy Cantell, Dan Cruickshank, Simon Jenkins, David Pearce and Margaret Richardson, with Binney (b. 1944) as chairman. Pearce was the only architect; all the rest were historians and/or journalists. SAVE was consciously different from all other conservation societies. It was unencumbered by ordinary members (having only a committee) and it became expert at generating publicity through press releases and reports on both individual threatened buildings and particular building types, such as industrial mills. It also became actively involved in the process of restoration by taking on threatened buildings, notably Sir Robert Taylor's Barlaston Hall in Staffordshire and Sir Gilbert Scott's church of All Souls, Haley Hill, Halifax.[52]

Resourceful, well-connected and brave, SAVE was very different from the established amenity societies and reinvigorated the conservation world. It also brought people together over sandwiches at the 'SAVE Lunches' held in Patrick Trevor-Roper's house in Park Square West. SAVE was also a pioneer in using broader arguments than those concerning aesthetic quality or historical importance, arguing, in the *SAVE Report* of 1975, that, 'Buildings – and not just historic ones, represent energy, labour and materials, which either cannot be replaced or can only be replaced at enormous cost. The fight to save particular buildings or groups of buildings is not the fancy of some impractical antiquarian. It is part of the battle for the sane use of all our resources.'[53] This led to the accusation, from Sir John Summerson, among others, that SAVE was totally uncritical about what it fought for and was therefore a menace.

This survey has concentrated on the principal amenity societies based in London whose architectural scope is defined by chronology. But it is important to recognise that there are many other independent organisations which have a specialist interest, such as the Cinema Theatre Association (founded in 1967), the Friends of Friendless Churches (1957), the new Chapel Society (1993) and, perhaps, the Ancient Monuments Society (1924). Founded by the architect and historian, John Swarbrick (1879–1964), for 'the study and conservation of ancient monuments, historic buildings and fine old craftsmanship', the AMS was, in effect, a northern branch of the SPAB until 1953 when it moved its base from Manchester to London.[54] There are also the bodies concerned with restoring particular buildings, like the Friends of Christ Church Spitalfields, whose membership overlaps with the principal amenity societies. This survey is, unfortunately, also English and metropolitan in bias, for it must not be forgotten that there are many local societies, civic societies and other bodies which fight hard for threatened buildings all over Britain. The Victorian Society has active Regional Groups while the Georgian Society for East Yorkshire was founded back in 1937. Honourable mention should also be made of the Ulster

Architectural Heritage Society, founded in 1967, and its admirable series of publications.

Scotland has been largely ignored here and really deserves a chapter on its own. In the early years of this century bodies like the SPAB and the National Trust were ambivalent about whether they were English or British in scope. The National Trust for Scotland was founded in 1931. Similarly, the Scottish Georgian Society was founded in 1956 and renamed the Architectural Heritage Society of Scotland in 1985 to make the wider range of its interest quite clear: 'Scotland is rich in natural beauty but it is not so well endowed with fine architecture that any more of it can now be wasted. Its mediaeval heritage is largely cared for by the government. There then follows the remarkable late development of the Scottish castle and from the seventeenth century to the end of the Victorian era, a stock of boldly detailed buildings in a variety of styles . . . These buildings are all now in danger . . . The Scottish Georgian Society is truly Scottish, not just another Edinburgh amenity group . . .'.[55] In fact, Edinburgh can boast the oldest of local societies in the Cockburn Association founded in 1875, while the New Glasgow Society was founded in 1969. Glasgow also has two societies devoted to protecting the work of local heroes: the Charles Rennie Mackintosh Society, founded in 1973, and the Alexander Thomson Society, established in 1991.[56]

In contemplating the architecture of postwar Britain (as opposed to England) it seems tragic that the two finest modern buildings in both Scotland and Wales are both in a desperate state: the Brynmawr Rubber Factory by the Architects' Co-Partnership is seriously threatened with demolition while the seminary at Cardross by Gillespie, Kidd & Coia is an obscene ruin. The sad fate of much of Scotland's best modern architecture is one reason why DOCOMOMO (Scotland) was set up in 1992. This is a local branch of the international working-party (established in Eindhoven) for Documentation and Conservation of buildings, sites and neighbourhoods of Modern Movement and one which objects to the assumption of DOCOMOMO (UK) to speak for north of the border.

DOCOMOMO (UK) was, after its inception in 1990, also resented by the Thirties Society for its narrow and partisan obsession with but one twentieth-century type of architecture. Indeed, the Thirties Society, as well as maintaining a resolutely catholic approach to style (defending the best of Modern Movement, classical, Art Deco or Tudor production), also led the way in campaigning for the protection of the best of postwar architecture. In Scotland, it was noted, it was theoretically possible for modern buildings over thirty years old to be listed, while in England the scope of the Department of the Environment ended firmly in 1939. This barrier was breached in 1987 when, apparently on the basis of a report submitted by the chairman of the Thirties Society, the first postwar English building was listed. This was Albert Richardson's Bracken House of 1955–9, ironically not 'Modern' at all, but a progressive traditional design that had been roundly condemned by the likes of Nikolaus Pevsner when it was built.[57]

In recognition of its increasing role in fighting for post- as well as pre-Second World War architecture, the Thirties Society at last rid itself of its problematic image and renamed itself the Twentieth Century Society in 1993. It now supports the systematic survey and listing of postwar architecture by English Heritage – the Historic Buildings and Monuments Commission – which was inaugurated by the government in 1983, while remaining anxious that unpublicised 'traditional' buildings of the 1950s and 1960s, such as Giles Scott's Bankside Power Station, are considered as well as famous 'Modern' ones. This policy has begun to heal the great breach between the architectural profession and (some) conservationists, as well as attracting the support of a much younger generation. However, it must be recognised that, as timid government ministers are well aware, an interest in protecting the best architecture of that most destructive decade, the 1960s, is not at all shared by a wider public. 'The simple truth about these architectural masterpieces,' maintains Auberon Waugh, 'is that they were never intended to last more than forty years. Like cheap motor-cars, they have obsolescence built into them, so that more work can be found for the next generation of architectural geniuses. There can be no excuse for preserving more than one of them for succeeding generations to laugh at'.[58]

As this terrible century draws to its close, what is striking is that the wheel of fashion is revolving more and more quickly, and that the interval between creation and revival is diminishing. Around 1900, the gap could be measured in centuries; in the 1990s it is but a few decades, and perhaps the most hated architecture today is the Post-Modernism of the previous – Mrs Thatcher's – decade, the 1980s. Soon, perhaps, conservation will catch up with the present, so nothing will be unfashionable and there will be no battles to fight – an alarming prospect, perhaps, until it is recognised that the immense built treasure of England's rich and varied architectural history continues to weather and decay or be mutilated and threatened by the stupid and the venal. There will always be much to do by those cursed with a passion for old buildings.

Meanwhile, one of the most extraordinary and cheering projects for the next Millennium is that to recreate the Euston Arch. The architectural historian Dan Cruickshank has discovered many of the original stones dumped in the River Lea and believes that, with these combined with much new stone, the murdered Doric propylaeum can rise again in Euston Square. If achieved, the resurrected Arch will both right a great wrong and stand as a symbol of the triumph of conservation.

6
Nationalising the country house

Peter Mandler

At the outbreak of the Second World War, the country house was at a nadir, both in its traditional role as the home of the great landowner, and in its modern role as a historic building worthy of preservation.[1] Socially and economically, the decline of arable agriculture and escalating rates of income tax and death duties on the rich had been breaking up the great estates for half a century, and breaking up country houses, too – over 5 per cent of the national stock of country houses was demolished between the world wars.[2] Politically and culturally, the country-house-owning class had been losing further ground over the same period. An increasingly democratic and egalitarian society no longer looked, as it had done in the mid-nineteenth century, to its historic landed class either for political leadership or for national symbolism. Country houses that a century earlier had been hailed as 'the mansions of the olden time' or 'the stately homes of England' were generally derided as white elephants, symbols of deservedly departed grandeur. Even the minority that did seek to honour and preserve vestiges of the national past – the pioneers of the conservation movement – almost universally preferred other heritage objects, less controversial and more consensual, such as ancient monuments, medieval churches or (best of all) bits of 'cottage' and 'village' England, from which the sturdy yeomen of the modern democracy (not the proud aristocrat) had sprung.

Nous avons changé tout cela. Today, not only has preservation been converted from a minority fad to a mainstream preoccupation, but the country house has moved well up the list of objects to be preserved. In many people's minds – among the general public as well as among cultural critics – the preservation of the English country house and the rise of heritage consciousness in the post-war period are of a piece.[3] This chapter seeks to explore the reasons behind, and the progress of, the 'nationalisation' of the country house, its rapid transformation from a private home into a public symbol, against the background of the broader preservation movement. It will be suggested that the circumstances of this sudden *volte-face* are not necessarily propitious for the long-term future of the country house. To understand why this should be requires an understanding first of the conditions preventing 'nationalisation' of the country house before the Second World War, and then a consideration of how – and how far – those conditions have altered since.

Private houses: to 1939

Given the spirit of *laissez-faire* that made British governments so reluctant to legislate for preservation, combined with the leading political role that great landowners played through the inter-war years, it is hardly surprising that country houses escaped legislative protection before 1939. At the insistence of landed politicians, the early ancient monuments acts excluded inhabited houses entirely as private property beyond the reach of any national claim. When antiquaries proposed to make such a claim in 1911, the Duke of Rutland dismissed it as 'a piece of massive impudence . . . Fancy my not being allowed to make a necessary alteration at Haddon without first obtaining the leave of some inspector!', and the resulting Ancient Monuments Act 1913 preserved the blanket exemption.[4] A decade later, the rogue peer Lord Beauchamp – he was both a Liberal and a homosexual – tried to lure country-house owners within the purview of State protection with the argument that '[t]he State should be prepared to recognise' – with grants and tax exemptions – 'the services of an owner who maintains on account of its historic artistic value a structure which is ill suited for modern requirements'. Such inducements had as yet little appeal to owners who in the 1920s had their own recipe – demolition – for structures 'ill suited for modern requirements'.[5] Although limited powers over inhabited buildings were granted to local authorities in the Town and Country Planning Act 1932, these powers were intended strictly to give towns the power to preserve their historic centres, and were in practice hardly ever employed. Even so, Lord Cranborne complained in *The Times*, 'It used to be said that an Englishman's house was his castle. It seems that this is no longer true in a town-planned area'.[6]

Such alarmism testifies more to the intransigence of country-house owners than to any real threat. There was not much public agitation for the preservation of historic buildings in this period, and what agitation there was would hardly have attached itself first to large country houses. Although, in the nineteenth century, country houses dating from 'the olden time' (the romantic age of the Tudors and early Stuarts) had been the objects of literary and artistic veneration and a surprising amount of tourism, such historical enthusiasms had been on the decline since the 1880s. A more democratic and materialist public came increasingly to see large houses, even those of 'the olden time', as symbols of excessive wealth and power. Reciprocally, owners of these houses began to withdraw them from public view and were, if anything, less rather than more likely to accept the public claims asserted by antiquaries. Substantially fewer country houses were open to the public in the 1930s than in the 1870s.[7]

In so far as country houses remained of public interest, it was as centres of enviable stretches of open space. Access to the countryside, especially near large towns, was one of the key points of conflict between aristocracy and people in the 1920s and '30s. Sometimes conflict could be resolved by purchase – many local authorities bought country houses in their grounds for use as public parks – but in these cases the public showed how much they cared for the houses by demolishing them, or turning them into refreshment rooms, or employing them as warehouses for museum collections. The historic-house museum as we know it today, where the house is as much the centre of attraction as its park, hardly existed before 1939. Of the 507 local museums in Britain in 1928, only sixteen were 'interesting historical buildings furnished so as to present the appearance of an inhabited house of the period', almost all of them town-houses.[8]

The educated minority that did care for historic architecture was not unaffected by the mounting anti-aristocratic feeling in society at large. Artists and architects had a deep-seated distaste for the classicism of the eighteenth century as too plain, but also too foreign and exclusive. Their preference for the vernacular styles of the fifteenth, sixteenth and seventeenth centuries – especially the small manor house or cottage – manifested itself in a range of new 'old English' buildings, as well as in the preservationist efforts of the Society for the Protection of Ancient Buildings. Thus when antiquaries showed a desire to protect inhabited houses, it was only houses dating from before the eighteenth century that they had in mind; 1700 was the terminal date of the brief given to the Royal Commission on Historical Monuments when it was appointed in 1908 to inventory the historic buildings of England. Similarly, in the early years of the National Trust, founded in 1895 to preserve places of historic interest as well as natural beauty, the historic buildings acquired were almost exclusively early in date and vernacular in style. The Trust's first country houses were small manor houses, medieval or Tudor, and its first large country house – Montacute, accepted reluctantly as a gift in 1932 – was Jacobean. The fact that there was a mini-revival in classical architecture at this time, largely confined to commissions for new country houses, only reinforced the link between classicism and exclusivity; the majority of architects did not have super-rich patrons, as did Sir Edwin Lutyens.[9]

For the same reasons, the very small group of people who did admire the typical (that is, classical) country house – a minority within a minority – tended to hail from landed backgrounds, and initially their cult was a private one. The politician Lord Curzon, who preserved two medieval castles, Tattershall and Bodiam, at his own expense and bequeathed them to the National Trust in 1925, also treasured his family seat, neo-classical Kedleston in Derbyshire, but never considered it as anything but a private possession. The one or two owners who, in the 1920s, deplored the mass demolition of classical houses as a national tragedy, and who, like Lord Beauchamp, felt legislative protection to be the lesser evil, were roundly denounced by both their peers and the public.

At this date, there was hardly even a concept of 'the country house', one which linked the mansions of the olden time with the quite different classical houses of the post-Civil War period. Christopher Hussey began to talk up such a country-house tradition in the pages of *Country Life* in the late 1920s, but it was then a view idiosyncratic to him and a small knot of fellow landowner aesthetes, who included the architect Lord Gerald Wellesley (later Duke of Wellington). When in 1936 Hussey and his friends persuaded the National Trust to take up the cause of the country house generically, the response was tepid at best. A young organiser, James Lees-Milne, was hired; government was asked to consider aiding owners, or at least exempting their houses from death duties; owners were offered the chance to remain in their houses while formal title passed to the National Trust, thus avoiding death duty on future successions. But neither government nor owners showed much interest. No tax concessions were forthcoming, and hardly any owners were interested in a scheme that had only public benefits. The few that were interested had ideological motives – the Liberal Lord Lothian (whose 1934 speech launched the scheme and who handed over Blickling), the socialist Sir Charles Trevelyan (who ultimately handed over Wallington) and the Liberal MP Sir Geoffrey Mander (who offered Wightwick Manor). The exception to this rule was the very wealthy but heirless Sir Henry Hoare, who handed over Stourhead in Wiltshire. By the time war broke out in autumn 1939, most sympathetic observers felt that the country-houses scheme had been a failure, and that, if the Second World War was to have the same social and political consequences as the first, the stately homes of England were on the brink of a final holocaust.

"This is my last warning, Charles. If you do not mend your ways I shall leave the estate to you instead of to the National Trust."

REPRODUCED BY PERMISSION OF PUNCH

Cartoon from *Punch*, 22 Jan. 1947: in the immediate post-war years, the grandest country houses were viewed by their owners more as burdens than as treasures.

Empty houses: 1939–53

To judge by *Brideshead Revisited*, Evelyn Waugh's elegy to the lost world of the country house, published in 1945, a holocaust did indeed ensue. Country houses, which had been largely untouched by the First World War, or at worst genteelly volunteered as hospitals, were requisitioned on a grand scale in the Second World War and adapted structurally to serve as hospitals, schools, warehouses, headquarters and barracks. Especially in the latter case, serious damage could be done to architectural features of which the average trooper knew and cared nothing – as was the fate of Brideshead.

When peace dawned, it was clear to everyone that country-house life *ante bellum* could never return. War damage could not be repaired due to shortages of building materials; the Bedford estate was fined even for knocking down part of Woburn Abbey in 1953. Nor could residence be resumed on a pre-war basis. Fuel and servants were in short supply for those who had the income to purchase such things, which, given very high marginal tax rates, few had. The election of a Labour government in 1945 cast further uncertainty over the economic functions of the country-house owner. Would agriculture come under State control? Would land development rights be nationalised? Would capital be confiscated? In these circumstances the country house seemed frozen by forces beyond control, and much later Lees-Milne compared it to Coleridge's 'sunny pleasure-dome with caves of ice', recalling also his frigid, desponding winter of 1946–7. Although Lees-Milne had clocked up some signal successes for the Trust's scheme during the war, scooping up Knole, Charlecote, Cliveden and West Wycombe, he felt that the scale of the problem was now well beyond the Trust's meagre resources, and that owners, so far from defending their homes, were now looking for the best terms on which to abandon them. Whereas owners had responded to post-First World War adversity by retreating into their bunkers, now the bunkers themselves were no longer tenable.[10]

On the bright side, the evident helplessness of the owners and the pathetic state of their houses began at this point to work a change of attitude. As the aristocracy lost its privileges and self-consciousness, public hostility declined, and large country houses could be perceived as pieces of art and architecture rather than as symbols of a social order. Scholars and preservationists who had hardly acknowledged the existence of the classical country house before the war found their sympathies and interest suddenly excited. Owners reciprocated with a new-found willingness to throw open their doors and archives. As a result, the country house and its collections played a central role in the remarkable flood of writing and broadcasting on architecture after the war: in Nikolaus Pevsner's *Buildings of England* series, for instance (appearing from 1951), or in John Summerson's classic text *Architecture in Britain 1530 to 1830* (1953), or in Howard Colvin's *Biographical Dictionary of English Architects, 1660–1840* (1954), or in innumerable broadcasts on architectural topics on the Home Service as well as the Third Programme by the likes of Pevsner, Summerson, John Betjeman, Hugh Casson and J. M. Richards. Few of these had shown much interest in country houses before 1939 and some, such as Pevsner, Summerson and Richards, had been almost exclusively identified with urban and

"You realize, I suppose, that this makes us Civil Servants."

REPRODUCED BY PERMISSION OF PUNCH

Cartoon from *Punch*, 14 May 1947: the National Trust's growing dependence on public funds for country-house preservation made it seem at the time like just another nationalised industry.

industrial architecture, so that younger modernists of the 1950s accused them of apostasy.[11]

How far did this experts' change of heart affect the general public? At first glance, not very far. While public hostility to the aristocracy specifically was tailing off, public hostility to great wealth in general was mounting; the result was the election of a Labour government in 1945 and the persistence of very high marginal tax rates and rationing. When asked, the public was no longer gleeful about country-house decay but not very sympathetic either. A common opinion was that country houses ought to be saved for efficiency's sake, not as cultural treasures but as big buildings suitable for use as 'Eventide Homes for workers', holiday centres, sanitaria, hostels or even as dance halls (as was said to be the case in Denmark).[12] The wartime success of the country-houses scheme was viewed with suspicion as 'a funk hole for death duty dodgers' and an attempt to publicise it after the war was met, Lees-Milne reported fretfully, with 'hostility, boredom, and criticism on the part of the Press that we were out of touch with the public'.[13]

Despite the more positive attitude of some owners and experts, therefore, the future of the country house looked very precarious indeed at the war's end. Lees-Milne felt that, apart from the restricted number of houses whose owners would consider passing them to the National Trust, the fate of most houses would be, if not demolition, then alternative use that preserved little or none of their historic or aesthetic value. Much hinged on the attitude of the Labour government. While most of its leaders shared the public indifference to the plight of the country house – and they had more important tasks to attend to – a few were alert to the effects that taxation policies were having on the great landed estate. Hugh Dalton, the Chancellor of the Exchequer, a lover of open space and a future President of the Ramblers Association, was particularly concerned that confiscatory taxation should not lead to the anarchic break-up of the countryside that had ensued after 1918. In his 1946 budget he created a £50 million National Land Fund,

> to buy some of the best of our still unspoiled open country, and stretches of coast, to be preserved for ever, not for the enjoyment of a few private land-owners, but as a playground and a national possession for all our people.[14]

Dalton's hope was that the purchases of the National Land Fund (NLF), coupled with forthcoming legislation establishing national parks and nationalising land development rights, would appropriate the great estates for public enjoyment. His concern, reflecting inter-war priorities, was strictly for open space, not for art or architecture (in which he showed no interest), but the National Trust was hopeful that some of this fund might be bent towards architectural preservation as well. It began to lobby Dalton hard to fund from the NLF Trust purchases of houses and estates that owners were unable to endow themselves, or, *in extremis*, to purchase country houses in addition to estates for State ownership. It felt that State-owned country houses would be dead museums, but better than no country houses at all.

Suddenly, in November 1947, Dalton was removed from the Exchequer – he had inadvertently revealed details of the budget to a journalist on his way to the House – and was replaced by Sir Stafford Cripps. Unlike Dalton, Cripps had no firm views on landed estates and, on the urging of Lords Esher and Crawford of the National Trust, decided that a long-term policy should be deliberately hammered out by means of an official inquiry. The Committee on Houses of Outstanding Historic or Architectural Interest was appointed in autumn 1948 under the chairmanship of the veteran civil servant Sir Ernest Gowers. It took evidence principally from owners and experts and reported in June 1950.

The Gowers Report is very important, not so much for influencing government policy – as we shall see, it proved politically inept – but rather for crystallising among its advocates a view of the country house's place in the culture. Although, perhaps because, only half the committee members had prior commitments to art and architecture, their report made far-reaching claims for the country house as a work of art and as a national treasure.[15] The report embraced the view advanced to it by the Duke of Wellington that 'the English country house is the greatest contribution made by England to the visual arts'; more, that 'these houses represent an association of beauty, of art and of nature . . . which is irreplaceable, and has seldom, if ever, been equalled in the history of civilisation.' Such rhetoric had before this date been pretty much confined to the pages of *Country Life*, but the report asserted, without much foundation, that the public was coming to share this view. Secondly, the report accepted the claim that owners or (in default) the National Trust were the best custodians of these national treasures, not the State. This claim, vigorously asserted in evidence by Christopher Hussey, was made not on the pre-war basis that owners should be allowed to enjoy their private property, but on Hussey's grounds that the cultural value of the house lay in its historic *ensemble*: not just the house, but its furnishings, collections, gardens, park, estate and family, in sum, a 'way of life'. Thirdly, therefore, the central recommendation of the report was that special tax reliefs and grants be allowed to country-house owners, more or less regardless of public access, to enable them to preserve their own homes. Only in cases where the owners chose voluntarily to abandon title but retain residence should the National

Trust be enabled to accept houses, and, even more rarely, only in cases where the owners chose to abandon their houses entirely should the State take ownership itself.[16]

Public reaction to the Gowers Report was muted at first: what comment there was expressed support for the idea of country-house preservation but, ominously, only the romantic – Tory *Daily Telegraph* backed subsidy to private owners.[17] The government to whom Gowers reported was aghast. Instead of the manageable proposal to take over or aid a representative sample of houses through the National Land Fund, Gowers was recommending blanket tax reliefs to 2,000 or more owners, at a cost (so the Inland Revenue estimated) of £10 million per annum. Instead of a plan which focused on public benefits, including access for ramblers and tourists and alternative uses of their houses, Gowers had turned the spotlight on to the plight of private owners, explicitly rejecting alternative use and downplaying even the possibilities for tourism.

The effect of the Gowers Report was double-edged. On the one hand, it shifted the range of policy options open to government decisively away from the forms of public ownership envisaged by Dalton. The National Trust scheme was now not the least but the most nationalised alternative under consideration. But on the other hand, neither a Labour government nor a vigorously egalitarian electorate could be expected to swallow Gowers's 'doles for dukes'. The government proceeded very cautiously. It prepared legislation making possible small maintenance grants to private owners in return for public access, but rejected tax reliefs except those that facilitated public or semi-public ownership (such as death duty concessions on gifts to the nation or the National Trust). Interestingly, when a Conservative government inherited these plans on coming to power in autumn 1951, it was, if anything, less enthusiastic. The minister responsible, David Eccles, though himself a connoisseur and member of the Georgian Group, was opposed not only to the public expenditure involved but also to the very idea of preservation. 'The fact is that the spacious way of life has changed,' he told parliament. 'No one can preserve all the outward manifestations when the life itself has taken on new forms . . . If we bent too much of our energies in trying to do so, that would, in my view, be a mark of decline in the nation.'[18]

The resulting legislation – the Historic Buildings and Ancient Monuments Act 1953, which remains the foundation of State preservation today – was correspondingly modest. It established Historic Buildings Councils (HBCs) for England, Scotland and Wales, composed of a mixed bag of experts and owners, to distribute repair and maintenance grants to the owners of historic buildings in return for public access. The English HBC had the lion's share of the money and nearly all the country-house work. The Treasury permitted modest increases in its expenditure in its early years, but as it got into its stride in the late 1950s the alarmed authorities froze its 'ration' at £400,000 per annum and, despite later increases, the ration shrank in real terms throughout the 1960s. About half of its budget was disbursed to country houses, and half of that to private owners (the remainder going to country houses owned by the National Trust, other charities or local authorities). Occasionally the Beaverbrook press kicked up a fuss about these 'doles for dukes', but normally the HBC did its work with little publicity and little opposition.[19]

The outcome of the post-war debate had been to encourage owners to defend their 'way of life' on their own, unhindered (if also mostly unaided) by the State. The prospect of widespread public or semi-public ownership of country houses receded. The system that Dalton had envisaged to bring landed estates into public ownership was also abandoned by Conservative governments after 1951. Development rights were effectively denationalised; the National Land Fund, which had been used sparingly to pass about a dozen country houses to the National Trust, was reduced in 1957 and hardly used at all after 1962. Between them, the experts and the Gowers Committee had defended the intact and inhabited country house from alternative use or public ownership, but in failing to achieve more positive results they had only placed the ball back in the court of the owners.

Open houses: 1953–74

To everyone's surprise, the owners managed pretty well on their own. When Waugh reissued *Brideshead Revisited* in 1959, he looked back on it as 'a panegyric preached over an empty coffin': the English aristocracy had preserved its identity and its houses to a degree unimaginable in 1945.[20] Of course Waugh exaggerated in 1959 as he had done in 1945. Aristocratic identity, especially among the younger ones who had seen war service, had changed considerably, not least by emerging from the stately isolation maintained before the war. It was this re-engagement with society, which helped to curry public favour, that was conducive to preservation of the historic house.

Many owners were unable or unwilling to resume residence after the war. They were often enormously relieved to have had this burden lifted from their shoulders. The ease and comfort of a smaller house or a London flat had proved

RCHME © CROWN COPYRIGHT

Bowood, Wilts.: south and west elevations of the main house (mainly by Henry Keene and Robert Adam, 1755–71); demolished 1955–6.

a pleasant novelty. Many came also to feel that the large house was ill-suited to the political realities of the new age: the landowner had to refashion himself as a businessman and entrepreneur and abandon the trappings of feudalism and *noblesse oblige*. This refashioning had two, countervailing effects on the country house. First, it did lead to further abandonment. The 1950s were the peak years of country-house demolition – at least another 10 per cent of the national stock went.[21] Other houses were ruthlessly cut down in size, as at Bowood in Wiltshire (the main block went, leaving only the orangery and stable block) and Woburn Abbey (which, illegally, lost its east wing, tennis court and riding school). Still others were sold off for institutional use as schools, colleges, hospitals and nursing homes. But secondly, owners were now more willing to contemplate uses in between the extremes of stately residence and abandonment. This could mean a hardheaded economic approach – partial conversion into flats, or use of the house as headquarters for the estate enterprise or lease for alternative use. For owners of historically or aesthetically important houses, it could also mean an attempt to exploit these qualities in the marketplace.

At first it did not occur to many owners that use might profitably embrace tourism and connoisseurship. Landowners' representatives submitting evidence to the Gowers Committee downplayed the possibilities of touristic access.[22] They were looking for tax concessions with the fewest possible strings attached, but they were also reflecting the pre-war aristocracy's prevailing view that the country house was a home, not a work of art and certainly not a national heritage. As the post-war generation succeeded, this view changed. The continued breakup of great estates meant that country-house owners were decreasingly part of a self-sustaining rural society, obsessed with agriculture and country sports. Increasingly their orientation became more urban and cosmopolitan. The burgeoning art and antiques market caused many to strike up relationships with auction houses and other centres of connoisseurship. The new enthusiasm shown by art and architectural historians helped; so did the proselytizing in landed circles of the Historic Buildings Councils, talking up tourism and offering as bait their helpful *douceurs*.

The 6th Marquess of Bath was not, strictly speaking, the pioneer of what came to be known as 'the stately home business'. Warwick Castle had been open to the public on a commercial basis, daily except for Christmas, almost every year (even in wartime) since 1885, and income from tourism had made the difference between penury and ease for successive Earls of Warwick. But there is no doubt that Lord Bath was the trailblazer of his generation. He had told Gowers that

> it was wrong in principle to consider any scheme of subsidising owners to live in their own houses . . . owners should help themselves and . . ., given vision and drive, many houses could be kept going in the same way as Longleat.

He had at that time already chosen not to live at Longleat, but not to abandon it, either; he was seeking to divide part of it into flats, and at Easter 1949 had opened it commercially to the public.[23] By the time that Gowers reported, among private houses there were as yet only a handful attempting to open on a commercial basis, although the National Trust was also now gingerly showing several of its larger houses. By the time the HBCs swung into operation, these pioneers had attracted many imitators, especially from 1951 when the Festival of Britain focused national attention on the economic benefits of tourism. Over 100 English country houses were open to the public in the Festival year, over 200 five years later, and nearly 300 ten years later, of which over 100 were privately owned.[24]

REPRODUCED BY PERMISSION OF THE MARQUESS OF BATH

Lord Bath at Longleat with one of his lions. Lord Bath was one of the first stately home owners to make his estate into a commercial visitor attraction.

Not many houses were able to attract the hundreds of thousands drawn to large, commercialised operations such as Longleat and Warwick, Lord Montagu's Beaulieu Abbey, or the ducal seats of Blenheim Palace, Chatsworth or Woburn Abbey. On the other hand, not many owners wished to follow this route. Most private houses open to the public were only open one or two days a week in the summer season. This was enough to qualify for HBC grant and, it was thought, not much was to be gained financially by opening the smaller country house further. The point was not to turn the house completely into a tourist attraction, but to gain the maximum benefit from tourism while continuing to use the house for other purposes, including part of it as a home. The idea that tourists wanted to see a home, emblematic of a 'way of life', shored up this practice.

Furthermore, tourism was only one of a number of options that owners were pursuing in the 1950s and 1960s. The 100 or so houses open to tourists were, of course, dwarfed by the hundreds that were not open, but remained the centres of estates.[25] These survived by other means, not so much agriculture (which limped along satisfactorily, but was inadequate to support the larger house) as the extraordinarily buoyant market for land (and, secondarily, for art). The Conservative position, successfully pushed by David Eccles in 1953, that the future of the country house lay in a deregulated land market and private enterprise, not nationalisation or even subsidy, remained the dominant one among both landowners and policymakers even after Labour was returned to power in 1964.[26] Landowners who had been despondent in the 1930s, because agriculture was failing, and in the 1940s, because State control loomed, were in the 1950s and 1960s much more optimistic. James Lees-Milne marvelled on visits in this period how buoyant were houses and families that had appeared to be on the brink of breakup during the war. This recovery did not depend upon tourism and connoisseurship, but by demonstrating the continuing vitality of country-house life in modern conditions, it helped to underpin the post-Gowers consensus that that 'way of life' could, and should, be preserved.

Thus by the 1960s a remarkable renaissance had been achieved. The old prejudices against the aristocratic lifestyle and against the classical styles associated with it had been largely erased. Those educated in art and architecture, including a section of the country-house-visiting population, were now devoted equally to Tudor gables, Palladian facades and (more tentatively) to picturesque Victorian skylines. What connected these disparate images was a continuous tradition of aristocratic country life, adding to houses and accumulating collections over generations, and surviving into the present day. No public commitment had been made to this heritage, apart from the small (and, in real terms, shrinking) HBC grant, but it seemed to be flourishing by means of private enterprise. Fewer houses were needing rescue operations via the National Trust. More houses were opening to the public.

Nevertheless, it would be wrong to exaggerate the rootedness of public attachment. Most country houses were surviving because of their owners' prosperity, not because public opinion was rallied behind them. The average day-tripper to the big showplaces such as Longleat or Chatsworth was not thought to be a loyal supporter. 'Arriving by the coach-loads at week-ends and in the holiday season,' wrote John Summerson in 1955, 'they pour into the house, through and out of it, and are probably little the wiser for anything they have seen or heard. Their great pleasure is in contrasts of grandeur and misery; they are touched, though inwardly gratified, by the collapse of privilege, and evidences of the descent are eagerly, whisperingly sought.' The smaller, select audience for the more aesthetic, less aristocratic house was more dedicated, but, Summerson feared, hidebound by class and intellectual snobberies. 'Such considerations put a brake on popularity.'[27]

As the nation's educational and material standards rose, there were opportunities to broaden the base of the country house's popularity. But not many owners were eager to grasp these opportunities, as Lord Montagu of Beaulieu complained in his 1967 'how-to' guide to the stately home business.[28] Even the National Trust, the membership of which rose steadily in the 1950s and 1960s with national prosperity, had its foot on the brake. Its traditional leadership was 'emphatically against any positive steps to enlarge the membership', fearing that too many visitors to its country houses would disturb their fragile atmosphere of serenity and good taste.[29]

A new generation of National Trust leaders emerged in the 1960s anxious to find an outlet for the booming membership's energies, and new departures in canal and coastline preservation were undertaken. But those responsible for these initiatives continued to feel stifled. John Smith, who initiated the canals campaign in 1958 in the hopes that 'it will bring about a spectacular increase in our membership', soon discovered that the 'men of taste' at the Trust's helm did not wish to become part of the mass-leisure business. He resigned his leadership position in 1964, bitter at the Trust's lack of energy, imagination and enterprise, which was cutting it off from the mainstream.[30] A few years later, another of the Trust's new enterprises spawned another rebel. Commander Conrad Rawnsley, grandson of one of the Trust's founders, had been hired in 1963 at John Smith's instance to run Enterprise Neptune, a public appeal aimed at purchasing substantial sections of the coastline. Rawnsley was an irascible character whose frictions with the Trust's leadership hardly stemmed solely from the latter's lethargy. But when these frictions led to Rawnsley's sacking in late 1966, and Rawnsley launched a public campaign against the Trust's elitism, his charges – though crudely phrased – rang a bell. Rawnsley called for a return to the ideals of the National Trust's founders, away from saving country houses for their owners and back to saving the countryside for the people. Since Rawnsley was in part appealing to the general public against the Trust's membership, elderly and privileged, it was easy for the leadership to persuade the members to reject his reform proposals. Subsequent internally generated reforms did lead to more rapid membership growth and a greater commercialisation of the Trust's country houses, such as Montagu had advocated, as well as further diversification of the Trust's activities, as Smith had urged. Yet by publicly repudiating criticism and engineering reforms oligarchically, the Trust's leadership ensured that its public image would remain into the 1970s pretty much as John Smith had described, snooty, nostalgic and unduly protective of its country houses.[31]

In that national mainstream for which Smith pined, the country house was still more of a curiosity than a treasure. The survival of great landowners was no longer much inveighed against but was viewed as a historical anomaly, motored by the adaptability and shrewd business sense of the class. The showmen responsible for the likes of Beaulieu and Woburn played up to this image, much to the annoyance of the more culturally serious stately home owner. A spate of books on the modern aristocracy, with attendant press publicity, reflected the characteristic late-'60s mix of iconoclasm and love of flair; so did the fashion for glamorous films set in stately homes, and yet not about them.[32] The public had come to tolerate the aristocratic 'way of life', even to admire it from a distance, but not yet to identify with it. It is notable that when popular interest in historic architecture did begin to intensify in the mid-1960s, it fixed not on country houses but on town houses. The great phenomenon of the 1960s from the point of view of preservation was the rise of the civic amenity society and the innovation of the urban conservation area in 1967. The Town and Country Planning Act 1968, which put a final stop to the demolition of listed buildings, was a product of this interest and not of any panic over doomed country houses. Similarly, the remarkable increase in the 'ration' allotted to the Historic Buildings Council for England – from £575,000 in 1969–70 to £2.25 million in 1973–4, well ahead of inflation – would not have been possible had 'historic building' still been equated with 'stately home'. As official preservationism came out of the closet and penetrated into the national consciousness, it also distanced itself from its Gowers-era roots.

Treasure houses: since 1974

As late as November 1973, writing in *Country Life*, Marcus Binney could worry that, amidst the revolution in public opinion favouring the preservation of historic buildings, there was 'a real danger that one type of building may be left behind – the country house'.[33] That worry was to dissipate rapidly in the next few years. A series

VICTORIA & ALBERT MUSEUM
The Hall of Destruction at the 1974 Victoria and Albert Museum exhibition, 'The Destruction of the Country House'.

of country-house *causes célèbres* were brought to public attention in the mid-1970s (mostly by the efforts of Binney, John Cornforth and others connected to *Country Life*) and evidently elicited intense sympathy. The simultaneous collapse of the 20-year land market boom, and the advent of a Labour government committed to raising taxes on capital, posed an immediate threat to hundreds of country houses. The arguments that had been advanced in vain by the Gowers Committee – for extensive tax reliefs to protect the 'way of life' sustaining historic houses – were revived in John Cornforth's report, *Country Houses in Britain: Can They Be Saved?*, and an exhibition at the Victoria and Albert Museum, *The Destruction of the Country House, 1875–1975*, both in autumn 1974. Unlike Gowers in 1950, Cornforth in 1974 met with a strong public response. The owners' lobby, the Historic Houses Association, collected 1.5 million signatures for a petition to parliament. After a bruising agitation, the government agreed in the following year to exempt privately owned historic houses and their contents from death duty (which now took the form of capital transfer tax (CTT)). It also permitted owners to set up CTT-exempt endowment funds, from which repairs and maintenance could be paid, or to hand over their entire estate to a CTT-exempt trust, while retaining residence and an interest. These concessions realised Gowers's chief proposals for sweeping tax exemptions for private property, and enabled owners to set up their own National Trust-style charities without abandoning title to strangers.

Scenting blood, the country-house lobby went further. Owners of historic houses were now protected from the worst of the tax bite, but houses abandoned by their owners remained vulnerable. A key case arose in 1977, when Lord Rosebery offered Mentmore, his Victorian house with impressive collections, to the nation for £2 million. The National Land Fund, theoretically available for such purposes, had long been virtually dormant, and the government claimed there was no money in the till for Mentmore. As a result of the agitation that was whipped up, the governnment reluctantly agreed to acquire three paintings, two pieces of furniture and certain minor objects for £1.4 million, a sum inflated by the public attention that the affair had by then received. In the aftermath, further public agitation forced the government to revive and reorganise the National Land Fund in 1980 as the National Heritage Memorial Fund, resuming the flow of abandoned houses into public or semi-public ownership.[34]

'Never have country houses been more in the limelight than today.' Marcus Binney's triumphant words of May 1978 reveal how much had changed in five short years.[35] This change in the national mood is hard to explain without benefit of the distance of time: disenchantment with the political left, environmental panic, the public's turn against modern architecture and planning, and imaginative propaganda by the country-house lobby were all factors. It would, however, be wrong to minimize the change in mood, or to melt it into the wider conservation movement.[36] Growing public interest in historic architecture, which had developed from the mid-1960s without much concern for the country house, began from the mid-1970s to fuse with the passions of *Country Life*. National Trust membership, which had grown healthily enough from 100,000 to 175,000 in the 1960s, took off to 850,000 by 1980 and 2 million by 1990. Country-house imagery became inescapable: on television in prestige series such as *Brideshead Revisited*, but also in advertisements for Japanese cars, in bookshops with the success of Mark Girouard's *Life in the English Country House* (1978) and its imitators, in fashion and interior decoration styles derived from country-house models. While the concern for conservation generally has been widespread throughout Europe (and beyond) since the 1960s, the romance with the aristocratic past seems to be a phenomenon specific to Britain, and in the closing years of the twentieth century it shows little sign of ebbing.

Given the widespread acceptability now of the 'way of life' understanding of the country house, it may seem perverse to conclude with some doubts about its long-term viability. Yet those doubts are voiced implicitly by the country-house industry itself. A recent report by the Historic Houses Association (HHA) concludes that the Gowers vision has not yet been effectively realised. The exemptions of the 1970s do not go far enough. Important houses such as Brympton d'Evercy in Somerset and Pitchford Hall in Shropshire have been sold by their historic owners. Great collections continue to be sold off piecemeal. Houses once open to the public are forced to close. The 'way of life' is under attack. New tax concessions are called for.[37]

PETER MANDLER

Even Warwick Castle, the first stately home to be commercialised as a tourist attraction by its aristocratic owners, has been abandoned by the Earls of Warwick – it was sold to Madame Tussaud's in 1978.

This perceived crisis, in the midst of plenty, points to some structural problems in the association of country-house preservation with country-life preservation, the association made by Gowers in 1950, fostered in the '50s and '60s by owners, and since the '70s by government. The fact is that, for all the magnitude of the country-house problem, it is more manageable than the country-life problem. The concentrations of wealth that historically have supported country houses cannot be maintained for ever. Nor is there a wider framework remaining to fix historic families in their houses. Each new generation is again vulnerable not only to tax but to bad fortune, changing values, the temptations of city life and professional pursuits. As the HHA report admits, old families are not replaced by 'neo-squires', either. Furthermore, while the public seems content to support the owners' 'way of life' to some degree today, its support is notoriously fickle and cannot be expected to continue forever, much less intensify as the HHA might wish.

Such concerns return us to the other preservation programmes bruited about in the 1940s: alternative use, or nationalisation in the true sense of the word, or museumisation. Might these not be more effective ways of rooting the country house permanently in the modern economy and in the national affection? The French châteaux offer an interesting comparison. English country-house lovers mock them as lifeless shells, lacking the *ensemble* of house, collection, park, estate and family that is England's gift to Western civilisation. And yet the châteaux may be more permanently secured because owners have been forced by political and economic circumstance to accept, even court, partial 'nationalisation'. Public funds have been available to private owners since the 1840s. In return, there are many more privately owned châteaux open to the public than country houses, nearly all open 6–7 days a week, many housing local museums and accommodating local functions and only incidentally providing residence. The long tradition of public attachment to the châteaux has insulated them from the crises and panics that have beset the country house over the past fifty years.[38] While it may be true that the country-house *ensemble* is England's unique possession, it may also be that the misguided attempt to save the *ensemble* is endangering the pieces that make it up.

7
How listing happened

Andrew Saint

Britain has a historical reputation for fetishising the rights of private ownership. For this reason, the protection of ancient monuments and historic buildings by the State developed here later and more hesitantly than among many other nations of Europe. And yet it is striking that Britain today enjoys one of the furthest-reaching legal systems of architectural conservation to be found anywhere in the world. The number of statutorily listed buildings, in particular, is remarkable. The usual figure cited for England, some 440,000 in 1994, refers to individual list entries, many of which cover several separate structures. If those separate structures or properties are individually counted, by some estimates the number can be raised to about 750,000.[1] That means three-quarters of a million English objects, from pillar boxes to palaces, which an owner cannot legally alter in any substance, inside or out, without consulting the local authority and submitting plans for listed building consent.

How did this happen? In particular, how did listing get started in the first place? For the growth of the system, once in place, may be less illuminating than the circumstances, experiences and emotions that led to the breaching of the landlords' defences in the 1940s.

The listing of individual buildings would never have taken hold in Britain or assumed the impetus it did, this chapter contends, had a wider political enthusiasm not gathered force from the 1920s to the 1940s about broader environmental issues – about the beauty of the countryside, the proper development of towns and suburbs, in brief, about planning. The irony is that the system slipped in under the Town and Country Planning Acts of 1944 and 1947 soon inhibited this very breadth of approach, which had been the key to getting listing accepted at the time.

* * *

A prescient book of 1905, Professor Baldwin Brown's *The Care of Ancient Monuments*, was the first to convey, by analysis of comparable European laws and institutions, how far Britain lagged behind its continental neighbours in legislating for the protection of its historic architecture and towns. One of the virtues of Baldwin Brown's approach was its inclusiveness. Monuments were at the core of his concerns. But from the measures he cited he was able to show that the issues of how to protect monuments merge into broader ones, encompassing not just antiquarianism and aesthetics but the whole appearance and management of cities, towns and landscapes. His book brings together laws dealing specifically with historical monuments, and general by-laws about the beautification and regulation of towns and cities – the rubric of 'aedilician' control, as he nicely called it.[2] In a paper given to the Royal Institute of British Architects in the same year, Baldwin Brown defined four areas in which he thought protective or restrictive measures by some arm of the State were needed to improve the modern city: the 'treatment of public edifices', especially those of an 'engineering character'; the building of new streets in connection with urban improvements; the laying out of new suburbs; and ancient monuments. Britain was doing something in all these areas, but Germany, France and Italy were doing more, said the Professor.[3]

The significance of this programme was that it linked the care of historic buildings to physical planning. Planning, though many people now forget it, was one of the great enthusiasms of the first half of the twentieth century. Still a highly intellectual, half-acknowledged concept at the turn of the century, planning developed into something akin to an obsession among the educated classes in the 1930s. From the first tentative national Planning Act of 1909, damaged in the legislative womb, to the almighty measure of 1947, the tide of planning swept big and small issues along with it. Ancient monuments and historic buildings were among the minnows caught up in the current.

When the first British monuments legislation was passed in the 1880s, this vogue for active physical planning had yet to make itself felt. All monuments laws imply lists, and so it was with the original Ancient Monuments Protection Act of 1882.[4] Attached to it, with cautious provision for enlargement, came a schedule of fifty monuments or groups of monuments, all prehistoric or Roman. So profoundly did parliament feel about private property that this was as much as the measure's promoters were able to achieve. And it was with the care of these most ancient, venerable and vulnerable national monuments that, in the first place, historians, antiquaries and archaeologists were naturally most concerned. Even medieval abbeys and castles did not come into the picture until the first additional Ancient Monuments Act of 1900. As for ancient churches and houses in use, almost every educated Englishman at the time agreed that these could, or at least ought to, be properly cared for by their owners. The infant Society for the Protection of Ancient Buildings (SPAB), for one, did not trust all those owners to do their duty, but it saw moral persuasion, lobbying and, if necessary, agitation as the means of redress, rather than the cumbrousness of law.[5] Even the scheduled monuments named were not directly protected by these early Acts. The government could merely acquire them, if owners cared to get rid of them, after which it handed them over to the Office of Works to look after them.

Acts of 1913 and 1931 significantly enlarged the scope of what had been laid down for ancient monuments in those of 1882 and 1900, but did not deviate from the principle that only uninhabited places and structures could be scheduled. More germane to the later emergence of listing proper were the three Royal Commissions on Historical Monuments (RCHMs) for Scotland, Wales and England, all created in 1908. Like those for Scotland and Wales, the English

RCHM was a separate, inventorising body charged with investigating and publishing monuments that might eventually be scheduled, county by county. Its independence from the Office of Works caused divergences which have never been resolved (and seem to be common in the inventorisation of monuments worldwide). The RCHM proffered full, objective, scholarly information to the growing band of experts in the Office of Works's Ancient Monuments Inspectorate. But it had no powers of scheduling itself, and its priorities for recording and publishing were not those of the inspectors. Above all, its progress was excruciatingly slow. In so far as the RCHM was meant to provide a national survey of monuments, it belonged to the emergent domain of official planning. In so far as its early county volumes tended (with honourable exceptions) to be disjointed and introverted repositories of fact, it clung to the methods of Victorian antiquarianism.

By 1931, when the last of the pre-war Ancient Monuments Acts was passed, much progress had been made, with over 3,000 ancient monuments scheduled and over 250 taken into active guardianship by the Office of Works. By now, enthusiasm for planning was far broader than it had been. With it came a stronger sense of the value of place, of total environments, and especially of the countryside. The protection of rural Britain from the consequences of democracy and the motorcar – from sprawl and from trippers – was a rallying cry among intellectuals of the interwar period. It led to the foundation of the Council for the Preservation of Rural England in 1926, followed quickly by equivalent bodies for Wales and Scotland.[6]

As luck would have it, the narrow focus of the monuments legislation on uninhabited sites such as barrows encouraged a crossover between nature conservation and monuments conservation – something that later was to get rather lost. As John Sheail explains in his book on inter-war conservation, three *causes célèbres*, Stonehenge, Avebury and Hadrian's Wall, dominated public debate about ancient monuments at this time. In each case the risk was not to the visible structure of these great monuments but to their natural settings and total archaeological environments. An ugly airfield blighted Stonehenge; there was talk of housing development at Avebury; and quarrying threatened a section of Hadrian's Wall. The 1931 Act aimed to protect the settings of monuments. Like all the pre-war legislation, it had few teeth. It depended upon the gentlemanly goodwill of landowners and, as a last resort, upon negotiated purchase. But the cases aroused broad public interest and a more profound sympathy for rural and historic preservation among politicians of all hues than had hitherto been manifest.[7]

The next phase of the struggle to extend preservation followed on shortly. This was the Town and Country Planning Act of 1932, the chief thrust of which was to encourage local authorities to designate planning schemes for specific areas, as had been mooted formerly in the Housing and Town Planning Act of 1909. Later, it became common to revile the 1932 Act as an utter failure. Sheail argues, pragmatically, that the introduction of active, interventionist, statutory planning was bound to be slow and bumpy. The 1932 Act was supposed to overcome unworkable provisions in the 1909 Act, but itself foundered on the rock of compensation, from which national planning was not to be rescued until 1947.[8]

For historic buildings, the significance of the 1932 Act was threefold. First, it drew into the picture a far larger and more recent potential class of structures than ancient monuments alone: above all, inhabited houses, at last freed from the landowning interest's half-century-old refusal to bring them into such legislation. This change of heart may partly reflect growing awareness of the struggles country house owners were having in keeping their mansions up, following the long agricultural depression, the growing burden of taxation, and the aftermath of the 1929 Crash. At a smaller scale, the SPAB and others had also been concerned by the growing loss of ancient timber houses in high-street redevelopments.[9] Secondly, the 1932 Act pulled this new class of buildings administratively into 'town and country planning', then under the aegis of the expanding Ministry of Health, not the Office of Works, where ancient monuments and hence the whole business of the government's role in preservation had been located up to this time. And lastly, it involved local authorities, hitherto bit-part players in preservation. Under Clause 17, local authorities could under one of their schemes 'schedule' houses or other buildings which were not to be demolished without permission. There were the usual powers of appeal which prevented these provisions from being too draconian. As it turned out, very few such schemes or orders were ever to be made. Setting aside problems of compensation, few local authorities had the will or the expertise to invoke Clause 17.

From the limited parliamentary debate of 1932 on this new departure, it seems that some legislators viewed Clause 17 as just a way of tacking historic country houses on to the ancient monuments legislation.[10] But others saw it as a prelude to surveying the whole country, not so much for its historic buildings *per se* as for everything of amenity and beauty, natural or man-made. Stafford Cripps, for instance, argued that the whole country must be covered by the new planning schemes, as had been intended by the Minister himself, Sir Edward Hilton Young, in previous, rather more ambitious Bills he had introduced as a backbencher. The implication was that these national assets would have to be itemised in detail. How that might be done was left in the air, doubtless because of the economic constraints so crushing in 1932.

It came up again, however, in February 1937, during what seems to have been the first free discussion of historic buildings in the House of Commons without a specific clause or measure.[11] This was brought forward on a motion of the architect-MP, Sir Alfred Bossom, who asked the government to enquire about the adequacy of its powers with regard to 'the destruction of beauty in town and country and the danger to houses of historic or architectural interest'. By now, the economic climate had improved; war loomed, but was not yet certain. There had been several demolition scandals, the National Trust was beginning to take on country houses, and Georgian architecture was coming into fashion. The 1932 Act, too, was plainly not doing what it was meant to. Bossom therefore wanted the government to appoint an advisory committee which would conduct a survey in order to:

FABER & FABER

Finchingfield village green, Essex as illustrated in W. H. Godfrey's *Our Building Inheritance* (1944). This was the kind of ensemble which was widely valued yet which the procedures instituted in the 1940s often failed to protect.

> reveal the monuments that could or should be saved; the villages, houses, cottages, churches, bridges, the hilltops, rivers, banks and woods, where roads should go and should not go, and where they should by-pass. In fact it could reveal the whole story of what we possess.[12]

This, he blithely thought, would take a year or two at most, after which a Bill could come before parliament and everything on the list would be protected.

In support of Bossom, Edward Keeling, who was to do most to secure effective listing in parliament seven years later, stressed the destruction of the countryside, paid tribute to voluntary bodies such as the National Trust and the Council for the Preservation of Rural England (CPRE), and insisted that 'beauty spots' must be designated in Bossom's survey as well as buildings. Josiah Wedgwood, the veteran Lib-Lab MP, offered his party's credentials:

> The Labour party are not usually considered conservative, but we are conservative when it is a case of conserving the natural beauty of England . . . in this case Socialism and Conservatism are bound together.[13]

In a debate with unusual breadth of reference, protective measures in France, Sweden and even Danzig were cited, and one MP recommended the statutory protection of wild flowers, as in the Cape Colony. The government spokesman, R. S. Hudson, countered all this by politely accepting the views of the speakers in principle, and by alluding to the efforts already being made by the amenity societies and to the powers available under the 1932 Act.

So as war again drew near, it was plain that there would be no quick change in the law. But equally there were clear signs of a growing demand abroad for effective measures through the planning process, to protect not so much historic architecture or buildings, as the whole, general beauty of England. New laws, and new lists to go with them, could not be delayed for ever.

* * *

The key piece of legislation for the establishment of listing in the modern sense was not, as is often said, the Town and Country Planning Act of 1947 but its predecessor, the Town and Country Planning Act of 1944. Framed under wartime conditions, the core of the 1944 statute was a kind of manifesto for the future on behalf of the new Ministry of Town and Country Planning. That Ministry had been set up a year earlier as a result of Lord Reith's attempts to restructure the departments responsible for planning and get them to play a forward-looking role in war and peace alike.[14]

Until the Second World War, the Ministry of Health looked after planning matters, while the Inspectorate of Ancient Monuments in the Office of Works ran and maintained the few hundred uninhabited buildings and ruins in national care. Now 'Works', hitherto a despised backwater of administration, suddenly took off, and became the vehicle of the rebarbative Lord Reith's ambitions when he joined the cabinet in 1940. Despite the fact that there was already a minister responsible for reconstruction (Arthur Greenwood), Reith was determined to make Works the focus of future physical planning in Britain. He had himself made 'Minister-Designate' and the Office became a Ministry. He brought in experts such as William Holford and John Dower, and commissioned the Scott Report on land use in the countryside and the better-known Uthwatt Report on compensation and betterment. In February 1942 he got his department further upgraded into the Ministry of Works and Planning. Then Reith suddenly lost his job, a casualty to Churchill's dislike. His plans were promptly rescrambled. In November 1942 the coalition government agreed to emasculate Works once more and assign the burgeoning planning boffins and their ambitions for a future Britain to a new Ministry altogether. So it was Reith's fellow-Scot, the less tortured W. S. 'Shakes' Morrison, who presided as first Minister of Town and Country Planning over the Control of Land Use Bill, as the 1944 measure was called in its preliminary stages.

This wartime tinkering with ministries was to have future reverberations for the administration of historic buildings. They were never more than a sideshow to grander dramas and arguments concerning the fair and orderly development of land (so marginal, indeed, that they receive no mention in J. B. Cullingworth's official history of land-use planning during the war). But the Reithian vision would have allowed their administration to be brought together within a single Ministry, in which practical expertise and planning powers reinforced one another. As it turned out, the 1944 and 1947 Acts perpetuated the old division between the Ministry of Health and the Office of Works in the new guise of the Ministry of Town and Country Planning and the Ministry of Works. That duality, inviting muddle and overlap, continues today in the split between the Department of Environment and the Department of National Heritage – with the added ingredient of a 'quango', English Heritage, thrown in for extra confusion.

How did historic buildings come into the 1944 Bill at all? There were two main elements to official thinking. One was dissatisfaction with the general provisions of the 1932 Act, which it was the purpose of the Bill to supersede. Historic buildings, we have seen, were there in Clause 17 of the 1932 Act. But the provisions for protecting them had not worked well – indeed, had hardly been employed, because of fears over compensation. During debate over the new Bill it was claimed that under thirty buildings had been protected by the 1932 Act;[15] it had certainly failed to prevent some egregious demolitions. Something had to be done about that. In the event, the greater proportion of parliamentary time on historic buildings during the passage of the Bill was spent not on listing, but on the drafting of clauses to improve the mechanisms for preserving buildings once their merit had been identified.

The other stimulus to legislative action on historic buildings was an indirect one: the once-in-a-lifetime chance created by the grievous bombing of Britain's cities in 1940–2. There was a consensus that the Blitz had triggered an opportunity for radical post-war planning improvements that must not be missed. Not that legislators and civilised people at large expected or wanted a *tabula rasa* in Britain's towns and cities, with everything swept away. The madness of the plan for London proposed by the juvenile architects of the MARS Group, to take the extreme pre-war example, suggesting that the metropolis should be refashioned *ab ovo* on lines even crazier than those of Le Corbusier's Plan Voisin for Paris, passed once it was realised that aerial bombardment amounted to something short of Armageddon. People were distressed by the historic destruction caused by bombs. And yet, scholars and sentimentalists apart, their distress was less than some might now care to project back upon them. Many welcomed the prospect of a fresh, post-war recasting of communities. To expedite this, they sought a guide – a list – to what ought to be kept and, where necessary, reinstated. In that way, when the experts came to lay their plans they would know without ambiguity or delay what to incorporate or skirt round; private owners, too, would be clearly apprised of what they were expected to keep.

Such thinking, then, lay behind the first expansion of national listing in Britain beyond the narrow category of scheduled monuments. Inventories that had any intellectual or academic merit in themselves could not be priorities in wartime. Volumes of that kind were already being produced at a snail's pace by the RCHM, but they were of little practical use for planning purposes. Instead, the lists were conceived as a workaday tool which official planners could have by their side as they refined their approach to the urban (and to a lesser extent, rural) landscape. The idea was not dissimilar to the proposition put forward by Bossom in 1937, but harder-edged, less sentimental; and there was no indication that natural features might be listed along with buildings.

By 1944, such a form of national listing was just becoming familiar. It had made its first appearance during the Blitz itself when, under the Ministry of Works' salvage scheme, over 300 consultant 'panel architects' were appointed on an *ad hoc* basis to make a list of what was worth keeping and ensure that buildings of value were not pulled down during the hurried wartime clearance after bombing raids.[16] This was how the system was explained in September 1942:

> The compilation of the lists has been made since the war and arose in this way. It was found that many buildings of interest were being neglected after damage by enemy action. The Ancient Monuments people considered the best method of ensuring their preservation, and it was decided to produce lists of buildings which were worth saving. This was done by co-operation with the RIBA, and some 300 Architects throughout the country have been appointed as Panel Architects. These Architects prepared the lists, copies of which were given to the Ministry of Home Security, who circulated them to the various ARP authorities. When a building gets damaged, the Borough Engineer reports it to the SRO [Senior Regional Officer] of the Ministry of Works, and also tells the Panel Architect. These architects are employed at 10/- per hour to supervise repairs. The list contains new buildings as well as old. Broadly, good buildings up to 1850 and exceptional buildings after 1850, e.g. the Manchester Grammar School appears on the list. The lists are being revised, but the revisions are not exhaustive.[17]

Despite the fairly generous range of dates, this earliest attempt at a national list was a necessarily makeshift response to crisis. It cannot have been aided by the fact that the bulk of the Ancient Monuments Branch which supervised it had been evacuated to Rhyl. Only areas under threat of bombing (and therefore distant from Rhyl) were covered. The Branch's SPAB traditions meant that villages and country towns could more easily be comprehended and dealt with than the larger towns and cities where bombing was worst. Nine categories were agreed upon, of which only the last, 'historic streets', made any reference to ensembles. There were no clear criteria or standards of expertise, and much variety of coverage. In London, preparation of the salvage list was devolved to the London County Council which was experienced in the field, had talked of inventorising the capital's historic buildings as far back as 1898, and had indeed begun its own systematic list in 1938 because of the growing toll of metropolitan demolitions.[18] Elsewhere the panel system was hit and miss, depending on the commitment and skill of private individuals, usually architects or surveyors still in practice but beyond call-up age. Dorset, for instance, was divided into five areas, with run-of-the-mill expertise in four of them but the energetic E. Wamsley Lewis covering Wareham, Purbeck and Weymouth.[19] Progress was naturally variable. By mid-1943, Exeter, Plymouth and Southampton were done, Yarmouth and Portsmouth were half done, but sorely damaged Canterbury was merely said to be 'in active preparation'.[20] William and John Harvey were hard at work on additional submissions for their fifteen Surrey parishes in 1943-4.[21] But, on the whole, the

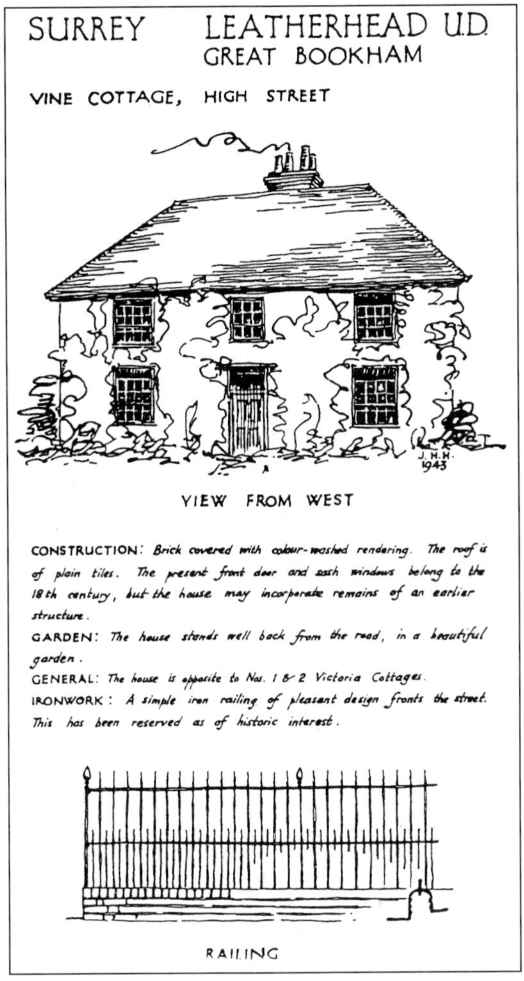

JOHN HARVEY

A sketch with accompanying description of Vine Cottage, High Street, Great Bookham, Leatherhead, Surrey, by John Harvey, one of the early listing investigators under the 'salvage' system; note the separate detail showing the railings.

work seems to have tailed off as the bombing died down, as the memorandum quoted above implies.

Two other types of wartime list should be mentioned, of which one was closely related to the salvage scheme. This was the compilation of the infant National Buildings Record (NBR), set up early in 1941 under the driving force of John Summerson (with government backing from Lord Reith) to record and document buildings in wartime danger.[22] As Walter Godfrey, its director, said: 'the first need is a list, in each district, of the buildings which are worthy of record'.[23] As a start, the first efforts of the official panel architects were sent in to supplement what might have already been published on luckier towns and districts, but Godfrey was 'anxious to amplify' them. By September 1942 the NBR had lists of buildings in 172 towns which it aimed to record, mainly by photography; sixty-seven towns had been covered, and twenty-one were in preparation. An exhibition of its work was shown at the National Gallery in June 1944. Despite this admirable record of activity, it must be remembered that the lists of the NBR (like those of the RCHM) had only indirect implications for preservation. Co-ordination between its own lists and the lists compiled by the panel architects was amiable but imperfect, with the more coherent NBR taking more than it gave.

The other type of wartime compilation worth mentioning related yet more sharply to hostilities. When the army occupied or the air force bombed foreign territory in North Africa and Europe, something had to be done about the

RCHME © CROWN COPYRIGHT

Nos 27–32 Southernhay West, Exeter, Devon, a late Georgian terrace of which only the facade remained after the air raids of 1942; photographed by Margaret Tomlinson for the National Buildings Record.

historic monuments and buildings on their trajectory. At the outset, the British armed forces were far less geared up to this task than the Germans and Italians, despite the well-known depredations of Goering. Charges of vandalism (allegedly falsified) followed the first British occupation of Cyrenaica. North Africa presented specifically archaeological problems. So the high-class archaeological team of Leonard Woolley, Mortimer Wheeler and J. B. Ward-Perkins was made chiefly responsible for getting things on to a better footing, by compiling lists and ensuring that captured monuments were safeguarded. By the time of the invasion of Italy, with its infinitely complex heritage, the British military possessed the bones of an archaeological organisation. This did not prevent serious looting and vandalism when Naples was reached, and reforms had to be made in November 1943. The Americans, too, were by now involved, a Harvard-based group having vainly tried to influence air forces by compiling lists and maps of historic buildings that they should endeavour to miss on bombing raids. The upshot of all this was that by the time of D-Day, a clear allied military structure existed for safeguarding historic monuments, buildings, fine arts and archives. Well-educated and well-briefed officers had agreed lists in their hands. They were authorised to work in forward positions, and knew what they were supposed to do and with whom they had to cooperate.[24]

The fruits of this experience abroad did not feed back entirely on to native soil until after the war. But it was vital first-hand education, and convinced many that Britain had to catch up with continental practice in the proper inventorisation and protection of its heritage. One of the Monuments and Fine Arts Officers in France, the painter-peer Lord Methuen, initiated a debate in the Lords on his return to air the subject of what could be learnt from French practice for the better protection of British country houses and domestic architecture generally.[25] Later, he published his experiences and drawings from France in the handsome *Normandy Diary* (1952), which is full of praise for the Beaux-Arts monuments administration.

* * *

These, then – the fruits of the salvage or panel system, of the National Buildings Record, and of the military Monuments and Fine Arts organisation – were the three efforts at listing historic buildings brought to birth by the Second World War. Those who worked on them tended to think of them as ends in themselves. But in the developing atmosphere of post-war planning, they became subsumed in a larger process. As Wamsley Lewis said of the panel system in 1943, 'the importance of these lists of buildings is now greatly increased, since they are to form an essential part of the data upon which the national plan for reconstruction is to be based'.[26] Better lists of historic buildings would be needed if the planners were to get ahead with their post-war work unimpeded and install the improved form of development control which the 1944 Town and Country Planning Bill was supposed to deliver.

It took a little time for the official planners, separated once again from the Ministry of Works by the reorganisation of 1943, to realise this. As first drafted, the 1944 Bill incorporated and amended the unsuccessful provisions of the 1932 Act for preserving historic buildings. But it took no account of how such buildings should be designated; nor did it ratify the official lists compiled under the panel system. The honour of making good this deficiency and lobbying successfully during the passage of the Bill for a proper national system of listing is due largely to the Georgian Group, specifically to its secretary, Angus Acworth, and to its deputy chairman, Edward Keeling, MP. Keeling, it will be remembered, had spoken in Bossom's debate of 1937. He had also orchestrated outcry in 1943 over the damage done by British troops at Naples and the revenge Baedeker raids.

The Georgian Group at this date was the *enfant terrible* of the amenity societies.[27] Founded in 1937, officially as a subcommittee to the Society for the Protection of Ancient Buildings, it chafed under the tweedy, Arts and Crafts traditions of its parent body. The SPAB was rural, professional, middle-class and mild-mannered; it had, by this time, close links with the Ancient Monuments Branch, which broadly was of the same ilk. The Georgians were, for the most part, different animals. They were modern, metropolitan, snobbish and quarrelsome; they cultivated the image of the educated amateur but were proficient at pulling establishment strings. Under the dashing leadership of Robert Byron, the early

FABER & FABER

The High Street, Lewes, East Sussex, a drawing from W. H. Godfrey's *Our Building Inheritance* (1944). The importance of such ensembles was stressed in the 1944 debates.

days of the Group had been much taken up with propagandising over the shocking losses of Georgian buildings in London: Waterloo Bridge, the Adelphi, Norfolk House, Mecklenburgh Square and, very nearly, Carlton House Terrace. Casework and publicity came first; forward thinking second. Nevertheless, early in 1939 a committee that included Acworth had drafted an abortive Architectural Amenities Bill, aimed at making good some of the deficiencies of the 1932 Act and including some sort of provision for listing.[28]

During the Second World War the Georgian Group scaled down its activities. It came to life again in 1944, with a new committee structure and Acworth in firm charge of policy. Working with Keeling, Dame Una Pope-Hennessy and Sir Alfred Beit, he laid out a clear set of objectives for the post-war Georgians, in relation to the public, to local authorities and to government. Later, Acworth enjoyed the reputation of a reactionary, but at this stage he was pro-planning and 'modern'. To Albert Richardson he wrote:

> Georgian architecture isn't ancient, it isn't medieval, it is essentially modern . . . the Group stands not only for the preservation of Georgian buildings of beauty and importance but also for the principles of the Georgian tradition in the architecture of town and countryside.[29]

The fifth report of the Georgian Group Policy Sub-Committee, 'The Georgian Group and Reconstruction', drafted by Acworth in June 1944, enlarged on this:

> . . . insofar as Reconstruction is based on the concept of a planned lay-out instead of on haphazard development of the type that has characterised the last hundred years, it must be warmly welcomed.

Acworth went on to quote Summerson:

> '. . . preservation in general is only of value when it is co-ordinated and related to a plan of positive development. The planned survival of old structures can enrich a town enormously. An unplanned snatching of isolated buildings from unplanned development will result in pathetic patchworks of obsolescence.' It seems to us that there is great scope for development of the Group's policy in this direction. Most valuable results might be obtained if the Group were invited as a matter of course to co-operate with Local Authorities in Reconstruction both by listing good Georgian buildings in their area and by advising them on their town-planning schemes so that these should provide, by skilful planning, for the retention of such buildings and, by proper zoning, for their appropriate use.[30]

It chimes in with such language that Patrick Abercrombie, doyen of British planners and an active member of the Georgian Group, should have addressed its enthusiastic annual general meeting in October 1944 on the tasks ahead.

Safe in the confidence that they were facing in the same progressive direction as the planners, Acworth and Keeling embarked on their scheme to amend the 1944 Planning Bill by regularising and extending the principle of listing. In his first parliamentary intervention on the subject, Keeling suggested that local authorities should compile the lists, and that until then all buildings dating before 1850 should be protected.[31] This was evidently unworkable. In September 1944 a conference was convened by the CPRE, chaired by Keeling and attended by all the main amenity bodies of the day. Acworth presented draft amendments to the Bill, including the all-important principle of a Ministry-compiled list of historic buildings. They were approved with few changes.[32] Keeling then got to work in parliament. His amendments were warmly endorsed by almost all speakers, accepted in principle by Henry Strauss (W. S. Morrison's architecture-loving parliamentary secretary), redrafted and added to the Bill at Report stage. Strengthened by an important change in wording (Strauss's version said that the Minister 'may' compile lists; the final version said he 'shall' compile lists) and with the extra proviso that he could 'approve such lists compiled by other persons' (so that the work of the panel system and the LCC could be incorporated), the Keeling amendments emerged as Clauses 42 and 43 of the Town and Country Planning Act 1944.[33]

The drift of the parliamentary debates on this subject in 1944 is striking in two respects.[34] First, as in 1932 and 1937, most of those who spoke in the Commons put their emphasis on places – set pieces or whole environments – rather than buildings. Strauss led the way by hoping that planning authorities would 'consider not only individual buildings but such important things as streets – to give an example, the high streets of Lewes, or Fareham or Burford'.[35] Keeling remarked that the panel architect's list for Aylesbury already included 'three or four squares and twenty streets'.[36] John Wilmot of Kennington wanted to know whether the environs of particular buildings could be protected, opining that it would be pointless to keep one side of Bedford Row if the other were demolished, and citing the effect of 'the awful Babylonian monstrosity in

Mornington Crescent' (the 'Black Cat' cigarette factory) on the crescent itself.[37] Colonel Greenwell from The Hartlepools was worried about the environs of Lincoln and Durham cathedrals; and so forth. The inter-war concern for environment and the rows over the surroundings of Stonehenge, Avebury and Hadrian's Wall had made their mark.

Secondly, there was debate on consultation and publicity. Some legislators – the landowning interest in the Lords, particularly – were alarmed at the prospect that buildings would be listed and protected from demolition or change without reference to their owners. Government spokesmen, both in 1944 and when the question came up again in 1947, stood firm on a clear and simple principle (though one increasingly muddied in recent years). The compilation of lists was for experts – and Keeling was adamant that there should be room over the years for revision and addition but not, without very good reason, for subtraction. It was also agreed in the course of debate that limited publication of the lists would be useful. The real public test of the lists would then come when someone wanted to alter or demolish a listed building. At that point (as under the 1932 Act) the local authority might or might not issue a preservation order, which would have to be confirmed by the Minister. In other words, the real arguments about a building's merits and destiny should take place when its future was a matter for practical concern. At the time even the most ardent proponents of listing and preservation anticipated that many old buildings would have to take their turn and succumb in the higher interests of national planning, as Abercrombie told the Georgians at their AGM.[38] That should not exclude them from the Ministry's new lists which, to gauge from loose comments, were expected to be sizeable in extent.

* * *

So far, so good. The principle of having an expert committee to supervise listing was agreed at a meeting chaired by Keeling in December 1944.[39] But with a war still on and Vls and V2s pockmarking the towns of the south of England anew, the listing provisions in the 1944 Act went into the pending tray. They were resurrected chiefly by Anthony Wagner, private secretary to 'Shakes' Morrison, crony of James Lees-Milne, Georgian Group member and future Garter King of Arms.[40] A shy man, Wagner seems to have had crucial influence on historic buildings policy between the 1944 and 1947 Acts. Under the 1945 Attlee government, Morrison was replaced by Lewis Silkin. But Wagner stayed for a few more years within the Ministry of Town and Country Planning and turned his attention to historic buildings. The expert committee of eleven appointed in October 1945 owed its membership largely to Wagner's suggestions and predilections, which tended towards scholarship and antiquarianism rather than modern planning. This marked a shift in emphasis. Significantly there was only one architect-planner among the new committee's members, the ubiquitous Holford; the rest were archaeologists, antiquarians and historians, notably John Summerson, whose contribution was to be critical. The committee was chaired by Sir Eric Maclagan, with Wagner as secretary, and first met on 6 December 1945.[41]

The Maclagan Committee drew up terms of reference. Churches and Crown buildings were to be included in the lists, even though the 1944 planning procedures did not apply to them. Grades of importance were assigned, not unlike the academic degrees with which members of the committee were comfortably familiar; a non-statutory category of Grade III was agreed for good, ordinary-looking buildings. Richard Garton, a Ministry of Works architect (and, according to his friend and colleague John Harvey, 'a many-sided artist . . . a musician of professional standing on the violin and the French horn . . . a painter in oils and a considerable water-colourist . . . a distinguished connoisseur both of wine and beer'), became Chief Investigator.[42] The first investigators appointed under him were all on a temporary basis, as it was assumed that the task would be finished in two years. For their operation Garton drew up a model manual, the *Instructions to Investigators* or 'grey book', drafted according to oral tradition with much help from Summerson.

The systematic investigation and listing of England's historic buildings began at the start of the new financial year, in early April 1946, and for a few short months went merrily forward. Then the first of many recurring crises struck over the rate and extent of listing. Already the Labour Party was intending a new planning Bill. The 1944 Act was proving unworkable, chiefly because of problems over compensation. Only Labour's full nationalisation of development rights could solve this problem and deliver the national, rational, interventionist postwar planning sought by the Ministry. This indeed was what the Town and Country Planning Act of 1947 achieved. In so far as it laid the ghost of government paying compensation for the restrictions placed upon an owner, either by listing a building in the first place or by refusing a scheme of demolition, alteration or extension later on, it was to free the whole process of protecting historic buildings from uncertainty and allow listing to carry on with confidence down to the present day. Even when development rights were denationalised by the back door under the Macmillan government, the refusal of listed building consent remained in ordinary circumstances exempt from the threat of compensation.

But in the first instance the Development Rights Bill, as the 1947 measure was called in its early stages, caused tremors in the infant listing inspectorate. The historic buildings provisions were to be consolidated. But with the threat of compensation not yet lifted and the planners eager to know where they stood, the civil servants drafting the Bill toyed with enshrining in the new measure some clear provision that the extent of listing would be small and finite. As one put it in September 1946, buildings ought only to be preserved if they are

> in a very limited category of superlative quality and possibly unique or . . . if they can be included in a rigid selection of representative specimens of their period or type. Some borderline buildings can be justifiably preserved if they can be put to good use. Even if the cost of going beyond that were not prohibitive, it is possible to preserve too many museum pieces.[43]

To find out what the scale of the problem might be, the government naturally wanted to know how the listing process was going on. The truth was, very slowly. By December 1946, Garton's staff was able to process 440 recommendations per week. He reckoned that a third of these would be cut out by the Maclagan Committee, but even so he estimated that with the present staff the task would take six years and there would be 130,000 items. After the harsh and prolonged winter of 1946–7, which slowed down and demoralised everyone in Britain, he was talking about seven years at the least, twelve years at the most. There were now thirty staff (some of them full time) and ninety local authorities had been covered, but twelve counties had not even been started.[44]

The Ministry's reaction to this was firm, and to be oft repeated in the future. Because the lists were intended as an element in the formulation of local authority development plans, which had to be produced within three years, even Garton's lower target of seven years was entirely unacceptable. A crisis ensued; Wagner was no longer there to ease the situation. The permanent secretary, Sir Philip Magnus, went off with Maclagan and Summerson to Cirencester and East Grinstead. They came back concluding that too much was being listed and in too high a grade, and suggested dropping Grade III recommendations to speed things up. The Maclagan Committee was divided. Summerson threatened to resign unless there was some reduction in listing; his obdurate old colleague, Walter Godfrey, from the National Buildings Record, said he would do the same if any fewer were included. In this interesting clash may be seen a division between the modern, discriminating art-history and pro-planning philosophy of the more progressive Georgians and the easier-going, inclusive, antiquarian and vernacular-orientated approach of the SPAB.[45]

In the event the matter was fudged, with the committee suggesting that rural areas and modern manufacturing towns could be deferred for the time being. This guidance allowed Garton to tell his superiors what they wanted, that under the new principles – already being called an 'accelerated programme' in 1947 – the lists would be ready in just two and a half years' time. But the new instruction seems to have been more or less a dead letter from the start 'because it was found to be impracticable'.[46] Both the authority and the permanence of the Maclagan Committee were in doubt, and indeed it met only occasionally after 1947; eventually it was replaced by the rather different Historic Buildings Council.

With the 1947 Act firmly on the statute book, the listing investigators were freed from the atmosphere of crisis and able to get on with their lengthy and absorbing task to the best of their abilities. Planning and listing were going separate ways again; and little more seems to have been heard of the incorporation of lists into local development plans. John Harvey, listing buildings once again in 1949 after his former turn of duty as a panel architect, found Garton scrupulous in attention to scholarship and detail and far from conceiving listing as a 'military operation'.[47] However, the Treasury was shocked to discover in that year that a task estimated at two years in 1946 should still be rolling along without prospect of conclusion.[48] The branch's staffing

PHOTOGRAPH BY WESTMORELAND STUDIOS, OXFORD

Conference of the investigators of buildings of architectural and historic interest, Oriel College, Oxford, 26 March 1949. For the names of those shown in the photograph, see below, p. 210.

suffered as a result, causing further delay to what by its very nature, we can see in retrospect, was bound to be a long-drawn-out process. The first survey of Britain's historic buildings was not to be completed in its entirety until 1970.[49]

This shaky start to the listing process had major consequences. The whole conception of listing drew gradually away from the urgencies of planning that had brought it to maturity. It became an end, and eventually a little industry, in itself, with its own cultural frame of reference, art-historical criteria and programme. This was perhaps inevitable; it was foreseen as early as 1946, when the Ministers of Works and Town and Country Planning exchanged views over whether historic buildings functions might not be better back with Works once the planning Bill was out of the way.[50] In the event, nothing was done. One can see why. Listing was, as it remains, umbilically connected to the planning process. But whereas in the wartime and immediate post-war years listing was meant to be a simple and positive tool wherewith planners would define and refine their land-use strategies, it soon developed a double edge. It was to become not just an inhibition against greedy private developers or philistine local authorities – the twin butts of parliamentary rhetoric in the 1940s debates on historic buildings – but a way of obstructing as well as promoting planned development, and, in due course, a weapon which the resourceful citizen could turn against the State.

Remnants of the first conception of listing as an *aide-mémoire* to the planning process remain down to this day. Notable among them is the unfriendly, rigid and skeletal nature of the official lists of historic buildings. In character these remain simple aids for planning departments instead of the independent inventories that they are in most European countries. Long ago they should have been turned into computerised inventories with attached provision for constant, informal updating and, above all, illustration.

The early crisis over the speed at which listing was proceeding also had the sorry effect of exacerbating the distinction between places (which the educated public at large had been so enthusiastic to protect) and specific buildings (which were straightforward to list and attracted the enthusiasm of the antiquarian-minded investigators). Once grading entered into the matter, and the Maclagan Committee had decreed first that 'ordinary' Grade III buildings were not to have statutory protection and then that they could be left out of lists altogether, there were bound to be difficulties over protecting groups of buildings, village scenes, and so on.

That there was the initial will to include them is proved not just by the parliamentary debates of 1944 but also by the tone of the original *Instructions to Investigators* compiled in 1946.[51] This in every way remarkable and highly philosophical document sets great store by the group, whether in the form of a planned unit (Royal Crescent, Bath, is cited) or 'accidental or pictorial architectural group'. The authors go into some detail to define different types of group further, and even go so far as to talk about the value of whole towns without, however, giving the investigator precise guidance as to what ought to be done about them:

> The preservation of the character of a whole town such as Conway or of the eighteenth-century character of Bath has a historical value almost of a different order from that attaching to the preservation of individual houses within these groups. From other points of view a single eighteenth-century building of moderate quality acquires extra value from being placed in an otherwise uninteresting wilderness of bleak modernity, but from this particular historical point of view the case is reversed and the maxim is 'to him that hath shall be added'.[52]

When it comes to the specifics of groups, the instructions are less cheering:

> There will probably be difficult borderline cases where investigators' feeling is that what is worth preserving somehow is a general character, in a street, town or quarter of a town, which is the cumulative effect of the grouping or repetition of a type of building, of which it is hard to say that any single specimen is more important than any other, and yet it is certain that some, if not too many, could without real loss be spared. It is the Ministry's view that, while such buildings as these ought to receive special consideration and protection, this should be given rather by simple notice from the Ministry to

> the Local Authority and by the normal exercise of planning control than by Statutory listing under Section 42 of the Act. Investigators are therefore asked to exclude from their draft Statutory Lists but to note on Supplementary Lists buildings which have in their view cumulative group or character value.[53]

All this was before the pressure on finishing the lists made itself felt and the supplementary lists receded into the background. The difficulty about groups was now serious enough for Garton in April 1947 to plead with his superiors for an amending clause in the new Bill to cover them, citing such examples as Castle Combe in Dorset, Finchingfield in Essex and Cavendish in Suffolk and arguing:

> The object of the legislation in Sections 42 and 43 [of the 1944 Act] is not only to protect individual buildings of special architectural merit, but to protect general pictures of groups of special and undoubted architectural merit, in which the elements comprising that picture cannot individually be said to possess architectural distinction.[54]

To judge from what we have seen, parliamentary and popular sympathy would have been on Garton's side. Yet he did not get his clause. Instead, buildings which under the original instructions might properly have been deemed of Grade III standards were often quietly bumped up to the statutory Grade II level for 'group value'. The rules were drafted vaguely enough to allow this.[55]

'Group value' continues today to be a recognised criterion of listing. But it is by any standards a poor and insufficient rubric under which to address the architectural and historical problem of place – of the cultural value of total built environments, planned or unplanned. This remained a difficulty unresolved up to the time of Duncan Sandys's Civic Amenities Act of 1967, which allowed for the designation of Conservation Areas. By then the political climate of planning was different. As amenity groups know to their cost, an unassailable system of protection parallel to that of the mechanisms for listing and listed building control set up in the 1940s could not be established. Listed building legislation has strong teeth, Conservation Area legislation has weak ones. Individual buildings on the whole do well under the British historic buildings regime; ensembles, even of charm or distinction, do badly, unless every single building is listed. Here is an anomaly – a critical cultural gap which remains to be filled.

ARCHITECTURAL REVIEW

Birkbeck Bank, Holborn, during demolition, 1965.

8
From comprehensive development to Conservation Areas

Sophie Andreae

An entertaining yet telling series of cartoons published in Osbert Lancaster's *Drayneflete Revealed* (1949) details in amusing fashion the changes that typically took place as towns and cities evolved in Britain. Twentieth-century Drayneflete is shown with a few key buildings from early periods, a mixture of Georgian and Victorian buildings and a few of the twentieth century. Only ten years on, the picture would have been vastly different, as the mania for comprehensive redevelopment took hold and historic towns and cities were ripped apart. In a speech at the Royal Academy Dinner in the summer of 1962, Viscount Hailsham – a prominent member of the Conservative government at the time – said:

> All the really artistically healthy societies of the world have been marked with a supreme artistic self-confidence . . . Mattocks and sticks of dynamite – no less, to clear away the rubble of the past, often of exquisite beauty, and to make way for new beauties in the future.[1]

He thus expressed sentiments which were being echoed in town halls and company boardrooms throughout the country, and by the architectural and planning professions.

Whether the view of Worcester across the Severn and towards the cathedral, or the appearance of the centre of Gloucester today, to name but two of literally hundreds of possible examples, represent any form of new beauty is something the public will continue to question. As this chapter will seek to demonstrate, the legislation to protect historic areas came late, and even when it came it lacked teeth for far too long. In Chapter 7, Andrew Saint illustrated how the preservationist measures that were put in place in the 1940s focused on the listing of individual buildings, considering masterpieces in isolation as opposed to buildings in their historic context. Conservation Area legislation did not arrive until the Civic Amenities Act 1967, and permission to demolish unlisted buildings in a Conservation Area was not a requirement until the Town and Country Amenities Act 1974.

Even today, Conservation Area status has its limits. Although there is control of demolition, alterations can, on the whole, be carried out. Cumulatively the effect can be devastating and the debate about the effectiveness or otherwise of

Article 4 Directions as a method of controlling alterations to buildings in Conservation Areas continues to rumble. Official views of what should merit Conservation Area status are sometimes at odds with local sentiment: should a residential area of, for instance, 1920s and 1930s houses qualify? Most local authorities would designate such areas today, not least as a result of local pressure to protect established environments and to prevent erosion of character and unsympathetic new development, but every now and then official eyebrows are raised and the question asked, 'Is the currency being devalued?'

There are now some 8,315 Conservation Areas in England.[2] It is fair to say that the number is unlikely to increase substantially, as virtually all historic town centres, older residential suburbs and village centres are now designated. Some will be extended, and some new ones designated, particularly around groups of buildings, such as farm buildings for instance, but the overall number is likely to remain reasonably constant. In fact, Conservation Areas are, on the whole, highly popular, particularly residential ones. Over 70 per cent of the area of the Royal Borough of Kensington and Chelsea is thus designated, and the figure for Westminster is even higher. Conservation Areas in commercial centres are inevitably more problematic. The City of London is perhaps the best example, where about 32 per cent of the Square Mile is designated, and yet within those areas whole swathes have been redeveloped in the relatively recent past – the No. 1 Poultry site being the most recent and notorious example.

In 1976 the Joint Committee of the National Amenity Societies published their report on the City of London, *Save the City*. One of its comments was that the City fathers, while keen to see the Wren churches preserved, were less than enthusiastic about many of the other old buildings that made up the fabric of the City. This type of preoccupation with individual masterpieces at the expense of context has coloured official thinking at local and government level for the past thirty years. Indeed, the attitude is very much alive today and is reflected in the policies being pursued by the Department of Health with its current large-scale disposal programme of former mental hospitals and associated sites.[3] These are coming on to the market, listed or not, to be sold to the highest bidder without regard to the historic interest of the site or the context of the buildings. Many will simply be demolished.

The Ministry of Defence is pursuing similar policies in its desire to rid itself of former barracks, munitions sites and naval buildings.[4] For example, the Penninsular Barracks in Winchester were perceived as a development opportunity both by the Ministry of Defence and the Crown Estate, the joint owners. Substantial demolition was viewed as the best option, followed by massive new development. The received wisdom was that a substantially cleared site would be likely to be infinitely more marketable than the site as it was when the military left, complete with all the main barrack blocks and ancillary buildings. It took a forceful campaign by SAVE Britain's Heritage in 1993–4, and their commissioning of an alternative scheme demonstrating how *all* the historic buildings on the site could be converted for residential use, to induce a change of heart in the Ministry of Defence. The site was finally sold and a

CIVIC TRUST

'Magdalene Street, Norwich, after treatment by the Civic Trust', this was the Trust's first street improvement scheme, begun in 1958.

developer is now implementing a scheme along the lines of the SAVE proposal. A protracted and expensive public inquiry has been avoided, as has the death knell of long-term abandonment and neglect. In a relatively short space of time the Ministry of Defence's 'white elephant' will have gained a new lease of life, and the centre of Winchester will have benefited immeasurably.[5]

What SAVE achieved in Winchester in 1994 would have been unthinkable in the 1950s, or even in the early 1970s. Yet it was in the 1950s that change began, and any assessment must begin with the Civic Trust, which gave a focus to the civic amenity societies which had begun to spring up in different parts of the country in the post-war period. The Trust was peculiarly the creation of Duncan Sandys MP, later Lord Duncan Sandys, who, as Minister for Housing and Local Government, had for some time been conscious that there was a need for a private body, separate from government, which could act as a kind of umbrella for the growing number of local civic societies around the country and arouse public concern for the state of the urban environment. The Trust's inauguration took place in the Great Hall of Lambeth Palace on 20 July 1957. Three hundred notable people attended and, after Duncan Sandys had explained the type of organisation he envisaged, those present came to the microphone one by one to lend support to the concept.[6]

From the outset, the Civic Trust saw its role as encompassing a broad spectrum. Its early leaflets stated that its priorities were: first, to encourage high quality in architecture and planning; secondly, to preserve buildings of distinction and historic interest; and, thirdly, to encourage the creation or improvement of features of beauty or interest. As early as 1958 Sandys set up the Civic Trust Awards Scheme. This has always focused on new architecture in traditional settings, as well as on restoration schemes.[7] Conferences were another early initiative. August 1957 saw the Trust's first conference on landscape architecture. A conference on trees in towns followed in 1958, and in the same year the Trust's first street improvement scheme was inaugurated in Magdalen Street, Norwich. Tidying up clutter, encouraging tree planting and improving the design of street lighting seemed to be major preoccupations. There was also the alarming tendency to brighten up old streets by painting buildings in pastel shades (a number of fine eighteenth-century brick buildings were spoilt in the process). July 1959 saw an exhibition entitled 'Better Towns for Better Living' organised by a group calling itself the Society for the Promotion of Urban Renewal, with grant aid from the Trust, which arranged for the exhibition to go on tour. In July 1960 the Ministry of Housing and Local Government held a conference at the Middlesex Guildhall on 'Rebuilding City Centre'. This was organised by the Trust, and demonstrates that the enthusiasm at that time for rebuilding and redevelopment was very much a part of the Trust's own ethos. Contemporary architects like Sir Basil Spence were, of course, numbered amongst the Civic Trust's trustees. It needs to be remembered that in the mid-1950s 'urban renewal' was an exciting term which had just crossed the Atlantic. There were then virtually no high buildings, few shopping centres and only eight miles of motorway.

When the Civic Trust was founded there were about 200 local amenity societies in existence. By 1960, 300 societies were registered with the Trust. By 1964 there were 500, and by 1967 the figure had risen to 600. From the outset, the Civic Trust issued a newsletter to civic societies; by the mid-1960s this had become a bi-monthly magazine, which in 1981 was given the title *Heritage Outlook*. The Civic Trust did a considerable amount to promote the formation of trusts in the 324 towns included in the Council for British Archaeology's 1965 list of historic towns, and by the time the Trust carried out a survey of societies in 1977, twenty years after its foundation, the astonishing growth in these local groups could justly be described as a 'movement'.[8] By then, the total membership of local amenity societies was just under 300,000. Perhaps unsurprisingly, there was a preponderance of such bodies in the south and south-east of England. Greater London, with local group membership of 46,633, outnumbered Scotland and Wales combined (27,677) and the counties of Surrey (24,356), Sussex (14,899) and Kent (14,349) outnumbered all the other regions of the Civic Trust (the north accounting for 12,166 individual members;

CIVIC TRUST

Proposed building for the 'Monico' site, Piccadilly Circus: the Civic Trust co-ordinated opposition to this banale and overscaled design.

Yorkshire and Humberside, 13,116; East Anglia, 10,758; and the West Midlands, 12,642). Norwich was singled out as the most active society, with 1,280 members, and the Civic Trust noted with regret that the only county town with no society at all in 1977 was Trowbridge.

It is a potential criticism of the Trust that its remit tended to be concentrated in the home counties and in prosperous London suburbs. In the Trust's 1977 overview it is interesting to note that although achievements in preserving buildings in traditional market towns feature, there is no mention at all of major industrial cities in the north, such as Leeds, Halifax, Huddersfield, Liverpool and Manchester. Deprived areas of London were also relatively neglected.

Yet the Civic Trust did play a significant role in the saving of three key sites in London. As early as 1959, the Trust took action over the proposed redevelopment of the so-called Monico site in Piccadilly Circus and co-ordinated the objectors' case. The Trust's main argument against Jack Cotton's scheme was that the replacement was unworthy and that, in any event, the design of the area should be considered as a whole and not redeveloped piecemeal. Despite having the support of the London County Council, Cotton's scheme was effectively defeated after a public inquiry.[9] There followed the proposed redevelopment of much of Whitehall, on which an inquiry was held in May 1966 at which the Trust was represented; this led to the scheme being abandoned. In 1971 the Civic Trust again played a significant part in defeating the redevelopment plans for Covent Garden. On the whole, however, the Trust did not engage directly in battles over particular sites, leaving it to local groups, the national amenity societies and later to SAVE to make the running.

However, the greatest achievement of the Civic Trust can be said to be its central role in the formulation of the 1967 Civic Amenities Act, which introduced the concept of Conservation Areas. This was very much the brainchild of Duncan Sandys himself. Sandys, who had steered the Clean Air Act and legislation on green belts through parliament, became increasingly concerned that the listing of individual buildings was not enough. The Civic Trust publication of January 1967, *Preserving the Architectural and Historical Scene*, provided the first full study of the Conservation Area concept, while it was Sandys himself who drafted the Act. He had come first in the private members ballot in 1966 and was able to bring forward the Bill as an all-party measure. It received Royal Assent in July 1967. As well as introducing the concept of Conservation Areas, the Bill also brought in legislation to preserve existing trees and to provide for the orderly disposal of rubbish and abandoned cars, which were then a not unfamiliar sight in backstreets. As Sandys had intended, the 1967 Act recognised the importance of preserving the harmony of whole areas, which might contain no single building of outstanding merit but which, taken as a whole, presented a scene of interest and charm.[10]

By the end of 1967 four Conservation Areas had been designated, the first being in Stamford. By the end of 1968 there were 138 outside London, fifty-two in London, five in Wales and twenty in Scotland. Between 400 and 500 were designated each year thereafter until 1973, and by mid-July of that year, when the Civic Trust did a count, there were 2,438. The Civic Trust was quick to spot that some authorities were more enthusiastic about designation than others. By July 1973 Kent had 198 Conservation Areas and Berkshire 101, whereas Herefordshire had only nine, Oxfordshire eight and the East Riding of Yorkshire only six. Towns reflected similar discrepancies. Bath had six, Chester one, York four, Gloucester eight and Oxford six, while many towns in the north had none at all (amongst these were Halifax, Blackpool, Oldham, Doncaster and Gateshead). Curiously, neither Ipswich nor Bury St Edmunds had designated any. Indeed, of the historic towns listed by the CBA in 1965 no less than six towns in England had no Conservation Areas even as late as November 1976, and neither did five towns in Wales (three of them in Radnorshire). By 1975 there were 4,004 areas designated nationwide, and by 1986, 5,868.[11]

Although the Civic Amenities Act was a private member's bill, the late 1960s also saw increasing interest in conservation by the Labour government then in office.[12] In 1968, the government commissioned studies of four historic towns, Bath, Chester, Chichester and York. The aim behind these was to provide not just a focus on the four towns concerned, but to provide a level of general guidance that might be applicable in other towns where a combination of run-down old buildings, traffic and pressure for new development posed problems.[13] At an official level, historic towns were still regarded as 'problems' and preservation was regarded as not merely unremunerative, but positively burdensome on owners. As it turned out, the reports were all very different. Colin Buchanan & Associates proposed a tunnel under the middle of Bath to ease traffic congestion. The Civic Trust applauded this idea and agreed that there was no scope in Bath 'as in many other cities for a conventional inner ring road through the "Victorian twilight areas"' – it is a sign of the times that most so-called 'twilight areas' would themselves now be Conservation Areas.[14] In his report on Chester, Donald Insall focused on the fabric of the buildings and argued the need for a national body to look after historic towns, in other words a national historic towns corporation. The study of Chichester was carried out by the County Planning Officer, Mr G. S. Burrows, and was much concerned with signs, shopfronts and infill schemes. Lord Esher took on York, and the York report is generally considered to be the most comprehensive of the four, with a section on the economics of conservation by Professor Lichfield.

At much the same time as the four town reports were commissioned, the debate was hotting up about public participation in the planning system. This culminated in the 1968 Town and Country Planning Act, which was arguably the most important piece of legislation since the Town and Country Planning Act of 1947. Part IV of the Act dealt with listed buildings and introduced the listed building consent procedure much as it is today. For the first time, local planning authorities were obliged to consider applications for listed building consent against criteria which were set out in the accompanying circular, including the importance of the building, its interest and condition, together with alternative uses for the site. Planning authorities were reminded that the number of listed buildings was limited and that there should be a presumption in favour of preservation, except where a strong case could be made out for demolition. This advice, which still holds true today, was further consolidated by Circular 8/87, which has only recently been replaced by *PPG 15*. Circular 8/87 contains perhaps the best apologia for the preservation of historic buildings ever to emerge from Whitehall.

The 1968 Act needs to be seen against the background of destruction that was already in full swing. As early as 1962 the Civic Trust was lamenting the fact that the statutory lists were far from complete.[15] Of 1,474 local authority areas, only 1,344 had been covered and only 1,020 lists issued. These early lists contained few buildings dating from later than 1800. In 1962, the Civic Trust pointed out that listed buildings were becoming scarce in industrial towns. Whereas Sheffield could boast sixty-two Grade II buildings on its list and seventeen Grade IIIs, Grimsby was down to one Grade II and five Grade IIIs. Notices to demolish listed buildings at this time were running at the rate of about forty-five a month. There had been 505 in 1959, 584 in 1960 and 550 in 1961. Since 1947, only 375 Building Preservation Notices had been made, of which only 261 were in force (covering 831 buildings, as some were terraces). The risk of being forced to undertake compulsory purchase discouraged many local authorities from using the Building Preservation Notice procedure at all, since there was no provision, short of such purchase, to encourage an owner to maintain his building. Indeed, both the government's sincerity and the validity of the listing legislation had been called into question by the decisions to demolish the Euston Arch in 1961 and the Coal Exchange in 1962.

The maximum fine for the demolition of a listed building without serving the requisite notice on the local authority and waiting two months did not exceed £100. Additionally, if an owner could argue that he had demolished a building because he considered it dangerous and its removal in the interests of health and safety, the demolition was not unlawful, provided notice was given to the local authority as soon as possible 'after the necessity for the work arises'. Closing Orders under the 1957 Housing Act were also used to remove old buildings. If a local authority thought a building unfit for human habitation on the grounds, for instance, of its standard of repair, or its defects from the point of view of damp, ventilation, drainage, or facilities for the storage or cooking of food, it could be closed down and demolished. The standards were so loosely phrased that it was left to each local authority to decide what should be included.

As well as providing clear criteria against which listed building consent applications should be judged, the 1968 Act also provided for the proper advertisement of applications and for formal consultation with the national amenity societies (the Society for the Protection of Ancient Buildings (SPAB), Georgian Group, Victorian Society and Ancient Monuments Society). Public consultation was henceforward a fundamental part of the process, as was referral to the Secretary of State in the event of a decision in favour of demolition.

The 1968 Act also introduced 'spot listing', a vital defence against premature demolition. The 1967 Civic Amenities Act and the 1968 Town and Country Planning Act were consolidated in the major Planning Act of 1971. Section 10 of the Town and Country Planning (Amendment) Act 1972 introduced exchequer grants for buildings in Conservation Areas. From 1973 to 1984 the Civic Trust helped to administer these grants. The 1968 Act also brought in the idea of Conservation Area Advisory Committees, again increasing the level of public participation. Yet what was still needed was greater control, particularly to protect unlisted buildings in Conservation Areas, and to encourage local authorities to evolve positive proposals for Conservation Area enhancement. In 1974 a Bill to provide this was brought in by Sir John Rodgers MP with the support of the then Secretary of State, Geoffrey Rippon. It had completed its Commons stage but before the Lords amendments could be considered a general election intervened. However, the incoming Labour administration was not opposed to the Bill and when Michael Shersby MP (Conservative) won first place in the ballot, the Bill was brought forward with the support of Anthony Crosland. The Bill became the Town and Country Amenities Act 1974, and for the first time control over demolition of unlisted buildings in Conservation Areas was provided.

Hence in the years around 1970, the legislative framework for conservation was significantly strengthened. Yet despite this, and despite all the good work of the Civic Trust, destruction still continued. It was only during the 1970s that this began to change, due to a shift of public perception and the beginnings of the widespread growth in interest in the conservation of historic buildings. The first book to protest about the horrific destruction that was devastating towns and cities all over Britain was Adam Fergusson's forthright work, *The Sack of Bath*, published in 1973. Subtitled 'A record and an indictment', this included a foreword by Lord Goodman, introductory rhymes by Sir John Betjeman and photographs taken by Lord Snowdon, amongst others. This was a campaigning book *par excellence*. Lord Goodman concluded that 'apathy, ignorance and even sheer philistinism are taking pride of place over cultivated knowledge and a genuine regard for aesthetic value', while, in the immortal words of the Poet Laureate:

Goodbye to old Bath. We who loved you are sorry
They've carted you off by developers' lorry.

BATH AND WILTS EVENING CHRONICLE

Calton Road, Bath, being demolished. An illustration from Adam Fergusson's *The Sack of Bath*, 1973.

Adam Fergusson detailed page by page the destruction of 'ordinary' streets and areas in Bath. Thirty years on, it seems hardly credible that swathes of sound Georgian housing bit the dust in a city that has always been internationally admired for its architecture and for the totality of its design. Yet, as Fergusson wrote: 'today "artisan Bath" is largely rubble'. The fights that the Bath Preservation Trust manfully engaged in – some won, but many sadly lost – are detailed, as is the conflict (echoes of which still survive today) between those who wish to conserve historic areas and those, like the members of the Royal Fine Art Commission who had strong views about Bath at the time, who consider that historic cities are enhanced and brought up to date by striking new buildings. In the 1970s (and, alas, still too often today, as at No. 1 Poultry) this dictum meant first of all destruction of fine old buildings on a central site, followed by the erection of a modern movement building, paying little or no regard to its neighbours, the street scene or the historic plan of the town or city.

The Sack of Bath graphically illustrated the complete myopia at official level towards historic areas. Following the 1947 Act which established listing, Bath had nearly 2,000 Grade I and II buildings. There were also a further 1,000 Grade III buildings which the Act stated were 'important enough to be drawn to the attention of local authorities and others, so that the case for conserving them can be fully considered'. It was these Grade III buildings that were wantonly destroyed. Any now surviving would, of course, be listed Grade II or above. The early Conservation Areas in Bath were confined to areas already famous and well protected by Grade I listings, like the Crescent or the Circus. Further evidence of the complete lack of appreciation of the historic architecture of Bath was highlighted by Fergusson in his comments about the Council's strategic 1960 development plan for Bath, in which the word 'Georgian' is mentioned only twice, and then in the context of historic buildings being millstones. 'One of the Corporation's problems', the document stated, 'is the preservation of fine examples of this period in the City'.[16]

Two years after the publication of Fergusson's book on Bath, Colin Amery and Dan Cruickshank published their important work, *The Rape of Britain*. This book was fundamental in alerting those interested in historic buildings and towns generally to the scale of destruction that was going on all over Britain. The book demonstrated that it was not just Bath that was suffering but virtually every market town up and down the country. The book emerged out of the respective authors' work at the *Architectural Review* and *Architects' Journal*. Thirty towns were described, with sketch plans showing town centres with the 'comprehensive development areas' dotted in and the routes of 'inner relief' roads clearly marked, and with illustrations showing the historic buildings that had already been demolished and those left to rot prior to demolition. The book identified the comprehensive development procedure, money and traffic as the principal causes of the destruction, together with the keen competition among towns for regional shopping centre status. The pressure for new offices in the centre of old towns was also highlighted.

The Rape of Britain was devastating, and its timing represented a turning point in attitudes to conservation. A few key victories by civic societies up and down the country encouraged them gradually to tackle the planners head-on. Indeed, the practical advice offered at the end of *The Rape of Britain* stressed the importance of amenity groups and the role that they could play. Mention is also made of the coverage given to historic buildings issues by the *Architectural Review* and the *Architects' Journal*, and there is no doubt that these two publications, together with *Country Life*, were the forum for the conservation debate at this time. Cruickshank and Amery lamented the 'often scanty and half-hearted treatment of conservation issues in the national press'.[17]

This was gradually to change, and the change was very much influenced by the arrival on the conservation scene of SAVE Britain's Heritage. SAVE was established in 1975 and Dan Cruickshank and Colin Amery were among its founder trustees. SAVE grew out of the impressive exhibition, *The Destruction of the Country House*, organised at the Victoria and Albert Museum in the winter of 1974 by Marcus Binney, SAVE's founder, who was then working for *Country Life*, and John Harris, then Curator of the Royal Institute of British Architects Drawings Collection. For the first time, people could see the extent of demolition of fine houses since the war. As part of publicising the exhibition,

Binney and Harris made sure photographs of lost houses were sent to local newspapers up and down the country. The exhibition organisers were overwhelmed by the response and interest in these local cases. Full-page stories were run, and more and more information was requested. Not only was it evident that people were interested in the subject; it suggested that if publicity could be given to buildings *before* demolition took place there could be a reasonable chance of encouraging owners to think again, or of persuading them to explore other options. SAVE thus came into being at the beginning of 1975 as a small ginger group whose aim was to publicise threats to historic buildings.

Its first task was to expose the true level of destruction going on, and what better year to do this than in European Architectural Heritage Year? From its beginning SAVE issued press releases about individual threats to buildings and quite quickly material began to come in from concerned individuals and amenity groups around the country. Towards the end of 1975, SAVE's first report was published. Lack of funds prevented publication as a booklet and the report was written for the *Architects' Journal*. SAVE's 'Heritage Year Toll' illustrated buildings both demolished and under threat. It recorded the alarming fact that in 1975 permission was being given to demolish one listed building a day – at precisely the time when official bodies throughout Europe were congratulating themselves that the heritage was generally appreciated and secure.[18] SAVE went on to publish further reports in architectural journals such as *Built Environment Quarterly* and *Building Design*, while issuing regular press releases about immediate threats, taking up cases from all over the country and helping local civic societies do battle for their buildings.

At that point, there did not seem to be a slot for conservation in the national press. However, this began to change when John Young, local government correspondent of *The Times*, expressed interest in using SAVE's material on the 'Court' page in that paper. Thereafter, so long as SAVE could provide a good photograph of a threatened building, regular coverage was given to SAVE press releases and reports. John Grigsby reported stories in the *Telegraph* (though seldom with pictures) and after a while the *Guardian* also began to give SAVE stories substantial coverage. This began with Donald Wintersgill's interest in the Mentmore affair, in which SAVE played a prominent role, while thereafter Martin Wainwright regularly featured threatened buildings and areas, particularly in northern towns. Television seemed to show little or no interest in conservation during the 1970s and early '80s, but magazines could usually be relied on to feature attractive buildings, and local newspapers continued to publish strong stories on local issues. Opposition voiced locally, backed up by some national coverage, was often a key factor in persuading a local planning committee to think twice about granting permission to demolish.

SAVE differed from the other national amenity societies in that, from the start, it was decided that its work should focus principally on publicity. It was not weighed down with statutory casework upon which it had to comment, as were the SPAB, Georgian Group, Victorian Society and Ancient Monuments Society. It did not, as a result, get any annual government grant and that is still the case.

SAVE

BRITAINS HERITAGE

SAVE BRITAIN'S HERITAGE

A typical SAVE leaflet, with its cover made up of a patchwork of newspaper cuttings relating to the group's campaigns.

A registered charity run on a shoe-string, it was able to choose its cases. These were often individual buildings, while on occasion it focused attention on types of building at risk. For instance, its first exhibition, *Off the Rails*, held at the Heinz Gallery of the RIBA in 1976, drew attention to the large numbers of decaying railway buildings. At the time, British Rail had no policy of conservation and no idea how many listed buildings or buildings in Conservation Areas it actually had in its care. Sir Peter Parker, then Chairman of British Rail, came to the exhibition. Shortly after, British Rail compiled and published a list of all its protected buildings. The Railway Heritage Trust eventually came into being in 1985 with an initial budget of £1 million and has done splendid work ever since in encouraging and grant-aiding conservation projects around the network.

From the beginning, SAVE aimed to show what was at risk. It also drew attention to what had already gone so as to establish some kind of benchmark for judging the present. Equally important were publications showing how buildings could be brought back into use through conversion and alternative uses. SAVE was (and is today) always anxious to demonstrate the benefits of conservation on a wider canvas. Key publications such as *Preservation Pays* by Marcus Binney and Max Hanna (1979) pointed up the link between preservation of historic areas and the economic benefits of tourism. SAVE's first town report was on Burnley in 1980. This began a series of some ten reports. The towns targetted still had major redevelopment proposals afoot or devastating road schemes. Titles included: *Leeds, Must Old Mean Bad, What! Conservation in Gateshead* and *Trowbridge: The Fastest Disappearing Mill Town in the West.* As the latter illustrates, good buildings in Trowbridge were still threatened by a longstanding and destructive inner relief road as late as 1985.

SAVE did not, of course, operate in isolation, and the major contribution made throughout the mid-1970s and 1980s by the SPAB, Georgian Group, Victorian Society and Ancient Monuments Society must not be overlooked. The annual reports of the Victorian Society throughout this period demonstrate the enormous effort being put into campaigns by voluntary societies. The Victorian Society's regional groups, particularly in the north, were especially successful. The emphasis here on SAVE is not intended in any way to underestimate the key roles played by others; it is simply to illustrate that publicity played a crucial part in changing the climate of opinion. Large numbers of ordinary people had been horrified at the scale of destruction in historic towns from the late 1950s onwards. Yet it was not until the mid-1970s that the voice of those concerned began not only to be heard but to influence directly official policy-making.

It was in this context that the later 1970s saw a coming together of initiatives from local bodies and from government. A case in point is presented by Building Preservation Trusts, the promotion of which was another of the Civic Trust's key contributions to the heritage scene. Although Hertfordshire County Council had established a trust in 1961 and Hampshire County Council set up its own grant scheme at about the same time (which evolved into the highly successful Hampshire Buildings Preservation Trust), European Architectural Heritage Year in 1975 saw the establishment by the government of an Architectural Heritage Fund from which Building Preservation Trusts could borrow funds at low interest in order to tackle repair projects which might otherwise be unviable. This implemented a recommendation made by the Civic Trust in its report *Financing the Preservation of Old Buildings*, again a Sandys initiative, which was prepared for the Department of the Environment in 1971.[19] Fifteen new Building Preservation Trusts (BPTs) were formed in or around European Architectural Heritage year, and by 1979 there were thirty-eight trusts operating nationally. A national Association of BPTs was formed in 1989 and there are now 148 trusts.[20]

Some of these organisations, like the Spitalfields Trust, used direct action to save buildings from demolition, persuading well-known architectural historians to occupy buildings moments before the demolition men moved in and thus embarrassing the owning property companies into rethinking their plans. Nos 5–7 Elder Street, Spitalfields, were saved in this way in 1977 (and received one of the first Architectural Heritage Fund loans): Mark Girouard and Colin Amery subsequently made the front page of the *Guardian* during their freezing occupation of the Central Foundation School Hall, also threatened with precipitate demolition, in December 1980.[21] The Derbyshire Historic Buildings Trust also did pioneering work rescuing the fifty-seven railway cottages by Francis Thompson near to Derby Station which were threatened by a road improvement scheme (sadly, British Rail demolished Thompson's station building in 1984). The Trust succeeded in getting the clearance order rescinded, acquired the cottages in 1979, and proceeded to restore all the cottages, dating from 1841, for resale. The Architectural Heritage Fund loaned £250,000 and the whole scheme cost £1.25 million, an astonishingly ambitious scheme for a small voluntary group.[22] More recently, inspired by SAVE's purchase of the derelict Barlaston Hall for a token £1 in 1981 and its subsequent restoration of the building with grant aid from government and other sources, various preservation trusts have been able to obtain and rehabilitate unwanted buildings in a similar manner.

A equally striking trend of the later 1970s was the increasingly positive attitude towards conservation taken in official circles. This is illustrated by the transformation at this time of the Historic Buildings Council (HBC), which had been set up in 1953 in the aftermath of the Gowers Report. Initially, the Council was mainly preoccupied with country houses, though it did offer grants for other kinds of buildings: for instance, one of its first repair grants in 1953 was for the medieval Gloucester Blackfriars, while in 1964 grants were offered for repairs to Kennet and Avon Canal and to the Dundas Aqueduct at Claverton, designed by the elder Rennie. Subsequently, the Council's reports show it acquiring increasing responsibilities in dispersing funds under the legislative initiatives of the late 1960s and early 1970s, for instance to outstanding Conservation Areas.

But in 1975–6 a really decisive shift occurred, which is signalled even by the format of the report for that year, which is very different in its presentation from its predecessors. Whereas they had been printed in the standard HMSO style of the day, now, for the first time, a photograph of a building appeared on the front cover while, inside, the report was printed on glossy paper and illustrated with photographs. Whereas the report from the previous year consisted of a mere four and a half pages reviewing the year's activity, followed by a list of grants and appendices, the 1975–6 report runs to no less than eighteen pages, including a contents page.

What caused the change? It can be linked directly to the change in chairmanship. The 1975–6 report was Dame Jennifer Jenkins's first report as Chairman of the Historic Buildings Council and her strong commitment to conservation and understanding of the issues runs through every page. Dame Jennifer had been active in the Ancient Monuments Society prior to her appointment, and she knew first-hand the scale of the problem the HBC needed to tackle. She saw quite clearly that the effect of grants, though vital, was limited. She perceived that the HBC could take on a much more active and proselytising role. She understood the importance of fighting for individual buildings but saw it as part of the wider battle to persuade reluctant local authorities that their heritage mattered, and to persuade the government that conservation was not a fringe issue. The timing of her appointment was significant as at precisely the same time the conservation movement was getting into gear.

Dame Jennifer's first report was quite clearly aimed at ministers and was a clarion call for a change of heart. Buildings at risk were illustrated and the new duties of the HBC in relation to historic gardens and Capital Transfer Tax exemption were mentioned; the report also provocatively stated that the government had accepted the principle of the need for state aid for churches in use and that the HBC was awaiting an announcement on the subject (in fact, state aid for churches was introduced in 1977, as the HBC report for that year noted with pleasure). The 1975–6 report stressed that the HBC now saw the priority as the establishing of conservation schemes in major historic towns and inner city areas. In a tone redolent of Dame Jennifer herself, and a very far cry from the officialese of earlier reports, ministers were urged to reconsider certain areas of public spending. The report argued that some capital schemes could surely wait: 'new car parks costing £35 million in 1974–5 are an example. Urgent repairs cannot'. The report ended with the words, '"Bull-dozer" redevelopment has demonstrably failed to bring the gains it promised: constructive conservation must now be seen as a real alternative'.[23]

The HBC reports continued in this forthright vein for the next few years, and this powerful rhetoric was designed to achieve a number of objectives. It sent a clear message to ministers that conservation was no longer a minority interest and that comprehensive redevelopment in historic towns had to stop. It also gave encouragement to local and national amenity societies to redouble their efforts to fight for key buildings. Part of this process involved persuading local authorities of the merits of area conservation. Dame Jennifer Jenkins herself travelled the country widely during her chairmanship of the HBC, meeting chief executives and chief planning officers. She was instrumental in encouraging them to enter into Town Schemes and in persuading them to tackle key buildings at risk with grant aid. Already, younger planning officers were more sympathetic to the preservation of buildings, although they were frequently very much in the minority in their departments, and this provided them with the support they often needed.

By 1981, Michael Heseltine was Secretary of State for the Environment and there were a number of individual cases in which he took a personal interest. In previous years, heritage matters had been relegated to the appropriate Under Secretary of State. These junior ministers had a tendency to change with unwelcome rapidity and there was a feeling among amenity societies that they were seldom in the job long enough to get a grasp of the complex issues involved. By contrast, Michael Heseltine demonstrated welcome interest in historic buildings and their fate. Marcus Binney, then Chairman of SAVE, was called to Marsham Street early on during Heseltine's tenure and asked to talk first-hand about what he saw as key issues.

SAVE had consistently maintained, as had other amenity groups, that the key to dealing with buildings at risk was to ensure that they were offered on the market at a reasonable price without undue conditions before consent to demolish was granted on the grounds of poor condition or lack of alternative use. For instance, there had been a number of notorious cases of buildings being offered through the Historic Buildings Bureau (the quarterly list of problem historic buildings in need of new owners that had been maintained by the Historic Buildings Council since 1954), yet whenever enquiries were made it would become obvious that there were so many binding conditions, or a lease was being offered that was unreasonably short, that prospective purchasers were deterred. This was, in some cases, a deliberate ploy by owners, who, having no use for a building themselves, could not envisage that sensitive and viable solutions were a possibility.

A case in point was that of Hasells Hall, a large and handsome eighteenth-century brick house in Bedfordshire, and the ancestral home of the Pym family. Virtually unused since the war, its condition was worsening, and it had featured a number of times in the Historic Buildings Bureau list. Kit Martin, who has since become well-known for his sensitive conversion of large country houses, had been interested in acquiring it, but was deterred by the very short lease and other onerous conditions. Although a minister at the time, Francis Pym applied for consent to demolish. It was refused following a public inquiry and in the event the house was finally sold to Kit Martin and is now happily restored.[24] The lesson of this case and others was not lost on the amenity societies who made their point to Michael Heseltine.

The HBC report of 1980–1 welcomed enthusiastically Heseltine's statement that he would not in future be prepared to grant consent for demolition unless every avenue had been pursued, and every effort made to find an alternative use, including offering a building on the market at a reasonable price and without restrictive conditions. This sentiment was clearly expressed by Heseltine in speeches and later incorporated into a government circular and then reiterated in

Circular 8/87. It gave key ammunition to all those fighting to save historic buildings, including junior planning officers and that new breed, conservation officers. It provided an unambiguous statement that they could put into their reports and reiterate at planning committee meetings. For the first time there was some kind of answer to the arguments traditionally put forward in favour of demolition, namely that a building had outlived its useful life or was uneconomic to repair. Though always subjective, such arguments frequently found favour with chief planning officers and planning committees for whom a cleared site had often represented an end to a problem. At last, by offering a building for sale the economics of conservation could be tested objectively, and time and time again what appeared to be a hopeless and desperate situation turned out to have a viable solution.

Michael Heseltine also endeared himself to those in the conservation world by visiting privately a number of controversial cases with which his department was dealing. He was known to have visited the former Billingsgate Fish Market, for instance, and there was much rejoicing when it was subsequently spot-listed. The City Corporation, however, were furious as they had been hoping to redevelop the site. The then City Surveyor wrote at the time that he thought the corrosive effects of fish juices might have weakened the iron structure irrevocably. He also sounded alarm bells – totally unfoundedly as it turned out – by claiming that there would be ground heave below Billingsgate when the large deep freezes in the basement were switched off. This type of apocalyptic response was typical from those still promoting controversial demolition proposals.[25]

Lastly, Michael Heseltine was the moving force behind the establishment in 1984 of the Historic Buildings and Monuments Commission for England, English Heritage, which took over the responsibilities formerly carried out by the HBC. The last HBC report, that for 1982–3, spelt out the guidelines that the HBC had developed to help it with its work over the thirty-year period of its existence. First, it stressed that members of the HBC were never selected for reasons of party allegiance and this was regarded as a strength. It stressed that the HBC had always had all-party support, emphasised by the inclusion of both government and opposition MPs. Members of the HBC, it stated, were chosen for their professional interests and experience and for their commitment to historic buildings. These attributes had enabled the Council to respond quickly, and as effectively as limited resources permitted, to new situations. The report recognised the widening appreciation of the historic environment. It noted with some satisfaction that the list of historic gardens in England was halfway complete and that grants would soon be available for large engineering structures. It stressed that the HBC saw grants for Victorian Liverpool as important as for Georgian Bath, for railway stations as well as historic houses, and it noted how greatly the base of political support for the heritage had widened in its thirty-year existence.

English Heritage produced its first glossy report in 1985. All had changed. Gone was the clear focus of Dame Jennifer Jenkins's Historic Buildings Council. Instead, the report consisted of eight pages devoted to the appointment of the new commissioners and general philosophy, followed by a substantial section on marketing, sales and promotion. Of course, this related to the properties in government care inherited from the old Directorate of Ancient Monuments, which the new body also incorporated. Since one of the purposes of setting up English Heritage was to promote these properties more effectively, it is perhaps not surprising that the focus shifted so dramatically. It was not until page 22 that conservation of historic buildings got a mention and then there was not much of depth. The 1986 report, no doubt to pacify concerned conservationists, saw historic buildings and gardens coming first, but again there was not much in the way of comment. There were lists of activities, numbers of listed building consent applications dealt with, and the first hint that the rules governing grant aid were being revised. This was later to affect not just historic houses which had long-term repair schemes running with HBC assistance, but also some of the longer-established town schemes and projects being carried out by Building Preservation Trusts. It was certainly arguable that by 1986 many of the key historic towns had definitely turned the corner and, with property values on the rise, grant aid could be a less crucial ingredient in getting neglected buildings repaired: but it sent a chill wind to those still battling against the odds to save worthwhile buildings from continued neglect. It was at about this time that English Heritage began to question the need for continued grant aid for cities such as Bath.

Yet it is questionable whether English Heritage had the focus of the old Historic Buildings Council. The organisation's early annual reports were full of comments about how English Heritage should 'develop more objective criteria in determining priorities' – the HBC decade from 1975 had never had a problem identifying and addressing the issues. In a section entitled 'campaigning' in the 1986 report is a reference to English Heritage making representations to the House of Commons Select Committee on the Heritage that was then sitting and which was to report in 1987. This was not campaigning as amenity groups understood it and it was small wonder that many observers at the time lamented the passing of the old HBC and saw its replacement as a bureaucratic monster, issuing reports full of pie charts and bar graphs, reluctant to engage in positive action. Encouragingly, however, February 1987 saw the publication of the first issue of English Heritage's *Conservation Bulletin*. This quarterly booklet, which is distributed widely to local authorities and those in the conservation world, has played a key part in disseminating information from the centre outwards. It has provided an important vehicle for professional staff within English Heritage to communicate with a wider public, and in particular to communicate with the growing number of conservation officers throughout England.

English Heritage's later annual reports focus on the casework undertaken, grants given and buildings at risk, together with all the organisation's other activities. Several years' time and much effort were spent analysing the percentage of buildings likely to be at risk in England but the study was unwieldy and its conclusions unremarkable.[26] The London Division, however, did publish its own Buildings at Risk Register for the capital in 1990, seeking advice from the boroughs and local amenity groups. This list, which has been revised in subsequent years, provided a valuable tool for focusing effort and for tackling problems of neglected buildings. It led directly to the targetting of grant aid towards threatened buildings in London, particularly in the East End. The rescue of St John's, Hoxton, and St Matthias, Poplar, for instance, together with many other buildings, is attributable directly to this initiative. In 1991 Jennifer Page, then Chief Executive, laid great stress on the need for English Heritage to improve its knowledge of the state of the historic environment. The emphasis was much less on direct action, with certain notable exceptions, and more on maintaining an overview. This remains the case today. But the climate of opinion is now supportive of conservation, with most areas likely to be eligible as Conservation Areas already designated, and list review filling the gaps in the statutory lists. Significant though the focus on listing post-war buildings is at the present moment, it will not involve the addition of vast numbers of buildings to the statutory lists as did the review of the Victorian period from the mid-1960s onwards.

In reviewing the period from 1975 onwards, however, it is important to recognise that those championing historic buildings did not have it all their own way. The Royal Institute of British Architects (RIBA) launched a rearguard action in the early 1980s, and RIBA Presidents such as Michael Manser and Owen Luder consistently made speeches vilifying the efforts of conservationists and arguing that conservation had gone too far. However, the Prince of Wales hit back at the architectural establishment in his well-reported speech at the 150th anniversary dinner of the RIBA in May 1984 and again in his Mansion House speech on 1 December 1987, parts of which were to be included in his TV programme and subsequent book, *A Vision of Britain* (1989).

Peter Palumbo (now Lord Palumbo) polarised opinion during his long battle to demolish the buildings on the Mappin and Webb site in the City of London. His original Mansion House Square scheme, which was the subject of the first public inquiry held in 1984, included a huge glass tower designed many years previously by the eminent but long-dead architect, Mies Van der Rohe. That this scheme got the support that it did from the architectural profession demonstrated all too vividly that the clean sweep approach to development was far from dead and still had its admirers. Amongst those giving evidence in support of the comprehensive redevelopment were well-known figures such as Sir Richard Rogers. They also included Sir John Summerson, representing the older emphasis on selective preservation of outstanding buildings as against 'group value', a concept with which he freely admitted that he always had difficulty. Even when the second inquiry loomed in 1988, Palumbo was able to rely for support on a galaxy of well-known architects who were prepared to see the whole area, including eight listed buildings, make way for a new building by the now late Sir James Stirling. SAVE had defended the existing buildings from the outset, commissioning the architect Terry Farrell to draw up a scheme illustrating how they might be viably rehabilitated. When the Secretary of State ruled in favour of demolition, SAVE bravely took his decision to the Court of Appeal and

SAVE BRITAIN'S HERITAGE

No. 1 Poultry, City of London: the buildings demolished after two public inquiries to make way for Lord Palumbo's redevelopment.

won. Sadly, the decision was overturned in the House of Lords and the long battle to save the Mappin and Webb site was finally lost.[27] However, it was made clear that the Secretary of State's decision in the No.1 Poultry Case was a one-off and would not set a precedent, as SAVE and others had seriously feared, and would not alter the general presumption in favour of preserving historic buildings and historic areas. At a time when property values, particularly in London, were soaring and major schemes for development were being proposed all over the capital (the King's Cross Goods Yard and the Spitalfields Market site, to name but two), this was reassuring news.

The heady days of the property boom of the late 1980s have gone, but, sadly, the threats today tend to be more insidious. Pressure for alterations continues to do untold damage to historic interiors (and exteriors) and the longer-term implications of change of use are seldom fully appreciated during the listed building consent application process. Equally, there is the temptation to gild the lily: all too many Conservation Areas have been treated to 'heritage-style' lighting and wall-to-wall paving in coloured, and often textured, paviors that spread like carpets across traditional roads and pavements, obliterating curbs and changes in level.

There is also the problem of unsympathetic alterations, for instance, the insertion of pseudo-Georgian doors and new windows. Sadly, Conservation Areas up and down the country have been ravaged by the new doors and windows syndrome and the legislation has not been adequate to prevent it. Article 4 Directions have often been difficult to get confirmed by the Department of the Environment, reflecting a lack of political will in a decade of burgeoning home ownership. The gradual erosion of historic character in the past fifteen years has been an issue that has been very difficult to tackle effectively. Total demolitions generate news but the gradual alteration of detail, which cumulatively can be so devastating, has been a hard subject for amenity groups to publicise. Not until the English Historic Towns Forum's 1992 report was the issue really been brought to the forefront.[28]

The issue that has yet to be tackled is the whole question of the growing abandonment of town centres as suburban living and out-of-town shopping – whether supermarkets or chain stores – kill off shops in traditional centres. This will probably not affect the best-preserved historic towns, which will continue to attract large numbers of people to live and work in them and visit them, so much as towns such as Bedford, which, despite the ravages of the era of comprehensive redevelopment, still retain a surprising number of their older buildings more or less intact. A similar case is of Faversham in Kent, a town where considerable conservationist efforts were made in the late 1970s and early 1980s, but which is now facing renewed decay. Places like these are now facing serious problems, with shops boarded up and upper floors empty. It is unlikely that a town can survive simply with banks and building societies. Getting people to live once again in towns such as these will be the conservation challenge for the late 1990s and beyond.

9

Open-air and industrial museums: windows onto a lost world or graveyards for unloved buildings?

Michael Stratton

Several of Britain's open-air museums have recently celebrated their silver jubilees.[1] For much of their history, they have aroused controversy among both museum professionals and building conservationists. They have been praised for spearheading innovative and lively approaches to interpretation, and for saving neglected local buildings. Critics have condemned them for inconsistent standards of conservation and curatorship and for taking buildings out of their local setting. Such architectural issues were strongly debated in the 1970s, while in more recent years open-air museums have become embroiled in the 'heritage debate' focusing on popular approaches to interpretation and public attitudes to the past.

Perhaps only now is it possible to attempt an appraisal of what open-air museums have achieved in terms of saving structures and explaining aspects of buildings, industrial processes and past ways of life to the public. Are they – or were they – spearheading the preservation of 'real' buildings and traditional skills, or do they represent the worst aspects of 'edutainment', 'fakelore' and the blurring of boundaries between historical credibility and the appeal to public nostalgia? Or are the hype and vitriol hardly justified by a relatively small number of museums and sites which are already mellowing into their landscape and into British cultural consciousness. This chapter will examine the evolution of open-air museums, focusing on Britain and especially those relating to industrial history. As well as briefly considering foreign antecedents, it will review subsequent developments in museum interpretation, in terms of the influence exerted by Colonial Williamsburg, Ironbridge and Beamish, and by outside ideas that are, in turn, influencing policy-making in open-air museums as they chase visitors in an increasingly competitive leisure market.

The picturesque and nationalist origins of the open-air museum

A brief historical overview can emphasise two key points. Open-air museums are not simply a modern by-product of increased leisure time and the appeal of easy-going history to the British public; they have an international pedigree refined over more than a century. Secondly, for most of that long period they have been conceived and judged in highly charged and nationalistic terms. Most were established to preserve and present a threatened aspect of regional or national culture and to help forge a sense of identity and achievement. The focus may be

Scandinavian folk life, the homestead roots of the United States of America or Britain's primacy in the Industrial Revolution. One needs to ask whether such worthy but potentially jingoistic aims retain any validity in a revisionist and more cynical age. If so, can they still be articulated through the colours of thatch and honest brickwork, and sounds of folk music and brass bands?

Dr Zippelius, one of the founder-figures of open-air museums, argued that they drew many of their key elements from landscape gardens of the eighteenth century. The aristocracy laid out and toured picturesque trails that took their guests to distant lands – Indian temples or Chinese pagodas – and back to a medieval world of Gothic grottoes. A recently restored example, Hawkstone in Shropshire laid out by Sir Rowland and Sir Richard Hill from the mid-eighteenth century onwards, featured a lion's den and a costumed hermit, now recreated by a high-tech hologram.

A more directly nationalistic approach developed in the nineteenth century, and was first apparent in displays at international exhibitions. Norway and Sweden showed examples of their national architecture at the Paris Exhibition of 1867. In the following decade Artur Hazelius developed a series of dioramas of Swedish life, which were shown at Paris in 1878. Awards given to the displays encouraged him to embark on collecting buildings from 1885, and to display them to the public from 1891 at Skansen Hill, Stockholm. The aim from the outset was popularist, to 'exhibit folklife in living style'. Lapps were brought in to care for reindeer and the programme of special events included dancing on midsummer's eve.[2]

The Skansen formula was highly successful and was taken up by other northern European countries anxious to reinforce their cultural identity. The Norwegian Folk Museum was founded in 1894, the Danish Frilandsmuseet in 1897, and The Netherlands Open-Air Museum at Arnhem in 1912. The 'Old Town' at Aarhus, Denmark gained its first re-erected house in 1909. In the same year, Henry Balfour, in his role as President of the British Museums Association, called for 'a National Folk Museum, dealing exclusively and exhaustingly [sic] with the history and culture of the British nation'.[3] A modern list of European open-air museums would show a marked concentration in Scandinavia, Russia and Poland. Britain would appear well down the league, while Mediterranean countries have hardly a proper open-air museum between them. Some other British museums, such as the Castle Museum in York, have a token re-erected building – in this case a stone-built watermill – to complement their indoor displays.

The United States initially explored its cultural roots not through open-air museums but period houses. Early in this century the Society for the Preservation of New England Antiquities created a network of house museums, still in their original location but with restored interiors and costumed guides. They were to be a key influence on Henry Ford in developing his village of re-erected buildings. Ford dedicated Greenfield Village in October 1929, on fields at Dearborn just outside Detroit. His aesthetic vision of recreating a small New England town allowed him to recapture the innocent world that his Model-T car had effectively destroyed. A Cotswold cottage was included to symbolise historic links with England. Nostalgia was combined with the celebration of the great heroes of American industrialisation by rebuilding houses and workshops occupied by Ford himself, the Wright brothers, Henry J. Heinz and Thomas Edison. In the words of Henry Ford, the aim of Greenfield Village and the adjoining museum was 'to show how far and fast we have come'; the tone was, and remains, vibrantly optimistic, the recurring theme being the merits of technology and the resourcefulness of the American people. The indoor museum hall was developed as a glorified attic with rows of cars, steam engines and sewing machines, some shipped out from Britain. It now pursues the broader remit of interpreting the impact of various technologies on American life.[4]

Ford's grand vision for Greenfield Village was outrun by John D. Rockefeller Jr's project to recreate Colonial Williamsburg, the capital of Virginia, over a decade of rapid development commencing in 1927. From the outset the aim was to create 'an authentic three-dimensional environment'. People and their way of life soon became the focal theme. From as early as 1932 'hostesses' or interpreters were dressed in period costumes.[5] Long-running criticism of Colonial Williamsburg as presenting a sanitised view of American history has been countered by recent projects, such as the lunatic asylum, with its stained and graffitied walls.

While European open-air museums, which now number around 450, moved towards a drier, more museological approach in the twentieth century, American curators increasingly saw buildings primarily as stage-sets for acted interpretation. Plimoth Plantation on the edge of Cape Cod Bay in Massachusetts has set the pace in 'living history'. The re-created village, first planned in 1956, has itself been largely rebuilt – at a rate of one building a year – as archaeologists and anthropologists gained a fuller understanding of the seventeenth-century settlers and their wood-and-thatch houses. Both the buildings and objects are replicas, allowing staff full play in demonstrating various activities. They can change the contents of the two dozen houses as new ideas emerge and so maintain the enthusiasm of the interpreters who adopt the grammar and accents of America's Puritan ancestors.[6]

British open-air museums and timber-framed buildings

Various projects to relocate timber-framed buildings were undertaken in Britain near the turn of the century. Two were moved to Bournville on the southern edge of Birmingham to add a period tone to Cadbury's garden suburb. Sir Philip Stott rebuilt three barns in the Cotswold village of Stanton, Gloucestershire, between 1906 when he bought the estate and his death in 1937. The first British open-air museum in Britain was established on the Isle of Man in 1938. Cregneash Folk Museum was based round a series of buildings set within a village, but none of them was relocated. The Welsh Folk Museum established at St Fagans near Cardiff was the first to draw more directly on Scandinavian precedent. Ideas were gleaned on an exploratory visit to Sweden in 1930 but development only commenced in 1951.[7]

Ulster gained its folk museum a decade later, in 1961. A clutch of regionally based museums were established in England during the sixties: Ryedale Folk Museum at Hutton-le-Hole, North Yorkshire in 1963, the Museum of East Anglian Rural Life at Stowmarket in 1965, Avoncroft Museum of Buildings at Bromsgrove in 1967 and the Weald and Downland Museum at Singleton near Chichester in 1969. Each had, and retains, its own idiosyncratic flavour. The Ryedale Folk Museum, for example has a site of less than three acres and was the initiative of just one man and his passion for the way of life on the North York Moors.

MUSEUM OF WELSH LIFE

Folk-dancing outside the Penparcau Toll-house from Aberystwyth, re-erected at the St Fagans Museum, South Wales, one of the earliest open-air museums in the British Isles.

These new ventures reflected a growing interest in vernacular, and in particular timber-framed, architecture, at a time of major threats to their survival from road widening and urban redevelopment. Freddie Charles was among those who saw a two-way link between researching timber structures and dismantling, moving and re-erecting them.[8] British open-air museums of buildings can be seen as a response to the mismatch between new-found knowledge among historians and conservationists and the adequacy of planning protection during the sixties and seventies. Multi-phase buildings, with their early timber structure obscured by later brick or plaster, were rarely listed. If threatened, their only hope might be removal and re-erection in an open-air museum. Early rebuilding projects gave architects and curators a much fuller understanding of timber-framed buildings. The finest of the three houses donated to the Weald and Downland Museum by the East Surrey Water Company, Bayleaf Farmstead from Bough Beech, Surrey, was re-erected in its original fifteenth-century form. Its dramatic open hall roused considerable interest in the form of late medieval and Tudor domestic architecture, so aiding the recognition and *in situ* preservation of other comparable structures.

Industrial decline and open-air museums

The concept of the open-air museum was adopted by industrial archaeologists as a means of saving and presenting artefacts and processes made redundant by the closure of canals, railways and traditional printshops, foundries and blacksmiths. Most of the pioneers in industrial preservation had been too independent of mind and smitten with wanderlust to be constrained by the boundaries and pedantry of museums. Arthur Elton recorded aspects of industry by documentary film in the 1930s. L. T. C. Rolt combined a love of steam engines and veteran cars with a nostalgic affection for the countryside, especially when seen from narrow, winding canals. Having laid the foundations of the canal preservation movement, he moved on to help establish Britain's first preserved railway, the Talyllyn in West Wales.[9] Scenes of industrial dereliction appealed to a broad spectrum of writers, historians and photographers. John Betjeman wrote of Dawley, set just above the Ironbridge Gorge: 'Dead collieries, branch railways, tileworks and iron foundries lie among waste heaps now and then left bare for a common . . . the district has a haphazard beauty especially when sun is setting over deserted brickfields and round shafts'.[10]

During the 1950s, local historians, who had initially dismissed industry for its rape of rural England, turned to study the landscapes of the West Midlands and the northern textile regions. Michael Rix published an article with the title 'Industrial Archaeology' in the *Amateur Historian* in 1955. A trickle of research and publication turned to a flood in the sixties, the regional volumes produced by David and Charles listing key sites across much of Britain. Public interest was heightened by concern at the loss of major monuments. The demolition of the Euston Arch in 1962 was followed by threats to nearby St Pancras Station and to Albert Dock in Liverpool.

Canal and railway preservation schemes prospered on amateur enthusiasm. The same combination of inventiveness and regional and national pride propelled the rapid development of four open-air museums devoted primarily to industrial preservation. Their founders, typically professionals, drew upon the precedent of St Fagans, Skansen and Arnhem, but also forged strong working ties with teams of local volunteers.

The Ironbridge Gorge Museum in eastern Shropshire and the North of England Open-Air Museum at Beamish were launched, if not actually opened, in the late 1960s. The Black Country Museum was established in 1975, after a series of temporary exhibitions had been mounted in Dudley Central Museum. The Chalk Pits Museum at Amberley opened in 1979. Their charitable status, with board members, trustees and appeal directors, gave them a dynamic – even radical – image a world apart from the dusty showcases and corridors of most contemporary national and local museums. Barrie Trinder has argued that their fashionability followed precisely from their roots in the Scandinavian open-air movement. 'Scandinavia meant good design (stainless steel dishes, smoked glass and Saab cars) . . ., a serious concern for the arts, and a life-style, which, in England, seemed blissfully hedonistic.' Open-air sites in the Low Countries also provided inspiration for the founders of the Ironbridge Gorge Museum through a visit of the director of one of the most important of these, Bokrijk, to England in 1965 and the perusal of guidebooks for other Belgian and Dutch museums.[11]

Planning considerations also played a part. The Ironbridge Gorge was included within the area of Dawley New Town, first designated in 1963 and later renamed Telford. The Development Corporation accepted the recommendation of a report drafted by John Madin in 1966 that the conservation of the Ironbridge Gorge could give a positive identity to the New Town.[12] Meanwhile the North of England Open-Air Museum had the support of eight local authorities in a region

IRONBRIDGE GORGE MUSEUM

Tollhouse, designed by Thomas Telford. This was relocated in the early 1970s from Shrewsbury to Blists Hill, as part of the Ironbridge Gorge Museum, Shropshire.

where the traditional economy and landscape of coal and shipbuilding was being swept away.

The philosophy of these new ventures was fluid if not ill-defined. The Ironbridge Gorge Museum was registered as a trust in January 1968, taking over the small company museum at Coalbrookdale but committed to developing a major open-air museum site. The forty-two acres of dereliction and woodland at Blists Hill were originally planned as a technology park, with steam engines and a blast-furnace surrounded by a flight of locks and a railway marshalling yard. A group of ruined cottages and a derelict colliery engine-house were demolished, but other structures such as the inclined plane, the foundations of the blast furnaces and the brickworks were to be consolidated *in situ*. Shortages of funds forced cut-backs in the original concept, while an alternative and more viable formula emerged in interpreting Victorian social history with modest workshops, shops and pubs rather than large-scale industry. Plans to remove and re-erect such prime Shropshire monuments as the charcoal furnace at Charlcot and the Telford aqueduct at Longdon-on-Tern were quietly filed away.[13] The director of

MICHAEL STRATTON

Rowley Station reconstructed at the North of England Open-Air Museum, Beamish, County Durham, in 1975.

Ironbridge, Neil Cossons, was encouraged to be less active in seeking redundant buildings for Blists Hill by more purist approaches that had come to hold sway in North America.

A comparable shift can be seen in the case of the North of England Open-Air Museum at Beamish, County Durham. Beamish arose out of the 'unselective collecting' of objects reflecting the life and work of ordinary people in the North East, led by Frank Atkinson as director of the Bowes Museum at Barnard Castle from 1958. Interiors of a chemist's shop and a miner's cottage were set up as 'tasters' in the stores which spread through twenty-two huts and hangars at Brancepeth. Durham County Council and seven other authorities gave their backing to the establishment of a museum showing 'every aspect of life in the past of the region'. Once established on land around Beamish Hall, to the south-west of Newcastle-upon-Tyne, volunteers started dismantling and moving buildings and machinery. A farm gin gan was brought from Ponteland and, in 1972, the Chophill No. 2 winding engine was moved from Beamish village. In that year, Frank Atkinson, by now the director of Beamish, summarised the reasons for relocating industrial monuments: their original sites may become incongruous, access and security may be inadequate, and buildings and structures could gain from being juxtaposed rather than many miles apart. A responding paper in 1973, by the deputy director at Ironbridge and a historian at Newcastle who had been involved in moving some of the machinery to Beamish, countered Atkinson's arguments and represented a marked shift in attitudes. They pleaded for any major monuments to stay *in situ*, so retaining their context and associated archaeology. The successful preservation of the Ryhope Pumping Station at Sunderland was quoted as an example.[14] Other academics and museum professionals agreed that it was difficult to re-create the landscape details – saggar walls, slag heaps and vegetation – essential for a full interpretation of the Industrial Revolution.[15]

Renewed attention was given to the merits of *in situ* preservation, already a long-established, if not highly developed, tradition within industrial archaeology. The largest waterwheel in Britain, Lady Isabella on the Isle of Man, had been restored as early as the 1920s. The Cornish Engines Preservation Society was formed in 1934. In the following year the Abbeydale steelworks in Sheffield was purchased by a trust and donated to the city.[16] Local initiatives became complemented by national programmes of conservation and documentation in the 1960s. Programmes of field research formed the basis of listing and scheduling, which in turn spawned further preservation projects. Small watermills, potteries and huge textile complexes were transformed into working industrial museums. The utopian cotton settlement of New Lanark, located on the banks of the Clyde south-east of Glasgow, was developed from 1785 by Richard Arkwright and David Dale but is most notable as having been a test-bed for the utopian ideals of Robert Owen. A conservation study undertaken in 1973 laid the foundations for a far-reaching programme embracing conservation, efforts to attract back commerce and residents, and interpretation for visitors. Gladstone Pottery in Longton, with the most complete surviving potbank in North Staffordshire, became a highly successful museum, while the nearby Chatterley Whitfield colliery was also preserved and opened to the public.

Removing and re-erecting buildings

It is difficult to present a detached viewpoint on the removal of historic structures to industrial or building museums. Most architectural historians and conservationists adopt, almost subconsciously, the purist stance expounded by the Society for the Protection of Ancient Buildings (SPAB) from at least as early as 1926, that 'the landmark must mark the land'. Any building has a spirit tied to the setting which is lost if the structure is dismantled and moved.[17] The SPAB was particularly vociferous in opposing the gathering together of various timber-framed buildings from across Coventry to create the heritage attraction of Medieval Spon Street.[18] Without doubt, this project resulted in a considerable loss of original fabric, infill material usually being completely discarded. It also encouraged a compartmentalised attitude towards urban conservation among the city fathers and planners, who accepted widespread redevelopment in other parts of Coventry. Those defending removal and re-erection argue that there is a long historical tradition of reusing and relocating timber-framed buildings, especially houses and windmills, complete or in part. Furthermore, relatively mundane buildings can be enriched in terms of their meaning and appreciation when grouped together within an open-air museum.

Most open-air industrial museums lacked clear collecting policies that could have prevented them encouraging the loss of buildings, and from taking on large structures that they lacked the resources to rebuild and display in an appropriate manner. In the context of the evolving appreciation of vernacular architecture and industrial archaeology in the seventies, open-air museums could be seen as an excuse for not preserving buildings in their original place. Local and national politicians could readily misinterpret the role of open-air museums and their collections. The MP for Anglesey stated in the House of Commons in 1961 that he regretted the fact that 'Almost every county, except unfortunately Anglesey, is represented by a building in the collection [at St Fagans] and I wish that one of the windmills in Anglesey could be removed to the museum'.[19]

With the hindsight permitted by more intensive listing of vernacular buildings, fears that open-air museums would denude the built landscape of Britain have proved exaggerated. During the peak period of growth in the first half of the seventies, when demolition consents for listed buildings were running at a rate of some 300 a year, eleven listed buildings were moved into open-air museums.[20] Proximity of a museum to a threatened unlisted building might tempt a local authority officer to adopt an *ad hoc* policy of quietly encouraging removal rather than submitting marginal cases for listing to the Department of the Environment. By the late 1970s most open-air museums sought to present a cautious and responsible approach. They insisted, at least in public, that removal should be the final option, to be invoked only if *in situ* preservation proved impossible. Other key criteria were whether the building could house a process or other form of interpetation, and whether it would attract more visitors to the museum. The acid test was increasingly whether there was adequate funding to ensure the re-erection of the building rather than risking it remaining as a pile of bricks and timbers vulnerable to the elements and to pilferage.[21]

Museums collecting timber-framed buildings sought, at least in their early years, to return structures to their original, often late medieval or Tudor, form. Later additions were removed, in disregard of the principle of buildings being an evolving, adaptable inheritance. Bayleaf Farmstead was shorn of its later doors, window and chimneys, and its brick infill replaced with wattle when it was re-erected at the Weald and Downland Museum. There is also a loss of context when buildings are set in a park-like setting. The Stryt Lydan barn re-erected at the Welsh Folk Museum in 1951 was also 'taken back' in time and built as a free-standing structure unrelated to any other buildings or any enclosures.

Criticisms that re-erected buildings were crude shadows of original structures have been tackled through improved standards of research, documentation and workmanship. Avoncroft and the Weald and Downland Museum could draw upon the approaches to recording timber-framed structures developed by the architect, Freddie Charles, and the architectural historian, Ronald Brunskill. Industrial museums were more likely to be concerned with stone or brick structures where there was no established benchmark of best practice. Initially, it seemed adequate to recreate walls and roofs using the original doors and windows and as many of the bricks and slates as could be reclaimed. A make-do attitude resulted from the use of staff with little experience of architecture, aided by employment teams from the Manpower Services Commission with questionable skills and levels of supervision. It was, and remains, too expensive to buy in specialist contractors to dismantle and re-erect buildings. When stone buildings were to be re-erected, as in the case of the Chophill winding-engine house at Beamish, quoins and other dressed stones were carefully marked and taken down, but the rubblestone that made up the bulk of the structure was simply tumbled, leading to damage and extensive loss. Subtle variations in colours and textures on different elevations and at different heights were lost. The use of pallets has reduced damage and allowed for more meticulous stone-by-stone or brick-by-brick approaches. Stuart Holm at the Black Country Museum pioneered the significant advance of numbering every brick, while Avoncroft led the way in relocating small buildings by crane and low-loader, so avoiding the need for any dismantling and re-erection.

BLACK COUNTRY MUSEUM

The Bottle and Glass Inn, relocated from Brierley Hill, and the hardware shop from Pipers Row, Wolverhampton, at the Black Country Museum, Dudley, West Midlands. The latter building shows the merits of 'brick by brick' reconstruction with the survival of its painted advertisement.

The Weald and Downland Museum has a research director, while at Ironbridge, an Archaeology Unit and the Ironbridge Institute (part of the University of Birmingham) have aided in formulating policies at Blists Hill. When a timber-framed building was moved from Little Dawley to Blists Hill, excavation on the vacated site uncovered the site of a bloomery, while an eighteenth-century iron-working site emerged under two farm buildings at Newdale after they had been dismantled in advance of opencast coal mining. Excavations have also been undertaken following the removal of buildings for the Museum of East Anglian Rural Life and for the Weald and Downland Museum, though the archaeological work is unlikely to have been undertaken by museum staff themselves. There is often a problem that curators and heads of interpretation are pursuing agendas divorced from the time-consuming and apparently pedantic approach of archaeologists. Museum staff need to have basic information on the form, function and possible technology related to a building, but cannot hope to present to the general public minutiae concerning phasing and buried finds.

Most museums have now developed policies on landscaping round their

MICHAEL STRATTON

Reconstructed buildings, including the sixteenth-century Manor House from Harome, at Ryedale Folk Museum, Hutton-le-Hole, North Yorkshire.

reconstructed buildings. By drawing on research by archaeologists they can respond to growing interest in modest gardens and vegetable plots, and in agrarian and industrial landscapes in general. In 1987 the Weald and Downland Museum started to create a garden, orchard and small woodland around Bayleaf House to provide an appropriate early sixteenth-century setting. Blists Hill has been zoned into an urban township, a heavy industrial zone and a wooded area, with a park being laid out in the first and the ecology of the woodland studied and protected. Nevertheless, many open sites still look rather unconvincing, being overtidy and having intrusive signage and bland, mown areas for special events.[22]

Progress has also been made with the interiors of reconstructed buildings. Timber-framed buildings were usually stripped out to their 'original' state. There was no possibility of providing original furnishings, so a bare minimum of replicas might be provided. Alternative approaches, such as their use as exhibition spaces, as at the Ryedale Folk Museum, are now recognised as a wasted opportunity, objects in glass cases and heavy timber frames doing little to complement each other. The most successful interiors are those where authentic furnishings can be used and a convincing atmosphere created through the presence of costumed volunteers engaged in appropriate activities. The cramped living room of the squatter's cottage or the engine house, with its smell of warm oil and soot, at Blists Hill have become strongly imprinted on many people's minds, inspiring them to further study of Victorian technology and domestic life.

There has been a subtle but significant shift in the aims and collecting policies of industrial open-air museums. The changes are in part a response to criticisms already discussed, but they are best understood in the broader context of the new world of visitor-led museology that evolved in the eighties. Independent museums of the 1970s, dependent on paying visitors for their survival, learnt to present their displays more brightly and to introduce a sense of vitality in tune with public taste. Many of the hallmarks of Ironbridge or Beamish – introductory audio-visual shows, furnished interiors and costumed interpreters – were to be taken up by the Madame Tussaud's Group or by Heritage Projects in the eighties. Over the past decade there has been a generally beneficial, but occasionally contentious, interplay between museums and heritage centres, running through to current development plans and applications for lottery money.

Theme parks and heritage centres

Polemical studies of heritage have branded open-air and industrial museums as a shallow nostalgic response to Britain's economic decline, with visitors tripping from one simplistic historical vignette to another. Robert Hewison implied that the idea of museums, exhibitions and costumed actors interpreting the past within contemporary cultural values was a new and unwelcome concept.[23] However, Western society has been playing games with history for centuries. Museums have, from their antiquarian onset, been in the nostalgia business, collecting the best relics of past ages and presenting them as being of worth for entrepreneurs, artisans and genteel women committed to self-improvement. Victorian pageants were a direct precursor of the war enactments presented at English Heritage castles as 'living history'. Horace Walpole and Sir Walter Scott had no doubts about the emotional draw exerted by historical sites, especially if they were Gothic and ruinous. Every display, building or enactment is subjective, and it is better to be honest about the constraints involved rather than trying to convey a self-righteous and bogus objectivity. The archetypal museum of art objects and stuffed animals is riddled with bias, simply through the choice represented by the objects on show, their categorisation into technology, decorative art or ethnography, and the highly selective information presented in captions. David Lowenthal has stated that 'The past is mostly erased or fabricated, consciously or otherwise, to supply a better heritage than people feel their forebears, or their enemies have left them'.[24]

The 1980s were the decade of heritage. The press gave detailed coverage to the latest heritage centre, the debate over charging for admissions and any in-fighting by the staff of national museums. Meanwhile 'heritage' became widely used as an adjective to help sell jewellery, picnic hampers and housing estates. The process that packaged Viking York into Jorvik, chocolate into 'Cadbury World' at Bournville, and the world of Queen Victoria into 'Royalty and Empire' at Windsor was condemned for trivialising history. Some of the criticism was justified. At the Wigan Pier heritage centre visitors can comfortably combine seeing a miner's widow mourning in front of a coffin with a trip on a sanitised section of canal and a pint in a neo-Victorian pub, without being confronted with the blunt and jumbled reality of a northern industrial town.

The problem with such heritage centres, perhaps for both their managers and their critics, was that the first, Jorvik, has proved a one-off and unrepeatable commercial success. Jorvik opened in the basement of a shopping centre in York in April 1984 and attracted almost 900,000 visitors in its first year. Having travelled in electronic cars through a recreated street of Viking York, visitors are able to see artefacts from the excavation on the site by the York Archaeological Trust. They are fascinated by being able to associate items of jewellery or clothing with the setting in which they were used and, many centuries later, excavated. Subsequent projects faltered either in terms of their high-tech wizardry or their content. The electronic cars for the 'Oxford Story' initially failed to cope with the steep gradients, while the 'Tales of Robin Hood' in Nottingham appeals more to a sense of hide-and-seek than history – visitors play at escaping the sheriff's arrows and ferocious wolves. The British public have voted with their cash for what it perceives as animated history rather than purely entertaining heritage.

Museum experiences

Heritage centres struck a raw nerve among museum curators. Rather than standing aloof, they either condemned them outright or ran headlong down the same road, introducing rides, actors and audio-visuals with only passing debate over the relevance of such expensive investments to their remit and their collections. Jorvik and other centres were perceived as a threat to their future; the President of the Museums Association condemned them for generating 'modern mythologies, deodorised and sanitised'.[25] Feelings of political and financial vulnerability seemed to exacerbate fears that the status of museums as storehouses and interpreters of history was being undermined. Designers who worked within Heritage Projects on developing Jorvik, 'Canterbury Tales' and the 'Oxford Story' have no aspirations to undermine the work of museums, seeing stage sets and dummies in a tradition not of museology but of entertainment, initiated by Madame Tussaud who toured Britain from 1802 with her collections of wax figures.[26]

The heritage agenda has now shifted yet again, from passive, high-tech entertainment to participation. The 1990s has been designated the decade of the cultured hobbyist, with people using their leisure time to develop their physical fitness, knowledge or a craft. Museum directors and managers have responded by converting their staid and sometimes dusty institutions into attractions buzzing with activity. The new-look museum combines exciting interactive displays with refurbished visitor facilities such as shops and restaurants. Investment may be linked with the introduction of charging and policies to ensure better 'customer care'.

The somewhat unlikely subject area where the high-technology experience first entered the museum world was warfare – perhaps because traditional displays were so inadequate or, one might argue more cynically, due to the ghoulish appeal of mock bombing raids and battles. The Imperial War Museum had its roots in a collection first displayed in the Crystal Palace in 1920, and transferred to a redundant lunatic asylum in south London in the 1930s. A rethink of the way that war should be interpreted was partly inspired by advances in military history, emphasising the experience of soldiers and civilians more than strategy and symbols of victory; the new approach is less directly orientated around the collections of military hardware, emphasising the universal influence of war during the twentieth century. The public, now paying admission charges, has been attracted in dramatically increased numbers by two heritage-centre style attractions. The 'Blitz Experience' has been an undoubted smash hit. From its opening in 1989 visitors have been queuing to sit in a cramped bomb shelter, to hear the whine and crash of bombs, and to grope their way out into a half derelict street scene. The experience, which runs forty-six times a day, is akin to a period episode of *EastEnders*; some critics and members of the public have shown just concern over the trivialisation of such a traumatic aspect of Britain's history. The follow-up attraction, the more simply presented 'Trench Experience', aimed to convey the squalor, fear and boredom of warfare during the First World War.[27] The central issue raised by these experiences is whether something as awful and emotive as twentieth-century warfare should be packaged and promoted as an attraction, to be squashed between a visit to Tower Bridge and a quiche and salad in the refurbished restaurant. One cannot deny that the sound sources, smoke generators and black boxes achieve a more vivid image of warfare than displays of glistening guns and Spitfires, but did the old-style museum generate a more contemplative and thought-provoking response among visitors than a media extravaganza that only succeeds if it engulfs all the senses?

The new-found popularity of the Imperial War Museum has guided the philosophy behind the huge new museum for the Royal Armouries at Leeds, due to open in 1996. Displays of armour are combined with medieval jousts in the incongruous dockside setting. The introductory leaflet invites us to 'step into the combat ring and take a lesson in foot combat, take aim and fire a shot in the shooting range and discover how crossbows and rifles really work . . . see weapons in action and handle them yourself . . . eat, drink and be merry'.[28]

Combining collections and innovation

The one distinguishing feature of any museum is that it holds objects for research and display to the public. It is not surprising, therefore, that some directors and curators have been urging a retreat from hands-on experiences or expensive audio-visual programmes to a renewed emphasis on ensuring that their collections are displayed to the best purpose.[29]

National Museums on Merseyside has played a pioneering role in bringing objects back out of storage for display in new-style glass cases and specimen drawers. In July 1986, the 'Art of the Potter' gallery was opened, outstanding items from the ceramics collection being displayed in appropriate tableaux settings, with two computer terminals providing further information on the pieces, their manufacturers and designers.

Following a series of temporary experiments, Merseyside Museums decided to build a Natural History Centre to encourage the general public to handle a large number of biological and geological specimens. The centre opened in 1987. It comprises an activity room with a children's area, and a collections room with thirty cabinets housing around 20,000 specimens. Visitors can examine rocks, fossils and spiders at close quarters through microscope cameras, and obtain further information from video discs. A team of demonstrators is on hand to answer visitors' questions and to safeguard the specimens. A visitor survey has shown the public response to be highly enthusiastic. Some visitors inevitably skip from fossil to fossil or from one computer terminal to the next, but the centre often answers specific enquiries, or serves to transform a vague interest into a developing enthusiasm. Visitors typically stay for at least half an hour, making appropriate reference through to the books in the small library.[30]

The enthusiasm of visitors to undertake modest programmes of personal discovery has encouraged museum staff to introduce more sophisticated and user-friendly computers, providing information that reinforces the experience of looking at and handling pictures or objects. The Sainsbury Wing at the National Gallery was opened in 1991 with a Micro Gallery, containing twelve touch-screen computers giving visitors access to a broad range of information on some 2,200 paintings in the collection.

High technology and the interpretation of industrialisation

Given the difficulty of interpreting historic buildings and living and working conditions, it is worth examining the extent to which high technology and the popular drama of the 'experience' has been applied to the world of open-air and industrial museums. None of the open-air museums relating to vernacular architecture and folk life has gone down the road of time-car rides, light-and-sound experiences or computer terminals. Such innovations have proved more alluring to museums tackling industry and industrialisation, partly because the subject has a natural affinity to technology and a sense of high drama.

Again, there are long and strong precedents. For over half a century science and industrial museums have used demonstrations to introduce movement and sounds into their otherwise hushed halls. The Chicago Museum of Science and Industry, from its opening in 1933, pioneered such features as full-size replica mine shafts, operational milking parlours and participatory and walk-through exhibits. Like most British science museums, it took a triumphalist view of the past, emphasising achievement and progress, with few twinges of regret for lost monuments or a lost way of life. An illuminated banner-heading: 'Tools that Made America Great' sets the theme of one gallery. The ordinary past tends to become forced out by the urge to display the first, biggest and most ornamental machines and products.

Many industrial museums have been criticised for their right-wing bias. Bob West saw them as, first and foremost, celebrations of technology, inventiveness and entrepreneurship – ultimately of capitalism.[31] Prime movers are hallowed like icons. Workers are seen as industrious and generally uncomplaining. Dead or declining industries gain the strongest coverage, being safer topics than car manufacture or waste disposal. When a chemical museum was established in Widnes it was given the positive title 'Catalyst', and a contemporary identity. One would not expect sponsoring firms to encourage exposure of appalling working conditions and pollution within their industry, but curators seem to adopt excessive self-censorship partly, one suspects, in pursuit of outside financial support.

What about the workers? The record of museums in covering the workforce in industry, their organisation and the experience of work has been patchy and generally half-hearted. Graphic panels tend to be turgid and didactic while period photographs convey a false impression of sepia-toned placidity. Costumed demonstrators can explain processes, but rarely convey the drudgery, danger or squalor of much manual work. All too many museums lapse unconsciously into cliched images – a power loom to symbolise the textile industry or a crawling child for coalmining – or give more attention to mangles and other symbols of domestic, rather than working, life.

The 'Engines of Change' exhibit at the Smithsonian Museum, Washington DC, developed in the late 1980s, was an early attempt to integrate the experience of work with developments in industrial technology, within a tightly focused historical framework. Videos, working models and reconstructed workshops outline stages in the transfer of technology, the de-skilling and discipline involved in mass-producing textiles and armaments, and the wage levels received by different types of worker. Some of the sections incorporate workshops and tools, which are demonstrated through interactive videos; other programmes emphasise the social consequences of industrialisation. 'Engines of Change' is multifaceted in its approach and thought-provoking, though in the last analysis too orientated around the American system of mass production to entertain any real doubts about the merits of industrialisation.

One can argue that every machine should be displayed within its social as well as its technological context, with captioning stating how much it cost, how many workers operated it and how many it maimed.[32] Captions can easily expand into a 'book on the wall' approach. The difficulties of interpreting ordinary people's lives in a museum context are exemplified by the example of labour history museums. During the 1970s several socialist local authorities sought to redress the balance of displays in established museum services, which typically ignored working-class life and celebrated achievements in technology and high art. The Museum of Labour History in Liverpool is angled round people rather than processes. The employment gallery looks at the heavy labour of dock workers and the stultifying nature of car assembly work. The major problem is the lack of exhibits, with the main sources of information being texts with contemporary quotations and opinions, and reproduced photographs. The longer-established People's Palace in Glasgow has the advantage of treating working-class life more broadly, embracing domestic life and working-class entertainment. By combining trade-union material with costume displays and football souvenirs, a lively interpretation is developed that has a clear resonance for local people. The museum commissions new work and organises a rich variety of temporary exhibitions.

Time-car rides in the Jorvik mould have been introduced to help interpret two industrial sites. The theme at New Lanark is the working and domestic life of a mill girl. At Chatham Dockyard the 'Wooden Walls' aims to show 'what it was really like in the eighteenth-century dockyard', largely through a recreation of Chatham, but animated with talking heads and a mechanical mouse.[33] Such 'experiences' can distract visitors from being able to appreciate dramatic buildings and landscapes. They may even be questionable as draws for additional visitors. The Black Country Museum invested in a £1 million underground experience called 'Into the Thick'. Heritage Projects created a replica Midlands coalmine in a series of buried concrete tubes, lined with imitation rock and coal, and with figures and light and sound effects to simulate life underground, complete with explosions and rock falls. 'Into the Thick' failed to emerge as a 'cult attraction' and may even confuse the strong identity of the museum proper with its carefully re-erected buildings and genuine canal tunnel.

Area interpretation and living history

Many of those committed to the preservation of the industrial heritage, or indeed heritage in general, and who do not have a vested interest in museums or heritage centres, see the key challenge for the 1990s as how to interpret real rather than reconstructed landscapes. The traditional threefold pamphlet or waymarked trail only appeals to those adept at map reading and tend to be suited best to pointing out aspects of architecture rather than broader historical themes. Audio trails may work well on English Heritage sites but are downright dangerous on busy streets.

America has led the way in area interpretation. The combination of role play with costumed interpreters has been applied to great effect at Lowell. Visitors to this New England mill town, designated a National Park in the 1970s, see an introductory audio-visual programme. It introduces a series of themes, such as relations between mill owners and workers, and between different ethnic groups, which are developed during tours round the mills and the water power system. Groups encounter costumed interpreters who act out a particular role. The actors avoid the social niceties characteristic of guided tours round country houses and achieve a sensitive consideration of aspects of political and social history.

In Europe several *ecomusée* projects have concentrated on landscape rather than object interpretation, but ideas and examples of excellence remain very thin across the United Kingdom. Ironbridge has grappled with the problem of explaining the landscape between its discrete museum sites, finding that detailed models – at the Museum of the River and more recently the Museum of Iron – prove both attractive and informative. The Trevithick Society is developing a network of sites relating to tin and copper mining in Cornwall. For the most part, museums have generally failed to act as bases for exploration – the Museum of Science and Industry in Manchester almost turns it back on the remarkable Castlefields area in which it is set, while the series of attractions at Portsmouth –

the *Victory*, the *Warrior* and the *Mary Rose* – seem to compete rather than contribute towards an appreciation of the dockyard itself. IDEAS Yorkshire, one of the successor firms to Heritage Projects, has been brought in by Portsmouth Naval Base Property Trust to develop an interactive exhibition to convey aspects of the operation of the yard, focused round the creation of the world's first dry dock 500 years ago.[34]

British open-air museums were developed primarily as collections of buildings, a characteristic that has proved to be increasingly incompatible with public interest in social history, clearly expressed in visitor surveys as a curiosity concerning 'the way that people lived in the past'. This schism has been exacerbated by the increased gulf between modern lifestyles – strongly influenced by central heating, supermarkets and videos – and traditions of the fireside, storytelling, vegetable growing and pig-rearing. Basic knowledge that could be taken for granted in the 1960s, such as the nature of coal as a source of heat, now take a higher role in the interpretative agenda than details of house plans and brick bonds. The importance of school groups to the revenue accounts of museums has provided a further impetus towards social history and brighter forms of presentation.

Most open-air museums have adopted elements of 'living history' from the United States, though restrained by British reserve and the expense of having fully trained actors in each building. Avoncroft and Ironbridge found that their most popular exhibits were those where a craft or a machine – from a windmill to a printing press – could be demonstrated. It was a short step to put the demonstrators in costume and to brief them in relevant aspects of social history. While the exhibits are still interpreted in third-person mode (without the demonstrator entering directly into a role) the animateur based at Blists Hill has developed a series of scenarios to be played out in the streets using actors on a first-person basis.

Open-air museums hold a strong card with their potential for reviving and demonstrating craft and industrial processes. Exhibit demonstrators have a productive role, while the visitor immediately has a topic for discussion rather than having to listen to a repeated talk about a particular exhibit. Products, from bread to candles and plasterwork, can be sold, so helping fund the demonstrator's salary and providing appropriate souvenirs. The Ironbridge Gorge Museum, having established a tile factory, then embarked on the more radical venture of making wrought iron using the furnaces, hammer and tools saved from the last works to operate in Britain, Walmsleys of Bolton. It has proved difficult to operate the wrought iron works on a regular enough basis for it to become a full visitor attraction and develop a market for the iron itself.

Some senior staff and commentators remain set against 'living history' within a museum context, emphasising the pre-eminent importance of the objects and the futility of trying to recreate the past. In the words of Robert Ronsheim: 'the past is dead, and cannot be brought back to life'.[35] Few would deny that buildings and objects should have primacy, but displayed in aspic they can present misinformation as well as representing a wasted resource. Open-air museums have the potential for enlarging the public's as well as the historian's knowledge of the past. By having to research the operation of a candle shop or a wrought iron works, staff can, as Barrie Trinder has put it, 'stimulate our visitors to ask themselves questions and to keep asking them when they leave our museum . . . an Open-Air Museum is a challenge to look at a past society in detail and in its entirety, to show that industrial growth cannot be explained simply as a series of technological developments, nor as just the achievements of heroic innovators or entrepreneurs, but in terms of society as a whole'.[36]

Objects, buildings and experiences

In reviewing where open-air museums sit within current museum and conservation practice, a start can be made by reviewing development proposals and applications to the National Lottery. None of the major applications relates to removal and rebuilding projects. Ironbridge and Beamish are preoccupied in making best use of existing resources and providing appropriate visitor facilities. In one of the first successful applications, the Ironbridge Gorge Museum has gained £400,000 to restore the *in situ* but largely derelict John Rose building, part of the Coalport China Works, as a youth hostel, restaurant and training workshops. The building that was most recently re-erected at Blists Hill is a restaurant. While the eating area is a careful reconstruction of a wooden pavilion – the Forest Glen from the Wrekin – it is backed by an all-modern kitchen and serving area, designed to fulfil current hygiene regulations.

Meanwhile Beamish is concentrating on developing the eastern section of its site as a recreation of the 1820s to provide an appropriate operational setting for its replica of the *Locomotion* steam locomotive. It is overlooked by Pockerley Manor, an *in situ* farmhouse, restored and interpreted in the context of the Regency period. The new building currently being erected as part of the 1820s project is a shed and workshop for the *Locomotion*. The structure, designed with public access in mind, is consciously larger than any engine shed of the period and built of breeze block faced with stone. The other major development project at Beamish is the urban area. Here a policy of brick-by-brick rebuilding has given way to a subtle facadism. The motor and cycle works uses equipment from garages in Cumbria and Herefordshire within a building made of second-hand materials and details collected over many years by the museum. The confectionery shop opposite is similarly a new design using elements from the collection, and designed with spaces and floors appropriate to handle groups of hungry chocaholics.

Only the more traditionalist open-air museums, focusing on vernacular architecture, are still re-erecting buildings in complete form, and even they are working through a backlog of donated buildings rather than risking the ire of conservationists by seeking out new projects. While the Black Country Museum, Ironbridge and Beamish have seen both award-winning success and financial stringency in fair measure, Avoncroft, the Weald and Downland and Ryedale seem to sail on relatively unruffled, with smaller numbers of visitors and with their buildings slowly blending into their setting. Weald and Downland plan to

MICHAEL STRATTON

The town at Beamish, showing newly erected rather than reconstructed buildings, incorporating architectural details from the museum's collection. The Beamish Motor and Cycle Works, on the left, was built in 1994 to recreate a typical Edwardian garage.

concentrate on re-erecting buildings held in store, concentrating on small projects that can be undertaken by the museum's own labour force. Avoncroft have quietly extended the boundaries of their remit by re-erecting first of all a prefab house of the 1940s and more recently a clutch of telephone kiosks. Meanwhile, Weald and Downland, Ryedale and Ironbridge have all invested heavily in new entrance and shop facilities.

Critics fear that some of the open-air museums are going soft. There certainly needs to be a clear boundary between the desirability of improving facilities and the packaging of a museum to the extent of blurring the borderline between historical interpretation and customer care. More research needs to be undertaken on the way that visitors work through buildings and demonstrations, and the attention they give to different forms of interpretation. The evaluation studies undertaken by Paulette McManus of the Natural History Museum suggest that visitors are stimulated by exhibits in fundamentally different ways according to their age, intelligence and, above all, by their company during a visit.[37] It is likely that they behave and respond in even more divergent ways in the more free-ranging but potentially confusing world of a reconstructed street or coalmine.

Meanwhile open-air sites have mellowed in the contexts of British museology and conservation. They are no longer a threat to the survival of buildings in the outside world, thanks to changed aims, shortages of funds and the extension of listing to embrace many vernacular and industrial buildings. Probably for better rather than worse, they are rarely at the cutting edge of new ideas for interpretation, such as touch-screen computers or other highly sophisticated interactive devices. Nevertheless, they have become a significant part of most people's consciousness – visited as a toddler, schoolchild and student, and as parent and grandparent. Children have found them highly rewarding in developing project work in a way inconceivable before the 1970s, while volunteers of all ages have gained new skills and found fulfilment. Open-air museums have contributed strongly to a broader sense of awareness of social history, and of local traditions and architecture. Their directors are now exploring future directions in their strategic plans. They emphasise the tasks of looking after and displaying the real objects and relocated buildings already in their care, rather than tackling major new challenges such as the major technologies and landscapes of the twentieth century. Maybe they, like us, can look back to the zealous, opportunistic and occasionally irresponsible dynamism of the late 1960s and '70s with a sense of achievement and even mild envy.

10
Bibliographical essay

This chapter surveys and evaluates the existing literature on the preservation of buildings, monuments and other relics of the human past in this country, and on ancillary issues relating to 'heritage' and its interpretation. Its emphasis will mainly be on recent and accessible secondary writings, although a few classic earlier texts will be singled out, especially ones that are (or ought to be) readily available. As will be seen, the literature is somewhat disparate and patchy in coverage, and few, if any, books give a satisfactory general overview. This is in contrast with the state of affairs in an area where developments have often closely paralleled those relating to historic preservation, namely concerning attitudes to nature and the origins of a conservationist approach to the natural world. Here there are some excellent general accounts of historical developments and of the current situation, including Keith Thomas, *Man and the Natural World: Changing Attitudes in England 1500–1800* (London: Allen Lane, 1983); John Sheail, *Nature in Trust: The History of Nature Conservation in Britain* (Glasgow and London: Blackie, 1976); and David Evans, *A History of Nature Conservation in Britain* (London: Routledge, 1992). There is also a polemical literature concerning nature conservation, paralleling that about historic preservation which will be surveyed below, including such books as Marion Shoard's *The Theft of the Countryside* (London: Temple Smith, 1980) and Richard Mabey, *The Common Ground: A Place for Nature in Britain's Future?* (London: Hutchinson, 1980; new edn, London: Dent, 1993).

Perhaps the most informative general account of the history of preservation hitherto extant is the historical section of Wayland Kennet, *Preservation* (London: Temple Smith, 1972), which combines various case studies with an informative canter through the history of earlier legislative and other changes and a detailed account of developments of the late 1960s and early 1970s. John Harvey, *Conservation of Buildings* (London: John Baker, 1972) also combines informative historical chapters with contemporary prescriptions, while a somewhat older work offering a longer timescale but tailing off as it reaches the twentieth century is Martin S. Briggs, *Goths and Vandals: a Study of the Destruction, Neglect and Preservation of Historical Buildings in England* (London: Constable, 1952); as its title suggests, this is as much about pre-conservationist attitudes as about the origins of modern ones.

In some ways, the most satisfactory syntheses hitherto have been multi-authored volumes. One classic, stimulated by an exhibition organised by the Victorian Society in 1970–1, is Jane Fawcett (ed.), *The Future of the Past: Attitudes to Conservation 1147–1974* (London: Thames and Hudson, 1976), the contributions to which include John Betjeman's 'A Preservationist's Progress' and Sir Nikolaus Pevsner's celebrated essay on 'Scrape and Anti-Scrape'.

ARCHITECTURAL PRESS

Sir John Betjeman, *guru* of the 1970s conservationist movement, being escorted past 9 Elder Street, Spitalfields, by Dan Cruickshank during the occupation of 1977. From Mark Girouard *et al.*, *The Saving of Spitalfields*, 1989.

Another useful and wide-ranging synthesis is David Lowenthal and Marcus Binney (eds), *Our Past Before Us: Why Do We Save It?* (London: Temple Smith, 1981), which ranges from historical studies to essays evaluating current trends in the preservation and exploitation of historic sites. An older and somewhat more erudite work that illustrates changing attitudes to buildings in various periods and from various points of view is Sir John Summerson (ed.), *Concerning Architecture: Essays on Architectural Writers and Writings Presented to Nikolaus Pevsner* (London: Allen Lane, 1968). Yet another essay-volume provides a wider view, with contributions on trends in various countries: Roger Kain (ed.), *Planning for Conservation* (London: Mansell, 1981).

A broader perspective is also offered by certain other general works on related topics, some of them ranging so widely that they are rather diffuse. Robert M. Newcomb, *Planning the Past: Historical Landscape Resources and Recreation* (Folkestone: Dawson, 1979) evidently owes its emphasis on landscape to the series of 'Studies in Historical Geography' in which it appeared, but in fact it has much on preservation more generally, and is specifically concerned with the tourist potential of historic sites. E. R. Chamberlin, *Preserving the Past* (London: Dent, 1979) is a chatty survey aimed at the general reader, while much more portentous is David Lowenthal, *The Past is a Foreign Country* (Cambridge University Press, 1985), a survey of man's relationship with his tangible past which ranges so widely as to be in danger of superficiality, although it contains much information and food for thought.

Turning to studies surveying the earlier developments in which modern attitudes to 'heritage' have their roots, tourism is well covered by two books: Esther Moir, *The Discovery of Britain: the English Tourists 1540–1840* (London: Routledge, 1964) and Ian Ousby, *The Englishman's England: Taste, Travel and the Rise of Tourism* (Cambridge University Press, 1990). The former has a series of chapters on topographical writers from the Tudor period to the Romantic era, while the latter is more thematic, surveying visits to literary shrines, country houses, ruins and wild nature. The second of these themes is dealt with in more detail in Adrian Tinniswood, *A History of Country House Visiting: Five Centuries of Tourism and Taste* (Oxford: Blackwell, and London: the National Trust, 1989) (although this tends to overemphasise the continuities rather than the discontinuities of the tradition); while a useful recent account of the eighteenth-century fashion for the picturesque is Malcolm Andrews, *The Search for the Picturesque: Landscape Aesthetics and Tourism in Britain 1760–1800* (Aldershot: Scolar, 1989).

The best general account of antiquarianism from our point of view is Stuart Piggott, *Ruins in a Landscape: Essays in Antiquarianism* (Edinburgh University Press, 1976), which includes studies of the origins of archaeological antiquarianism in the seventeenth century and of the county archaeological societies which were to flourish in the Victorian period. It also deals with the role of Sir Walter Scott, on whom see also various of the studies collected in Alan Bell (ed.), *Scott Bicentenary Essays* (Edinburgh: Scottish Academic Press, 1973) and Clive Wainwright, *The Romantic Interior: the British Collector at Home 1750–1850* (New Haven and London: Yale University Press, 1989). Another pioneer, John Carter, has at last received the study he

The Gothic Revival's precise – if doctrinaire – interest in medieval architecture is illustrated by this plate from J. H. Sperling, *Church Walks in Middlesex; Being an Ecclesiologist's Guide to the Ancient and Modern Churches in that County* (London, 1843).

deserves in J. M. Crook, *John Carter and the Mind of the Gothic Revival* (London: Society of Antiquaries, Occasional Papers, 17, 1995). The popularisation of antiquarianism in the Victorian period, on the other hand, is a topic which has not yet received the attention that it merits, though a good deal of relevant information will be found in Sir Roy Strong, *And When Did You Last See Your Father? The Victorian Painter and British History* (London: Thames and Hudson, 1978).

More specifically on Victorian attitudes to medieval buildings, an account of the influential Cambridge Camden Society and its impact on church restoration will be found in J. F. White, *The Cambridge Movement: the Ecclesiologists and the Gothic Revival* (Cambridge University Press, 1962), while a new perspective on church building is offered by Chris Miele, '"Their Interest and Habit": Professionalism and the Restoration of Medieval Churches 1837–77', in Chris Brooks and Andrew Saint (eds), *The Victorian Church: Architecture and Society* (Manchester University Press, 1995), pp. 151–72. On attitudes to restoration, a more detailed study is S. T. Madsen, *Restoration and anti-Restoration: a Study of English Restoration Philosophy* (Oslo: Universitetsforlag, 1976), while a wider-ranging study of this theme is to be found in Wim Denslagen, *Architectural Restoration in Western Europe: Controversy and Continuity* (English translation, Amsterdam: Architectura and Natura Press, 1994: originally published in Dutch in 1987).

For a more general account of Victorian attitudes see Charles Dellheim, *The Face of the Past: the Preservation of the Medieval Inheritance in Victorian England* (Cambridge University Press, 1982), although this is unduly preoccupied by the rather artificial 'paradox' that the Victorians were perfectly capable of combining a fascination with their medieval past with a confidence in the future. Among the case-studies that this contains, some deal with the Society for the Protection of Ancient Buildings, background to Chris Miele's account of which will be found in most biographies of Morris, perhaps notably E. P. Thompson, *William Morris: Romantic to Revolutionary* (revised edition, London: Merlin Press, 1977) or more recently Fiona MacCarthy's *William Morris: A Life* (London: Faber, 1994). A further account of the SPAB which complements Chapter 2 from a different perspective is Chris Miele, '"A Small Knot of Cultivated People": William Morris and the Ideologies of Protection', *Art Journal*, 54 (1995), 73–9.

Various accounts from different viewpoints exist of Sir John Lubbock and the 1882 Ancient Monuments Act. The best study of the Act and the developments that stemmed from it is Christopher Chippindale, 'The Making of the First Ancient Monuments Act, 1882, and its Administration under General Pitt-Rivers', *Journal of the British Archaeological Association*, 136 (1983), 1–55. An alternative view is provided by Tim Murray, 'The History, Philosophy and Sociology of Archaeology: the Case of the Ancient Monuments Protection Act (1882)', in Valerie Pinsky and Alison Wylie (eds), *Critical Traditions in Contemporary Archaeology* (Cambridge University Press, 1989), pp. 55–67, which is insightful, though it is somewhat sidetracked by its preoccupation with placing the measure in the context of the sociology of knowledge. On the first inspector appointed under the Act, see M. W. Thompson, *General Pitt-Rivers: Evolution and Archaeology in the Nineteenth Century* (Bradford-on-Avon: Moonraker Press, 1977), and Mark Bowden, *Pitt Rivers: the Life and Archaeological Work of Lieutenant-General Augustus Henry Lane Fox Pitt Rivers* (Cambridge University Press, 1991). See also Andrew Saunders, 'A Century of Ancient Monuments Legislation 1882–1982', *Antiquaries Journal*, 63 (1983), 11–33.

A further development of the late nineteenth century, the foundation of the National Trust, has been the subject of a plethora of writings, and, partly for this reason and partly because its remit is only partly concerned with buildings and monuments, it has been relatively neglected in this book. Most recent are two histories brought out to celebrate the Trust's centenary: Jennifer Jenkins and Patrick James, *From Acorn to Oak Tree: the Growth of the National Trust 1895–1994* (London: The National Trust, 1994), and Merlin Waterson and Samantha Wyndham, *The National Trust: the First Hundred Years* (London: The National Trust/BBC Books, 1994). Neither of these goes into as much detail as John Gaze, *Figures in a Landscape: a History of the National Trust* (London: Barrie and Jenkins, 1988), while an older account of the rise and progress of the Trust is to be found in Robin Fedden, *The Continuing Purpose: a History of the National Trust, its Aims and Work* (London: Longmans, 1968; second edition retitled *The National Trust, Past and Present*, London: Jonathan Cape, 1974). A flawed but interesting attempt at a revisionist account of the Trust's early history is Graham Murphy, *Founders of the National Trust* (London: Christopher Helm, 1987); this stresses its founders' preoccupation with the countryside, in implicit criticism of their successors' concern with country houses, a tension which is further elaborated in Paula Weideger's recent critique of the Trust, *Gilding the*

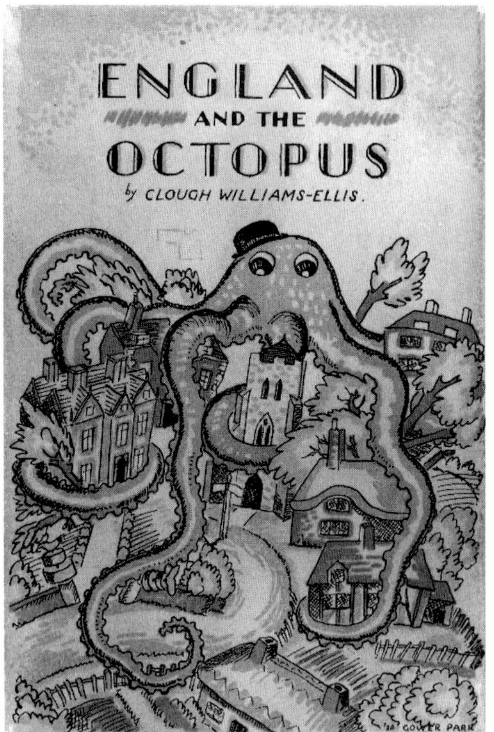

The illustrated dustwrapper of Clough Williams-Ellis' *England and the Octopus* (London: Godfrey Bles, 1928).

Acorn: Behind the Facade of the National Trust (London: Simon and Schuster, 1994). It is also worth singling out an excellent biography of one of the founders: Gillian Darley, *Octavia Hill: a Life* (London: Constable, 1990).

A key early twentieth-century preservationist work is Gerard Baldwin Brown, *The Care of Ancient Monuments* (Cambridge University Press, 1905), but developments of the first two decades of the century have as yet received little retrospective attention, other than in general books like Kennet's *Preservation*. Virtually the only exception to this is the useful account of the London Survey in Hermione Hobhouse, *London Survey'd: the Work of the Survey of London 1894–1994* (London: Royal Commission on Historical Monuments, 1994). On trends in the 1930s, and particularly the interest in rural planning noted by Andrew Saint in Chapter 7, see John Sheail, *Rural Conservation in Inter-War Britain* (Oxford: Clarendon Press, 1981). A sense of the underlying anxiety about such matters at the time is well given by the books of Clough Williams-Ellis, both his prescient *England and the Octopus* (London: Geoffrey Bles, 1928), and the collection of essays by various celebrities that he edited, *Britain and the Beast* (London: Dent, 1937), a book which sold widely and which often turns up second-hand.

One inter-war development worth noting here is the foundation of the National Trust for Scotland, which was somewhat different from its English counterpart in having a clear interest in townscape from the outset, as seen in its early activity at Culross, though this was combined with the custodianship of areas of countryside. A succinct account of the history of the Trust will be found in R. J. Prentice, *Conserve and Provide: a Brief History of the National Trust for Scotland* (National Trust for Scotland [*c.* 1971]), which provides information not to be found in the more popular and descriptive accounts by Robert Hurd, *Scotland under Trust: the Story of the National Trust of Scotland and its Properties* (London: A. & C. Black, 1939), and Iain Crawford, *Held in Trust: the National Trust for Scotland* (Edinburgh: Mainstream Publishing, 1986).

Title page and frontispiece of *The Bombed Buildings of Britain*, edited by J. M. Richards with notes by John Summerson (second edition, London: Architectural Press, 1947). The frontispiece shows St Paul's through the ruins of the City; the drawing of a burnt-out house in Bath on the title-page is by John Piper.

The other chief preservationist initiative of the 1930s was the founding of the Georgian Group. On this, Gavin Stamp's account in Chapter 5 may best be supplemented by reading Robert Byron's mordant *How We Celebrate the Coronation* (London: Architectural Press, 1937; originally published in the *Architectural Review*) – which perhaps deserves to be reprinted as a preservationist classic. A perspective on the Group in terms of attitudes to Georgian London in the twentieth century as a whole will be found in the 'Epilogue' added to the 1988 edition of Sir John Summerson's *Georgian London* (London: Barrie & Jenkins, 1988), while further information is available from the special issue of the *Architects' Journal* devoted to the Group on 31 March 1982.

The impact of the Second World War and the destruction that it entailed is vividly recorded in such illustrated books published at the time as James Pope-Hennessy and Cecil Beaton, *History Under Fire: 52 Photographs of Air Raid Damage to London Buildings 1940–1* (London: Batsford, 1941); J. M. Richards and John Summerson, *The Bombed Buildings of Britain: a Record of Architectural Casualties 1940–1* (London: Architectural Press, 1942; extended 3rd edn, 1947; originally based on an *Architectural Review* special number for July 1941); and William Kent, *The Lost Treasures of London* (London: Phoenix House, 1947). The thinking of the wartime and post-war period is also illustrated by books attempting to instil a new appreciativeness towards historic architecture as a whole, such as W. H. Godfrey, *Our Building Inheritance: Are We to Use or Lose It?* (London: Faber, 1944), in this case by one of those responsible for the listing system, as indicated by Andrew Saint in Chapter 7. For the work of the National Buildings (later Monuments) Record, the best introduction is *Fifty Years of the National Buildings Record 1941–91* (Beckenham: Trigon Press, in conjunction with the Royal Commission on Historical Monuments, 1991), with its Scottish equivalent in *N.M.R.S. 1941–91: National Monuments Record of Scotland Jubilee: a Guide to the Collections* (Edinburgh: Her Majesty's Stationery Office, 1991). Andrew Saint's account of the origin of listing may be supplemented by the special issue of the *Transactions of the Ancient Monuments Society* in 1993 devoted to the origins of the system and to the relisting then recently completed, while for a work that sketches the intellectual developments which encouraged the concentration on individual buildings as against broader groups which listing institutionalised, see David Watkin, *The Rise of Architectural History* (London: Architectural Press, 1980).

As for the National Trust's efforts to acquire country houses during and after the war, the best account of these is given by its chief agent, James Lees-Milne, both in his three volumes of diaries, *Ancestral Voices, Prophesying Peace* and *Caves of Ice* (London: Chatto & Windus, 1975, 1977, 1983), and in his subsequent memoirs, 'The Early Years of the Country House Scheme', in Gervase Jackson-Stops (ed.), *The National Trust Year Book 1976–77* (London: Europa, [1977]), pp. 81–7, and his P*eople and Places: Country House Donors and the National Trust* (London: John Murray, 1992). As far as the changing post-war ethos of the country house is concerned, the key document – as Peter Mandler indicates in Chapter 6 – is the *Report of the Committee on Houses of Outstanding Historic or Architectural Interest* chaired by Sir Ernest Gowers (London: His Majesty's Stationery Office, 1950), which led to various changes, including the setting up of Historic Building Councils for England, Wales and Scotland in 1953.

Whatever was going on in the countryside in the post-war era, in towns there is no escaping the unavoidable tension between preservation and the ethos of comprehensive redevelopment which dominated these years. A good account of the latter is given by Lionel Esher in *A Broken Wave: the Rebuilding of England 1940–80* (London: Allen Lane, 1981); it was little mitigated by the sedulity for better standards in design fostered by the Civic Trust from its foundation in 1957, as outlined in Esher's *The Continuing Heritage: the Story of the Civic Trust Awards* (London: Franey, 1982). Of early reactions to such developments there is as yet no comprehensive account, but a taste may be obtained from the columns of the *Architectural Review*, for instance the 'Outrage' issue edited by Ian Nairn in June 1955, or J. M. Richards's article, 'The Euston Murder', which excoriated official apathy over the destruction of the Euston Arch, in ibid., 131 (1962), 234–8 (reprinted in Peter and Alison Smithson, *The Euston Arch and the Growth of the London Midland and Scottish Railway* (London: Thames and Hudson, 1968)). It is also salutary to read the early reports of the Victorian Society, on which Gavin Stamp draws in Chapter 5; this particular group deserves a full-scale history. As far as official thinking on such matters is

DAN CRUICKSHANK

Illustration from *The Rape of Britain* by Colin Amery and Dan Cruickshank (1975), showing the impact of road-building on Salisbury.

concerned, the turn-around which occurred *c.* 1970 is well described in Kennet, *Preservation*, since the author himself instigated a number of the measures brought into effect at that time. Perhaps the best index of the change that now began to come over government attitudes is to be found in the lavish publication by the Ministry of Housing and Local Government, *Historic Towns: Preservation and Change* (London: Her Majesty's Stationery Office, 1967), which even included a full-page photograph of the Euston Arch as an example of the unnecessary damage that the urban fabric had suffered in the preceding years.

Despite this, however, destruction continued in the early 1970s, particularly by local authorities, and this inspired a reaction signalled by a plethora of books published at that time. Perhaps most poignant, in view of the significance of the city involved, was Adam Fergusson, *The Sack of Bath: a Record and an Indictment* (Salisbury: Compton Russell, 1973; reissued as *The Sack of Bath – and After* with an epilogue by Tim Mowl, Salisbury: Michael Russell, 1989). Yet Bath was only the tip of an iceberg of destruction, as was illustrated most clearly in Colin Amery and Dan Cruickshank, *The Rape of Britain* (London: Paul Elek, 1975); although crudely produced from typewriting in the manner of the 1970s, this work was evocative in its juxtaposition of before and after photographs and its angry text. A similar book was Tony Aldous' *Goodbye Britain?* (London: Sidgwick and Jackson, 1975), like both of the former furnished with a foreword by Sir John Betjeman, very much the *guru* of the assertion of preservationist sentiment at this time. As far as London was concerned, similar feelings were expressed by books ranging from Hermione Hobhouse, *Lost London: a Century of Demolition and Decay* (London: Macmillan, 1971) – a beautiful production whose impact was slightly dulled by its inclusion of buildings destroyed by bombing as well as those wantonly torn down for development – to Christopher Booker and Candida Lycett Green, *Goodbye London: an Illustrated Guide to Threatened Buildings* (Glasgow: Fontana, 1973), a more sensationalist action guide.

A more general work capturing the mood of crisis was Patrick Cormack, *Heritage in Danger* (London: New English Library, 1976; reissued in revised form, London: Quartet, 1978), while there are also various books dealing with specific struggles which during the 1970s cumulatively led to a change in policy. To a disproportionate extent, these deal with events in London: the saving of Covent Garden is dealt with from different points of view in Robert Thorne, *Covent Garden Market, its History and Restoration* (London: Architectural Press, 1980) and Brian Anson, *I'll Fight You For It: Behind the Struggle for Covent Garden* (London: Jonathan Cape, 1981); while on Spitalfields see Mark Girouard, Dan Cruickshank *et al., The Saving of Spitalfields* (London: Spitalfields Historic Buildings Trust, 1989). Outside London, studies dealing with specific cities include David Palliser, 'Preserving our Heritage: the Historic City of York', in Richard Kimber and J. J. Richardson (eds), *Campaigning for the Environment* (London: Routledge, 1974), pp. 6–26; J. S. Curl, *The Erosion of Oxford* (Oxford: Oxford Illustrated Press, 1977); and Gordon Priest and Pamela Cobb (eds), *The Fight for Bristol: Planning and the Growth of Public Protest* (Bristol: Bristol Civic Society and the Redcliffe Press, 1980).

Undoubtedly, as Sophie Andreae indicates in Chapter 8, books like these signalled a turning of the tide in favour of preservation as far as public opinion was concerned. Indeed, the year 1975, which was declared European Architectural Heritage Year, is often seen as pivotal, and it is symptomatic that this was taken as the starting date for a survey of recent trends organised as an exhibition at the Royal Academy in 1989: this resulted in a book-length publication, David Pearce, *Conservation Today* (London: Routledge, 1989), which celebrates the record of conservation and restoration in the intervening years in an almost complacent tone.

If the 1970s were a time of crisis for the urban fabric, the same was also true of other parts of the built environment. One, as Peter Mandler shows, was the country house. Despite the impact of the Gowers Report, and despite the entrepreneurial skills displayed by some stately-home owners – entertainingly retailed in book form by Lord Montagu of Beaulieu in *The Gilt and the Gingerbread: or How to Live in a Stately Home and Make Money* (London: Michael Joseph, 1967) – destruction had continued remorselessly. The alarm bells were set ringing by a significant report by John Cornforth, *Country Houses in Britain: Can They Survive?* (London: *Country Life* for the British Tourist Authority, 1974) – which searchingly analysed the problem and suggested various strategies for dealing with it – and, more spectacularly, by a dramatic exhibition at the Victoria and Albert Museum, in association with which a book was published: Roy Strong, Marcus Binney and John Harris (eds), *The Destruction of the Country House 1875–1975* (London: Thames and Hudson, 1974).

An account of the subsequent controversy over the dispersal of the contents of the Rothschild mansion at Mentmore, and the resulting establishment of the National Heritage Memorial Fund – aimed to replace the underused and ineffective post-war National Land Fund as a means of protecting such ensembles when they came under threat – is provided by Arthur Jones, *Britain's Heritage: the Creation of the National Heritage Memorial Fund* (London: Weidenfeld and Nicholson, 1985). Some idea of the subsequent work of the Fund will be found in the lavish catalogue published in conjunction with an exhibition of objects bought and buildings restored through the Fund's largesse held at the British Museum in 1988–9, *Treasures for the Nation: Conserving our Heritage* (London: British Museum Publications, 1988). An even more lavish, similarly titled compilation had appeared three years earlier, Gervase Jackson-Stops (ed.), *The Treasure Houses of Britain: Five Hundred Years of Private Patronage and Art Collecting* (Washington, DC: National Gallery of Art, and London: Yale University Press, 1985); this commemorated an exhibition held at Washington which celebrated the country house as the quintessence of British culture and which was mainly made up of privately owned objects remaining *in situ*. Indeed, some cynically saw that publication as almost a kind of glossy sale catalogue, and dispersals have continued, as is documented in Michael Sayer and Hugh Massingberd, *The Disintegration of a Heritage: Country Houses and their Collections 1979–92* (Norwich: Michael Russell, 1993). Even if this book may reflect special pleading, published as it was under the auspices of the Historic Houses Association, this indicates a degree of instability in the concept of the ensemble of privately owned country houses with intact contents which Peter Mandler signals in Chapter 6.

The 1970s also saw attention drawn to specific categories of buildings in need of greater attention, not least by the pressure group SAVE Britain's Heritage, which Sophie Andreae discusses in Chapter 8. One of these, as she indicates, was railway architecture: this was the subject of an important exhibition in 1977 with an associated publication entitled *Off the Rails: Saving Railway Architecture* (London: SAVE Britain's Heritage, 1977), which flagged up the deplorable conservationist record of British Rail at that time. SAVE was to follow this up two years later with a fuller celebration of the architectural heritage of the railway: Marcus Binney and David Pearce (eds), *Railway Architecture* (London: Orbis, 1979). Two further publications dealt with churches, of which an increasing number were being declared redundant at that stage: Marcus Binney and Peter Burman, *Churches and Chapels: Who Cares* (London: British Tourist Authority and *Country Life*, 1977), and *Change and Decay: the Future of our Churches* (London: Studio Vista, 1977), the latter associated with a further exhibition at the Victoria and Albert Museum in 1977. The related question of nonconformist places of worship was addressed in Ken Powell, *The Fall of Zion: Northern Chapel Architecture and its Future* (London: SAVE, 1980), while in 1978 SAVE drew attention to a further category of neglected buildings, this time industrial ones and their place in the landscape of the Pennines, in *Satanic Mills* (London: SAVE, [1978]). Various of SAVE's reports on specific buildings and towns are referred to in chapters 5 and 8, while a full account of the various campaigns in which it has been involved will be found in Marcus Binney and Marianne Watson-Smyth, *The SAVE Britain's Heritage Action Guide* (London: Collins and Brown, 1991) (an earlier synopsis appeared in Marcus Binney, *Our Vanishing Heritage* (London: Arlington Books, 1984)). The group's continuing work is illustrated by its more recent championship of a new category of buildings in need of help in *Deserted Bastions: Historic Naval and Military Architecture* (London: SAVE, 1993).

A further development of the 1970s was an attempt to see conservation in a broader economic context, trying to foresee threats to historic buildings and neighbourhoods before they became acute, and to make constructive plans for their long-term viability. This approach had originally been signalled by the 1967 document *Historic Towns: Preservation and Change*, which has already been referred to; it was further promoted by the studies of four ancient towns – Bath, Chester, Chichester and York – commissioned by Lord Kennet and written respectively by Colin Buchanan & Associates, Donald W. Insall & Associates, G. S. Burrows and Viscount Esher and published under the general title of *A Study in Conservation* (London: Her Majesty's Stationery Office, 1968). As far as London was concerned, a comparable initiative came from the amenity societies in the form of David Lloyd (ed.), *Save the City. A Conservation Study of the City of London* (London: Society for the Protection of Ancient Buildings, Georgian Group, Victorian Society and Civic Trust, 1976; republished jointly with the Ancient Monuments Society, 1979), while a further significant publication of 1980 was *Britain's Historic Buildings: a Policy for their Future Use* (London: British Tourist Authority): this was the report of a working party under the chairmanship of Lord Montagu of Beaulieu, set up by the Historic Buildings Council for England during the regime of Jennifer Jenkins, the significance of which Sophie Andreae stresses in Chapter 8.

Revealingly, *Britain's Historic Buildings* was published by the British Tourist Authority; they also collaborated with SAVE in publishing *Chapels and Churches: Who Cares*, and this collaboration was taken further by a tellingly titled joint publication by the chairmen of that Board and of SAVE, Max Hanna and Marcus Binney, *Preservation Pays: Tourism and the Economic Benefits of Conserving Historic Buildings* (London: SAVE [1979]). This took it for granted – rightly or wrongly – that the cost of rehabilitating old buildings would be paid for by the extra revenue that they would raise from tourist use. As such, this formed part of the preoccupation with 'heritage' as a source of leisure provision which has increasingly characterised the 1980s, and it is into this context that the growth of visitor attractions surveyed by Michael Stratton fits. A useful book describing some of the more innovative of such experiments is Kenneth Hudson, *Museums of Influence* (Cambridge University Press, 1987); further information is best sought in booklets put out by specific museums, such as Rosemary Allen and Peter Lewis, *Beamish: the Making of a Museum* (Beamish: the North of England Open Air Museum, 1991). Indeed, what might be seen as the ultimate accolade to this new approach to the past was paid by the 1987 *Report of the House of Commons Environment Committee on Historic Buildings and Ancient Monuments* (3 vols., London: Her Majesty's Stationary Office, 1987), the evidence presented to which forms a fascinating view of the state of affairs at that point: for the committee declared itself basically satisfied with its findings, but urged that more should be done to exploit the potential of the heritage as a tourist attraction, thus enabling it to earn its keep and reducing its dependence on the public purse.

It was perhaps only to be expected that all this would inspire a backlash. A pioneering work from this point of view was Martin Wiener, *English Culture and the Decline of the Industrial Spirit 1850–1980* (Cambridge University Press, 1981), which saw the preoccupation with preservation in the period around 1900 as one of many symptoms of the malaise affecting English society at that time. A more frontal attack on the contemporary state of affairs seems to have begun in Australia rather than in Britain, in Donald Horne, *The Great Museum: the Re-Presentation of History* (London and Sydney: Pluto, 1984), a caustic attack on the preoccupations of tourists to the Old World. It was soon to catch on here, most notably in Robert Hewison, *The Heritage Industry: Britain in a Climate of Decline* (London: Methuen, 1987), a brief but hard-hitting excoriation of what the author saw as the symptoms of a sick, past-worshipping country, though his work is almost a self-fulfilling prophecy in its *a priori* presumption of the incompatibility of 'heritage' with a forward-looking society, which is hardly borne out by his occasional international comparisons with countries such as the United States and Japan.

A slightly earlier work on a related theme was Patrick Wright, *On Living in an Old Country: the National Past in Contemporary Britain* (London: Verso, 1985), which tried to probe at the hidden values underlying preservationist concerns, and which shows some insight, though its message is somewhat obscured by a baggage of post-Marxist theory. This is mercifully jettisoned in Wright's more recent books on related topics – *A Journey through the Ruins: the Last Days of London* (London: Radius 1991) and *The Village that Died for England: the Strange Story of Tyneham* (London: Jonathan Cape, 1995) – in which he uses telling detail to write more reflectively (if, ultimately, somewhat inconclusively) on the relationship between the past and the present in this country today.

If Wright's trajectory has been from scepticism to reflectiveness, a contrasting course has been pursued by Sir Roy Strong, who, as Director of the Victoria and Albert Museum in the 1970s, had presided over the very awakening of public concern about heritage which has already been referred to. In his *Lost Treasures of Britain: Five Centuries of Creation and Destruction* (London: Viking, 1990), however, Strong aligned himself with the heritage sceptics, combining an account of episodes of destruction and recreation in the past – as at the Dissolution of the Monasteries or after the Civil War – with a monitory epilogue warning how the contemporary preoccupation with preservation was in danger of stifling such creativity.

It is symptomatic of the popularity of 'heritage' that such views have become commonplace, especially in academic circles and in the more intellectualist echelons of journalism. Such writings have been salutary in revealing the extent to which values might be embedded in conservation of which those promoting it were unaware, though they have frequently said as much about the prejudices and preoccupations of their authors as about the phenomenon they attack. Most involved in heritage matters (like the public) have tended to ignore them, but one can at last recommend a robust, if rather diffuse, response to them in Raphael

Samuel, *Theatres of Memory*, vol. 1: *Past and Present in Contemporary Culture* (London: Verso, 1994).

For better or worse, 'heritage' is with us in the 1990s, and there is an increasing, rather technical literature on its different aspects which it seems better to categorise in general terms than to try to describe in full. First, there is a literature of 'heritage interpretation', presided over since 1975 by the Society for the Interpretation of Britain's Heritage (now renamed 'Interpret Britain'), perhaps the most substantial publication of which has been David Uzzell (ed.), *Heritage Interpretation* (2 vols., London: Belhaven Press, 1989). In the archaeological sphere, related publications include Henry Cleere (ed.), *Archaeological Heritage Management in the Modern World* (London: Unwin Hyman, 1989), while the publishers Routledge have launched a series on 'The Heritage: Care–Preservation–Management', evidently in response to a proliferation of university and polytechnic courses dealing with 'heritage management' and related themes. Early titles in this include Peter Fowler, *The Past in Contemporary Society: Then, Now* (London: Routledge, 1992), together with such studies of the ethos of museums as Kevin Walsh, *The Representation of the Past: Museums and Heritage in the Post-Modern World* (London: Routledge, 1992): though some such volumes have been a little vacuous or modish, it is to be hoped that the series will settle down to a worthwhile future.

Secondly, there is a literature on planning and its links with the 'heritage', of which the most useful volume so far to appear is Michael Ross, *Planning and the Heritage: Policy and Procedures* (London: Spon, 1991), a comprehensive, if slightly complacent, account of current legislation in relation to listed buildings and Conservation Areas. A similar work is Ruth Richards, *Conservation Planning: a Guide to Planning Legislation Concerning our Architectural Heritage* (London: Planning Aid, 1990), and others may be expected, particularly as the legislation regarding listing and Conservation Areas is revised and refined.

Thirdly, there is a literature concerning the practicalities of conservation. Here, English Heritage has produced some useful publications, while another source is Donhead Publishing, whose current list includes such valuable items as Peter Burman (ed.), *Treasures on Earth: a Good Housekeeping Guide to Churches and their Contents* (London: Donhead, 1994), as well as a series of conference proceedings on related topics and even (from 1995) a *Journal of Architectural Conservation.*

Finally, for information about continuing threats to the built environment, probably the best sources are the annual reports and the more frequent newsletters published by the SPAB, Georgian Group, Victorian Society and Twentieth Century Society, which retail the successes and failures of their casework. A more sustained call for a change in policy in a key area is the English Historic Towns Forum's *Townscape in Trouble: Conservation Areas – the Case for Change* (London: Butterworth, 1992), while for an example of a polemic dealing with conservationist policy in one particular town, see Timothy Mowl, *Cheltenham Betrayed* (Tiverton: Redcliffe Press, 1995). One can predict confidently that debate on this and similar issues will continue for the foreseeable future.

Appendix

Key events in the history of preservation in Britain

1845	Protection of Works of Art and Scientific and Literary Collections Act
1854	Public Statues Act. Commissioners of Works made guardians of London statues
1865	Commons Preservation Society founded
1877	Society for the Protection of Ancient Buildings founded
1882	Ancient Monuments Protection Act. Provides for a schedule of significant antiquities, mainly prehistoric, which could be taken into public guardianship
1895	National Trust founded
1900	First use by London County Council of powers granted to it in 1898 to purchase buildings, and publication of first volume of London Survey under its auspices
1900	Ancient Monuments Protection Act. Extends the range of antiquities covered by the 1882 Act
1908	Royal Commissions on Historical Monuments for England, Wales and Scotland founded
1913	Ancient Monuments Consolidation and Amendment Act. Makes provision for list of ancient monuments considered worthy of protection, and for preservation orders. Churches and inhabited houses excluded. Ancient Monuments Boards established
1931	National Trust for Scotland founded
1931	Ancient Monuments Act. Authorises local authorities to set up preservation schemes to protect monuments and their surroundings
1932	Town and Country Planning Act. Extends similar provision to inhabited buildings and groups of buildings
1937	Georgian Group founded
1937	National Trust country-houses scheme inaugurated

1938	First open-air museum in Britain opened: Cregneash, Isle of Man
1941	National Buildings (later Monuments) Record established
1944, 1947	Town and Country Planning Acts. As part of a wide-ranging package of planning measures, provision made for compilation of comprehensive list of buildings worthy of preservation, the owners of which were required to give notice to the relevant authorities of their intention to alter or demolish them
1950	Gowers Report on Country Houses
1953	Historic Buildings and Ancient Monuments Act. Minister of State, advised by Historic Buildings Councils, empowered to order grants for repairs and maintenance of buildings of outstanding interest and their contents
1957	Civic Trust founded
1958	Victorian Society founded
1967	Civic Amenities Act. Empowers local authorities to identify and declare 'Conservation Areas'
1968	Town and Country Planning Act. Alters position so that owners of listed buildings wishing to demolish or alter them have to seek explicit permission for this, rather than serving notice of their intentions. Spot-listing introduced. Crown buildings listed for first time
1969–87	Resurvey of historic buildings for listing; interwar buildings first listed in 1970
1971	Town and Country Planning Act. Further powers granted, including compulsory purchase
1972	Field Monuments Act. Introduced a system of 'acknowledgement payments' to landowners with scheduled monuments on their land
1972	Town and Country Planning (Amendment) Act. Funds provided for conservation schemes, especially in 'outstanding' Conservation Areas
1974	Town and Country Amenities Act. Toughens protection of Conservation Areas by requiring that demolition or radical alteration of buildings within them be sanctioned by relevant planning authority
1975	European Architectural Heritage Year

1975 SAVE Britain's Heritage founded

1979 Ancient Monuments and Archaeological Areas Act. Initiates system of grant of consent for archaeological sites similar to that for listed buildings, and introduces concept of 'archaeological area', where developers obliged to allow access to archaeologists

1979 Thirties (later Twentieth Century) Society founded

1980 National Heritage Memorial Act. Appoints Trustees authorised to give financial assistance for the acquisition, preservation or maintenance of land, buildings, or structures deemed important to the national heritage

1984 English Heritage and Historic Scotland formed, taking over role of Historic Building Councils and Ancient Monuments Boards

1987 Circular 8/87 issued, key statement of government conservation policy; thirty-year rule introduced, under which any building over thirty years old could be considered for listing

1990 *PPG 16* (Planning Policy Guidance Note 16, Archaeology and Planning). Insists on proper consideration being given to all archaeological remains in the planning process

1990 Planning (Listed Buildings and Conservation Areas) Act. The basis of current law in the field

1993 National Lottery Act. Grants made from lottery funds have already had a major impact on 'heritage' spending

1994 *PPG 15* (Planning Policy Guidance Note 15, Planning and the Historic Environment). Major government restatement of conservation policy

Contributors

SOPHIE ANDREAE, born 1954, worked for SAVE Britain's Heritage from 1976 to 1988, first as its Secretary and latterly as its Chairman. She was Head of the London Division of English Heritage from 1988 to 1993. She currently sits on various heritage committees, including the Fabric Advisory Committee of St Paul's Cathedral, and has recently been appointed to the Royal Fine Art Commission.

TIMOTHY CHAMPION, born 1946, is Professor of Archaeology at the University of Southampton, with a particular interest in the management and preservation of archaeological remains. He is President of the Prehistoric Society, and a member of English Heritage's Ancient Monuments Advisory Committee.

JOHN EARL, born 1928, joined the LCC Historic Buildings Section in 1956. Apart from four years with the Ministry of Public Buildings and Works, working on royal palaces, he remained with the Section and its successor (the Historic Buildings Division) until the GLC was abolished in 1986. From 1986 to 1995 he was Director of the Theatres Trust, a statutory body charged with the protection of theatre buildings.

MICHAEL HUNTER, born 1949, is Professor of History at Birkbeck College, University of London. He is an established authority on the history of ideas in the seventeenth century, and he has a longstanding interest in historic preservation. His publications include the co-authored *Avebury Reconsidered* (1991) and a study of the origins of preservationist attitudes which appeared in *Our Past Before Us* (1981).

PETER MANDLER, born 1958, is Reader in Modern History at London Guildhall University. His most recent books are *After the Victorians*, a collection of biographical essays on twentieth-century intellectuals, edited with Susan Pedersen and published by Routledge in 1994, and '*The Stately Homes of England*': *the English Country House and the National Heritage since the Eighteenth Century*, to be published shortly by Yale University Press.

CHRIS MIELE, born 1961, received his doctorate from New York University's Institute of Fine Arts in 1992, and now works as a historian in the London Region of English Heritage. He is currently editing a collection of William Morris' writings on architecture for Sheffield Academic Press and is one of a team of curators for the Morris retrospective to be held at the Victoria and Albert Museum in 1996.

ANDREW SAINT, born 1946, is Professor of Architecture at the University of Cambridge. He worked for the Greater London Council on *The Survey of London* from 1974 to 1986 and for English Heritage's London Division from 1986 to 1995. He is Chairman of the Victorian Society's Buildings Sub-committee and the author of several books.

GAVIN STAMP, born 1948, is a Lecturer in Architectural History at the Mackintosh School of Architecture, Glasgow School of Art. He joined the Victorian Society in 1966, has been the Chairman of the Twentieth Century Society, formerly the Thirties Society, since 1983 and is the founder and Chairman of the Alexander Thomson Society. He gave evidence (against) at the public inquiries on the Poultry site both in 1984 and 1988 (see pp. 153–4).

MICHAEL STRATTON, born 1953, is a Lecturer in Conservation Studies at the Institute of Advanced Architectural Studies, University of York. He was formerly Programme Director of the Ironbridge Institute. He has written books on architectural terracotta, car factories and power stations.

Notes

Chapter 1

1. *Cultural Trends*, issue 15, 1992 (London: Policy Studies Institute, 1992), p. 25.

2. English Heritage, *Grants 1993–4* (London: English Heritage, 1994), p. 5.

3. *The Times*, 17 Nov. 1993.

4. See J. H. Plumb, *The Commercialisation of Leisure in Eighteenth-century England* (Stenton Lecture, 1972, Reading: University of Reading, 1973), reprinted in Neil McKendrick *et al.*, *The Birth of a Consumer Society* (London: Europa, 1982), pp. 265–85; Janet Minihan, *The Nationalisation of Culture: the Development of State Subsidies for the Arts in Great Britain* (London: Hamish Hamilton, 1977), especially chs. 2–4.

5. See especially J. A. R. Pimlott, *The Englishman's Holiday: a Social History* (London: Faber and Faber, 1947).

6. Cf. Minihan, *Nationalisation of Culture* (n. 4). On eighteenth-century taxation, see J. H. Brewer, *The Sinews of Power* (London: Unwin Hyman, 1989).

7. Christopher Chippindale, *Stonehenge Complete* (London: Thames and Hudson, 1983).

8. See Michael Hunter, *John Aubrey and the Realm of Learning* (London: Duckworth, 1975); H. M. Colvin, 'John Aubrey's *Chronologia Architectonica*', in Sir John Summerson (ed.), *Concerning Architecture* (London: Allen Lane, 1968), pp. 1–12.

9. See Hunter, *John Aubrey*, especially pp. 202f.; J. M. Crook, 'John Britton and the Genesis of the Gothic Revival', in Sir John Summerson (ed.), *Concerning Architecture* (London: Allen Lane, 1968), pp. 98–119.

10. Peter J. Ucko *et al.*, *Avebury Reconsidered* (London: Unwin Hyman, 1991), p. 257.

11. *Gentleman's Magazine*, 58 (1788), 689–91.

12. G. L. Gomme (ed.), *Gentleman's Magazine Library: Architectural Antiquities*, Part 1 (London: Elliot Stock, 1890), p. 11 and *passim*. See also J.M. Crook, *John Carter and the Mind of the Gothic Revival* (London: Society of Antiquaries Occasional Papers, 17, 1995).

13. Cf. Crook, 'John Britton' (n. 9), p. 118.

14. See Stuart Piggott, 'The Origins of the County Archaeological Societies', in his *Ruins in a Landscape* (Edinburgh: Edinburgh University Press, 1976), pp. 171–95. See also Philippa Levine, *The Amateur and the Professional: Antiquaries, Historians and Archaeologists in Victorian England 1838–86* (Cambridge University Press, 1986).

15. See Clive Wainwright, *The Romantic Interior: the British Collector at Home 1750–1850* (New Haven and London: Yale University Press, 1989).

16. See Peter Mandler, *The Stately Homes of England* (New Haven and London: Yale University Press, in press).

17. See Michael Hunter, 'The Preconditions of Preservation: a Historical Perspective', in David Lowenthal and Marcus Binney (eds), *Our Past Before Us: Why Do We Save It?* (London: Temple Smith, 1981), pp. 22–32, on pp. 24, 27–8.

18. Quoted in Christopher Chippindale, 'The Making of the First Ancient Monuments Act, 1882, and its Administration under General Pitt-Rivers', *Journal of the British Archaeological Association*, 136 (1983), 1–55, on pp. 8–9: Dickens's reference to a single person alludes to Lubbock's role at Avebury: see below.

19. J. M. Frew, 'Richard Gough, James Wyatt and late Eighteenth-century Preservation', *Journal of the Society of Architectural Historians*, 38 (1979), 366–74, especially p. 373.

20. See Chris Miele, '"Their Interest and Habit": Professionalism and the Restoration of Medieval Churches,

1837–77', in Chris Brooks and Andrew Saint (eds), *The Victorian Church: Architecture and Society* (Manchester University Press, 1995), pp. 151–72.
21. John Ruskin, *The Seven Lamps of Architecture* (2nd edn, Orpington: George Allen, 1880; reprinted, New York: Dover, 1989), p. 197.
22. Joan Evans, *History of the Society of Antiquaries* (London: Oxford University Press for the Society of Antiquaries, 1956), pp. 309–12.
23. Martin Wiener, *English Culture and the Decline of the Industrial Spirit 1850–1980* (Cambridge University Press, 1981).
24. Chippindale, 'Ancient Monuments Act' (n. 18), pp. 4f.
25. On this context to the National Trust see the valuable work of Lord Eversley, *Commons, Forests and Footpaths* (revised edition, London: Cassell, 1910).
26. C. R. Ashbee (ed.), *The Survey of London: Being the First Volume of the Register of the Committee for the Survey of the Memorials of Greater London, Containing the Parish of Bromley-by-Bow* (London: LCC, 1900), pp. xviii–xxv.
27. *Art Treasures for the Nation: Fifty Years of the National Art-Collections Fund* (London: Thames and Hudson, 1953), Introduction by the Earl of Crawford and Balcarres, pp. 5f.
28. *Parliamentary Debates, Lords, 1912*, vol. 11, 30 April 1912, col. 876.
29. H. G. Hutchinson, *The Life of Sir John Lubbock, Lord Avebury* (2 vols., London: Macmillan, 1914), i, 150.
30. Chippindale, 'Ancient Monuments Act' (n. 18), especially pp. 25–6, 28.
31. G. Baldwin Brown, *The Care of Ancient Monuments* (Cambridge University Press, 1905), p. 150 and *passim.*
32. Earle to the First Commissioner of Works, 12 Jan. 1927, PRO WORK 14/2312. I am indebted to Peter Mandler for this reference.
33. An earlier analogue is perhaps provided by the acute sense of the past of observers like Aubrey, stimulated by the epoch-making changes in the years from the Dissolution of the Monasteries to the Civil War. See Hunter, *John Aubrey* (n. 8), especially pp. 165–6; see also Margaret Aston, 'English Ruins and English History: the Dissolution and the Sense of the Past', *Journal of the Warburg and Courtauld Institutes*, 36 (1973), 231–55.
34. Quoted in Baldwin Brown, *Care of Ancient Monuments* (n. 31), p. 154.
35. See Michael Ross, *Planning and the Heritage* (London: Spon, 1991), pp. 87–9; Victorian Society Report on Listing of Historic Buildings [1991], especially app. B.
36. See Arthur Jones, *Britain's Heritage* (London: Weidenfeld and Nicolson, 1985), especially ch. 15: 'Does the Treasury Govern Britain?'
37. Sir Robert Witt, *The Nation and its Art Treasures* (London: William Heinemann, 1911), p. 32.
38. C. Williams-Ellis, *England and the Octopus* (London: Geoffrey Bles, 1928), p. vii.
39. Clapham, 'Anniversary Address', *Antiquaries' Journal*, 23 (1943), 87–97, on p. 95. On Clapham and listing, see Angus Ackworth and Sir Anthony Wagner, 'Twenty-five Years of Listing', *Architectural Review*, 148 (1970), 308–10.
40. Hewison, *The Heritage Industry* (London: Methuen, 1987), p. 84 and *passim*. For other works with a similar message, see Chapter 10.
41. Strong, *Lost Treasures of Britain* (London: Viking, 1990), pp. 215f.
42. The commentator who comes closest to self-parody in this respect is Kevin Walsh, *The Representation of the Past: Museums and Heritage in the Post-Modern World* (London: Routledge, 1992).
43. Nick Merriman, *Beyond the Glass Case: the Past, the Heritage and the Public in Britain* (Leicester University Press, 1991), especially ch. 3.
44. Samuel, *Theatres of Memory* (London: Verso, 1994), especially pts. 3 and 4.
45. See Robert Thorne, 'Conserving the Present', *History Today*, Sept. 1994, pp. 10–12.

Chapter 2

1. Drawn from tables in 'Survey of Church Building and Church Restoration. 1840–1875', *Parliamentary Accounts and Papers*, 58 (1876), 52–210. See C. Miele, '"Their Interest and Habit". Professionalism and the Restoration of

Medieval Churches 1837–77', in C. Brooks and A. Saint (eds), *The Victorian Church: Architecture and Society* (Manchester University Press, 1995), pp. 151–72, on pp. 156–60.

2. Owen Chadwick, *The Victorian Church* (2 vols., London: Adam and Charles, 1966, 1970).

3. As discussed by C. Miele, 'Real Antiquity and the Science of Gothic Architecture', in C. Brooks (ed.), *The Study of the Past in the Victorian Age* (Oxford: Oxbow Books, forthcoming).

4. C. Miele, 'The Gothic Revival and Gothic Architecture: The Restoration of Medieval Churches in Victorian Britain' (PhD thesis, Institute of Fine Arts, New York University, 1992), pp. 339–86.

5. Miele, 'Gothic Revival' (n. 4), pp. 487-531.

6. Miele, '"Their Interest and Habit"' (n. 1), pp. 161–3.

7. G. E. Street, 'On the Restoration of Ancient Buildings', *The Builder*, (1861), 389.

8. SPAB Minutes, SPAB Archives, 25 July 1878; 5 Aug., 30 Sept., 14 Oct., 11 Nov. 1880; 23, 30 July 1885; 14, 28 Jan., 4, 25 Feb. 1886.

9. P. Levine, *The Amateur and the Professional: Antiquarians, Historians and Archaeologists in Victorian Britain* (Cambridge: Cambridge University Press, 1986), app. 5.

10. For a discussion of Morris's intended audience see C. Miele, '"A Small Knot of Cultivated People". William Morris and the Ideologies of Protection', Art Journal, 54 (1995), pp. 73–9, on p. 75.

11. *The Collected Letters of William Morris*, ed. N. Kelvin (Princeton University Press, 1984) [hereafter 'Kelvin'], vol. i: 1848–1880, letter no. 1, 417, 10 July 1877. Morris asked Ruskin for permission to reprint the lines from 'The Lamp of Memory' condemning restoration.

12. See above, p. 4. See also J. M. Crook, *John Carter and the Mind of the Gothic Revival* (London: Society of Antiquaries Occasional Papers, 17, 1995).

13. See, for example, an anonymous article in *Archaeologia Cambrensis*, 1 (1846), 364–8. At about the same time Robert Willis was coming to similar conclusions. A. Buchanan, 'Robert Willis and the Rise of Architectural History' (PhD thesis, University College, London, 1994), especially app. B. See also Miele, 'Gothic Revival' (n. 4), pp. 105–21.

14. Miele, 'Gothic Revival' (n. 4), pp. 125–40.

15. Kelvin, 1, 393. See also *The Athenaeum*, 31 March 1877. For details of what actually was done at Tewkesbury see A. Jones, *Tewkesbury* (Chichester: Phillimore, 1987), pp. 164–71.

16. First Agenda Paper, SPAB Archives.

17. A draft was sent to Rosetti on 3 April. Kelvin, 1, 391.

18. Kelvin, 1, 404. Also copy of letter to Bishop of London from G. Cavendish-Bentinck, 19 June 1877, City Churches file, SPAB Archives.

19. G. Cobb, *London City Churches* (rev. edn, London: Batsford, 1989), pp. 123–8.

20. Kelvin, 1, 406, published 4 June. See also Kelvin, 1, 407 and 411 (7 June and 22 June, respectively).

21. Canterbury I, 1876–1896, SPAB Archives, letters dated 23 June, 4 July and 9 August 1877. See also *The Athenaeum* 7 July 1877, pp. 22–3.

22. *Macmillan's Magazine*, July 1877, pp. 136–42, 228–37.

23. M. Girouard, 'The Architecture of John James Stevenson, part I', *The Connoisseur*, 184 (1973), 166–74, on p. 167.

24. *RIBA Sessional Papers*, 1876–7, pp. 219–25, on p. 219.

25. 'On the Recent Reaction of Taste in English Architecture', *Building News*, Volume number (1874), 689. M. Girouard, 'The Architecture of John James Stevenson, part II', *The Connoisseur*, 185 (Feb. 1974), pp. 106–12.

26. *RIBA Sessional Papers*, 1876–7, pp. 242–52.

27. In a letter to his close friend George Howard, Morris denied that the SPAB had been behind Stevenson's piece. Kelvin, 1, 414.

28. The Committee on the Conservation of Ancient Monuments and Remains, founded by Scott and others in autumn 1864, had tried to promote a recording project in the winter of 1865–6. Miele, 'Gothic Revival' (n. 4), pp. 481–2.

29. Miele, 'Gothic Revival' (n. 4),

pp. 473–82, and '"Their Interest and Habit"' (n. 1), pp. 161–3.
30. For example, 21 April 1877, p. 258, and 16 June 1877, pp. 391–2.
31. Ibid., pp. 393–4.
32. 24 August 1877, p. 176.
33. Vol. 2 (1877), pp. 446–70.
34. Agenda Paper, SPAB Archives.
35. SPAB Minutes, 13 Sept., 11 Oct. 1877.
36. The matter was referred to the SPAB from someone in the Lincoln Diocesan Architectural Society, which visited the Minster on 10 July 1877. *Associated Architectural Societies. Reports and Papers*, 14 (1877–8), vi–viii.
37. Southwell file, SPAB Archives, correspondence from August to December 1877.
38. Southwell file, 18 June 1878.
39. Kelvin, 1, 393.
40. *Building News*, 19 September 1879, pp. 331–2.
41. 27 October 1877, p. 229.
42. The best published account of this campaign is to be found in P. Ferriday in *Lord Grimthorpe* (London: John Murray, 1957), pp. 76–122.
43. SPAB Minutes, 20 Nov. 1879.
44. *Architect*, 11 Aug. 1877, p. 77.
45. G. Murphy, *Founders of the National Trust* (London: Christopher Helm, 1987), pp. 25–33.
46. SPAB Minutes, 5 Feb. 1880. Christian and J. L. Pearson filed affidavits with Tebbs asking Grimthorpe to produce detailed plans, SPAB Minutes, 11 March.
47. SPAB Minutes, 29 April 1880.
48. St Albans file, SPAB Archives, letters dated 5 and 7 Dec. 1881.
49. Kelvin, 1, 585.
50. As emerged in subsequent weeks, care of the building was actually the responsibility of the Ministry of Public Instruction. Documents relating to this campaign, including letters of support, are split between St Mark's, Folder B, 1879–80, SPAB Archives, and British Library, Add. MS 38,331, Papers Presented by Henry Wallis, St Mark's in Venice Committee.
51. Letter to Henry Wallis, British Library, Add. MS 38,331, fols. 56 and 57. See also F. Sharp, 'A Lesson in International Relations: Morris and the SPAB', *Journal of the William Morris Society*, 10 (Spring 1993), pp. 9–14.
52. Their first report appeared in 1882. Copy in Guildhall Library, Corporation of London, Pam. 854. The executive committee featured many of the same names as the SPAB's. The national Society for Protecting the Memorials to the Dead was founded about this time.
53. SPAB Minutes, 3 Jan. 1878, 29 May 1879. No example of this form has come to my attention, and I suspect it was not completed.
54. *First Annual Report of the SPAB*, p. 9.
55. SPAB Minutes, 10 Oct. 1878.
56. SPAB Minutes, 30 Aug. 1877.
57. Undated note attached to SPAB Minutes for 13 Sept. 1877.
58. SPAB Minutes, 27 Sept. 1877.
59. SPAB Minutes, 13 June 1878.
60. SPAB Minutes, 27 June 1878.
61. Irthlingborough file, SPAB Archives, 10 Sept. and 16 Oct. 1883.
62. SPAB Minutes 25 Feb. 1886; SPAB Archives, St Helen's Bishopsgate file, correspondence between Hellier Gosselin and Thackeray Turner.
63. SPAB Minutes, 13 June and 11 July 1878.
64. SPAB Minutes, 23 Jan. 1878. Wardle's motion calling for a printed code of conduct for the local correspondents was approved at this meeting. I have never seen one.
65. Occupied from 7 Nov. 1878.
66. A decision to take *The Builder*, *The Architect*, and *Building News* on a six-month trial period was first approved at a meeting of 11 April 1878. SPAB Minutes.
67. SPAB Minutes, 18 Sept. 1884.
68. SPAB Minutes, 24 Oct. 1878.
69. See *The Architect* for 7 and 28 July, 22 Sept. 1877, pp. 11–12, 48, 163, respectively.
70. It did so in 1883 for Llandanwg Church near Harlech in Wales.
71. Stratford-on-Avon Church, 1881. The firm wrested control of the project from William Butterfield. Later that year Bodley refused to discuss his plans for Frodsham Church with the Society, although in 1887 Webb was able to exercise some influence on Bodley's plans for Wellow Church near Bath.

72. Chesterton Church.
73. Edington Church.
74. Framlingham Church, although the parties disagreed over several points.
75. Knapton Church in 1881.
76. Fairford Church in 1886. Here Morris wrote out a detailed specification for the repair of the ancient glass.
77. SPAB Minutes, 13, 20, and 27 Jan. 1881.
78. 42 and 43 Vic. Amended in select committee, and read for the third time on 22 July. Clauses 20–22 deal with the disturbances to City Churchyards. Clause 27 extended protection to St Mary-at-Hill and clause 32 to St Leonard Eastcheap.
79. See letter to Wyndham, dated 11 March 1880, 'Tisbury' file, SPAB Archives. Wyndham was a Tory MP and one of those most active on the Society's behalf in parliament.
80. According to Gavin Stamp Sir George Gilbert Scott's drawings of *c.* 1874 were used as contract drawings in 1880. John Oldrid Scott made designs for the refitting in 1879. The papers relating to this case have not survived in the SPAB's casework archives, and I am indebted to John Newman for drawing my attention to it. For further information on Sir G. G. Scott, see Gavin Stamp's edition of his *Personal and Professional Recollections* (Stamford: Paul Watkins, 1995).
81. *The Beautiful World* (The Journal of the Society for Checking the Abuses of Public Advertising), 1896, pp. 16–18. This meeting took place on 31 January 1896. Reprinted in C. Miele (ed.), *Morris on Architecture* (Sheffield Academic Press, 1996).

Chapter 3

1. W. Kennet, *Preservation* (London: Temple Smith, 1972), pp. 21–30; A. Saunders, 'A Century of Ancient Monuments Legislation 1882–1982', *Antiquaries Journal*, 63 (1983), 11–33, on pp. 11–14; C. Chippindale, 'The Making of the first Ancient Monuments Act, 1882, and its Administration under General Pitt-Rivers', *Journal of the British Archaeological Association*, 86 (1983), 1–55; T. Murray, 'The History, Philosophy and Sociology of Archaeology: the Case of the Ancient Monuments Act 1882', in V. Pinsky and A. Wylie (eds), *Critical Traditions in Contemporary Archaeology* (Cambridge University Press, 1989), pp. 55–67.
2. S. Piggott, 'The Origins of the English County Archaeological Societies', *Transactions of the Birmingham and Warwickshire Archaeological Society*, 86 (1974), 1–15, reprinted in his *Ruins in a Landscape* (Edinburgh University Press, 1976), pp. 171–95.
3. D. Weatherall, 'From Canterbury to Winchester: the Foundation of the Institute', in B. Vyner (ed.), *Building on the Past: Papers Celebrating 150 Years of the Royal Archaeological Institute* (London: Royal Archaeological Institute, 1994), pp. 8–21.
4. A. Way, 'Introduction', *Archaeological Journal*, 1 (1845), 1–6.
5. *Parliamentary Debates, Commons, 1845*, 3rd series, vol. 81, 27 June 1845, cols. 1329–34.
6. T. D. Kendrick, 'The British Museum and British Antiquities', *Museums Journal* 51 (1951), 139–49.
7. Report of the Select Committee on National Monuments and Works of Art, 1841, 416, *Parliamentary Papers*, 6, 437.
8. Evidence of J. Britton, Select Committee Report (n. 7), question 1947.
9. D. E. L. Haynes, *The Portland Vase*, 2nd edn (London: British Museum, 1975), pp. 11–12.
10. Chippindale, 'First Ancient Monuments Act' (n. 1), pp. 18–33; Saunders, 'Century' (n. 1), pp. 13–14; M. W. Thompson, *General Pitt-Rivers: Evolution and Archaeology in the Nineteenth Century* (Bradford-on-Avon: Moonraker, 1977), pp. 58–74; M. Bowden, *Pitt Rivers: the Life and Archaeological Work of Lieutenant-General Augustus Henry Lane Fox Pitt Rivers, DCL, FRS, FSA* (Cambridge University Press, 1991), pp. 95–102.
11. D. Murray, *An Archaeological Survey of the United Kingdom: the Preservation and Protection of our Ancient Monuments* (Glasgow: MacLehose, 1896).
12. B. H. St J. O'Neil, 'The Congress of Archaeological Societies', *Antiquaries Journal*, 26 (1946), 61–6.

13. J. P. Williams-Freeman, *Field Archaeology as Illustrated in Hampshire* (London: Macmillan, 1915).
14. M. Thompson, 'The Origin of "Scheduling"', *Antiquity*, 37 (1963), 224–5.
15. G. Baldwin Brown, *The Care of Ancient Monuments* (Cambridge University Press, 1905).
16. Reports showing the systems adopted in certain foreign countries for the preservation of ancient monuments, 1912–13, Cd. 6200, *Parliamentary Papers*, 68, 1.
17. Report of the Joint Select Committee of Lords and Commons on the Ancient Monuments Protection Bills, 1912–13, 360, *Parliamentary Papers*, 6, 345.
18. *Parliamentary Debates, Lords, 1912*, vol. 11, 30 April 1912, col. 886.
19. *Parliamentary Debates, Lords, 1913*, vol. 14, 24 June 1913, cols. 672–3.
20. *Parliamentary Debates, Commons, 1913*, vol. 56, 12 Aug. 1913, cols. 2459–60.
21. *Parliamentary Debates, Lords, 1912*, vol. 11, 30 April 1912, cols. 871–2.
22. Ibid., col. 873.
23. Evidence of G. H. Duckworth, Select Committee report (n. 17), questions 707–12.
24. Evidence of A. F. Major, Select Committee Report (n. 17), question 246.
25. Marquis of Curzon and H. A. Tipping, *Tattershall Castle, Lincolnshire: a Historical and Descriptive Survey* (London: Cape, 1929).
26. *Parliamentary Debates, Lords, 1912*, vol. 11, 30 April 1912, col. 883; *1913*, vol. 14, 28 May 1913, col. 434.
27. M. Wiener, *English Culture and the Decline of the Industrial Spirit 1850–1980* (Cambridge University Press, 1981); R. Colls and P. Dodd, *Englishness: Politics and Culture 1880–1920* (London: Croom Helm, 1986); D. Lowenthal, 'British National Identity and the English Landscape', *Rural History*, 2 (1991), 205–30.
28. *Parliamentary Debates, Lords, 1912*, vol. 11, 30 April 1912, col. 872.
29. House of Commons Bill, 1914, 151, *Parliamentary Papers*, 1, 129.
30. J. Sheail, *Rural Conservation in Inter-war Britain* (Oxford: Clarendon Press, 1981).
31. V. Cunningham, *British Writers of the Thirties* (Oxford: Oxford University Press, 1988), pp. 211–40.
32. O. G. S. Crawford and A. Keiller, *Wessex from the Air* (Oxford: Oxford University Press, 1928).
33. D. N. Jeans, 'Planning and the Myth of the English Countryside in the Interwar Period', *Rural History*, 1 (1990), 249–64.
34. Cited by W. J. Keith, *The Rural Tradition* (Hassocks: Harvester, 1975), p. 216.
35. O. G. S. Crawford, 'Editorial', *Antiquity*, 3 (1929), 1–4, on pp. 2–3.
36. Sheail, *Rural Conservation* (n. 30), pp. 48–62.
37. Sheail, *Rural Conservation* (n. 30), pp. 57–60.
38. *Report of the Committee of Enquiry into the arrangements for the protection of field monuments 1966–68*, Cmnd 3904 (London: HMSO, 1969), para. 36.
39. W. F. Grimes, *Excavations on Defence Sites: vol. 1, mainly Neolithic and Bronze Age*, Ministry of Works Archaeological Report, no. 3 (London: HMSO, 1960).
40. A. Williams, 'Canterbury Excavations, September–October 1944', *Archaeologia Cantiana*, 59 (1946), 64–81.
41. W. F. Grimes, *The Excavation of Roman and Medieval London* (London: Routledge and Kegan Paul, 1968), pp. 92–117.
42. B. Jones, *Past Imperfect: the Story of Rescue Archaeology* (London: Heinemann, 1984), pp. 14–29.
43. Royal Commission on Historical Monuments (England), *A Matter of Time: an Archaeological Survey of the River Gravels of England* (London: HMSO, 1960).
44. *Report on Field Monuments* (n. 38).
45. C. M. Heighway (ed.), *The Erosion of History: Archaeology and Planning in Towns* (London: Council for British Archaeology, 1972).
46. Jones, *Past Imperfect* (n. 42), pp. 50–61.
47. *Parliamentary Debates, Lords, 1978–9*, vol. 398, 20 Feb. 1979, cols. 1779–80.
48. C. Eccles, *The Rose Theatre* (London: Hern, 1990).

Chapter 4

1. In compiling this account I have relied heavily on three sources: (i) an undated research note made by an ex-colleague in the GLC Historic Buildings Division (HBD), Frank Kelsall, now filed in English Heritage London Region (Historians Section) papers. See also his article 'Listing and the London County Council', *ASCHB (Association for Studies in the Conservation of Historic Buildings)* Transactions, 10 (1985), 48–9; (ii) my own work done for the Introduction to *Historic Buildings in London* (HBIL) (London: Academy Editions, 1975), at a time when I could find most of the documentary evidence I required in active HBD files; (iii) the phenomenal memory of another ex-colleague, Kenneth S. Mills, who worked in the LCC's Historic Records and Historic Buildings Sections from 1949 onward.

2. G. Baldwin Brown, *The Care of Ancient Monuments* (Cambridge University Press, 1905), pp. 31, 32.

3. See Chapter 3.

4. C. R. Ashbee, 'Introduction' to *The First Volume of the Register . . . Containing the Parish of Bromley-by-Bow, Survey of London* (London: P. S. King for the LCC, 1900), p. xxxv: 'The objective [of the register] is not so much the making of a *paper* record as the preservation of the things recorded.' Ashbee's Introduction is a wide-ranging philosophical and polemical essay on the preservation of old buildings and open spaces and the creation of civilised housing conditions by municipal action.

5. John Gwynn, *London and Westminster Improved* (London: Gwynn, 1766; reprinted Gregg, 1969).

6. Ibid., pp. 126–7: 'it ought to be repaired before it is too late, but with a most scrupulous adherence to its original form'. The whole passage is worth reading in the light of the Society for the Protection of Ancient Buildings Manifesto of 1877 and modern conservation charters.

7. Temple Bar was recorded by the Society. The preservation of the Bar *in situ* or on another site was much discussed before it was dismantled and removed to Hertfordshire in 1878. One solution proposed a broad, rusticated archway spanning Fleet Street, with the Bar re-erected on top.

8. Edwards, *History of London Street Improvements 1855–1897* (London: LCC, 1898), p. 162.

9. William Haywood, *Report to the Special Committee upon Improvements of the Honourable the Commissioners of Sewers of the City of London on the Traffic and Improvements in Public Ways of the City of London* (London: for the Commissioners, 1866), pp. 105–6.

10. Edwards, *Street Improvements* (n. 8), p. 57.

11. William Morris, Manifesto of the Society for the Protection of Ancient Buildings, 1877.

12. N. Kelvin (ed.) *Collected Letters of William Morris* (Princeton University Press, 1984), i, no. 563 (25–30 April 1879); HBIL (n. 1), pp. 9–10.

13. G. L. Gomme, 'Preface' to Ashbee (ed.), *Survey of London*, vol. 1 (n. 4), p. iii, and see Kelsall (n. 1).

14. Gomme, loc. cit., p. iv.

15. C. R. Ashbee, *The Trinity Hospital in Mile End: An Object Lesson in National History* (London: Essex House Guild and School of Handicraft for the Committee for the Survey of the Memorials of Greater London, 1896). Ashbee's attribution of the almshouses to Wren and Evelyn does not stand up. They were designed and built in 1695 by William Ogbourne. In every other respect, the Guild-produced volume, with its hand-made paper covers, fine printing, lithographs by Max Balfour and drawings by Matt Garbutt, Ernest Godman and J.Allen, was exemplary. The authoritative account of the origins and development of the Survey of London is Hermione Hobhouse, *London Survey'd* (London: RCHM, 1994).

16. Gomme, 'Preface' (n. 13), p. iv.

17. Ashbee, *Survey of London vol. 1* (n. 4), p. xxxv.

18. *Proposed Demolition of Nineteen City Churches: Report by the Clerk . . . and the Architect of the Council* (London: LCC, 1920). The architect said that the churches constituted 'some of the most interesting monuments of the City of London and their architectural beauty and historical

associations render them worthy of preservation'. Attention was drawn to the fact that in twelve cases the rebuilding cost of the existing churches (after the Great Fire) had been met in large part from public money (the tax on coals).

19. Kelsall (n. 1). The earliest official guides to the plaques, commencing with the *Indication of Houses of Historic Interest in London* (LCC, 1907) are prefaced by the Council decision of 22 Nov. 1901, followed by several pages of historical notes on each of the plaques so far erected. The later LCC and GLC Blue Plaque Guides, dealing with hundreds more plaques, simply give details of their inscriptions. Later prefaces, however, give an account of the development of the scheme, set out the criteria used in evaluating suggestions and describe the variations which have occurred over the years in the design of the plaques.

20. G. L. Gomme, *London in the Reign of Victoria* (London: Blackie, 1898), p. 141.

21. HBIL (n. 1), pp. 10–11.

22. Marie P. G. Draper and W. A. Eden, *Marble Hill House and its Owners* (London: GLC, 1970), often mistakenly shelved as a *Survey of London* monograph. See also HBIL (n. 1), pp. 11–12. The purchase of Marble Hill and other lands 'to regulate the erection of buildings which may be detrimental to the view from Richmond Hill' was included in the London County Council (General Powers) Act 1902. The house itself (1724–9, by the Earl of Pembroke and Roger Morris, probably derived from designs by Colen Campbell) was not mentioned in the Act. Its restoration to the original design in 1965–6 was one of the first historic buildings projects to be completed by the GLC.

23. HBIL (n. 1), p. 13. It became the Geffrye Museum in 1914.

24. HBIL, pp. 12–13. *Survey of London* monograph no. 8 is a record of Crosby Place prior to demolition. Godfrey's account of the reconstruction can be read in Alfred W. Clapham and Walter H. Godfrey, *Some Famous Buildings and their Story* (London: Technical Journals, n.d.). See also Hobhouse, *London Survey'd* (n. 15), pp. 21–3.

25. HBIL (n. 1), Introduction, p. 9.

26. 1840 by George Porter. The story of its acquisition and restoration by the Council is recounted as a recent achievement by Raine Dartmouth (then Countess of Dartmouth) in *Do you Care about Historic Buildings? The Work of the Historic Buildings Board of the Greater London Council* (London: GLC, 1971).

27. *The Site of the Globe Playhouse, Southwark* (London: LCC, 1921) also carried an appendix with a conjectural reconstruction which, by following the evidence of the most reliable contemporary view of London, by Hollar, comes closer than many later attempts to the conclusions reached after lengthy inquiry in the Bankside reconstruction now (1995) in progress. Following established practice, the drawings published in the 1921 report are signed by the Council's architect, G. Topham Forrest.

28. Reginald Minton Taylor seems to have been involved in the Council's first major restoration project. For Winmill's work for the Society for the Protection of Ancient Buildings (SPAB) see Joyce M. Winmill, *Charles Canning Winmill, An Architect's Life by his Daughter* (London: Dent, 1946). Susan Beattie, *A Revolution in London Housing: LCC Housing Architects and their Work* (London: GLC and the Architectural Press, 1980) is the essential introduction to this outstanding team of architects. See n. 33.

29. Edwards, *Street Improvements* (n. 8), pp. 251–60.

30. Ibid. pp. 253 and 255–6 (for the RIBA's views).

31. Kelsall (n. 1).

32. Sir Laurence Gomme and Philip Norman (eds), *Survey of London Vol. 3, the Parish of St Giles-in-the-Fields (Part I) Lincoln's Inn Fields* (London: LCC, 1912), pp. xv and xvi.

33. Now at GLRO. See also HBIL (n. 1), ill. p. 126. The drawings are initialled by Reginald Minton Taylor. Notes and colour washes indicate precisely what was retained and what was new work.

34. For information about Quirke, Farrar, Armitage and the work of HB Section in the postwar years I am grateful to Kenneth Mills.

35. Nationally the initial lists took more than twenty years to complete. Before the last was issued the first resurvey of London was already being undertaken. See Martin Robertson *et al.*, 'Listed Buildings: The National Resurvey of England; The Background', *Transactions of the Ancient Monuments Society*, 37 (1993), 21–94, on pp. 24, 25.
36. Richard Edmonds, chairman of the LCC Town Planning Committee in F. H. W. Sheppard (gen. ed.) *Survey of London Vol. 26: the Parish of St Mary Lambeth (Part Two: Southern Area)* (London: LCC, 1956), p. v.
37. Designed by Norman Harrison to complement the Thomas Archer house and the flanking wings by Sir Edwin Lutyens.
38. Too numerous to list in full but, in addition to the National Provincial Bank and Westbourne Terrace, named in the text, the following might be mentioned: the Pantechnicon, Motcomb Street (Joseph Jopling, 1830), the Lyric Theatre, Hammersmith (Frank Matcham, 1895) and a success achieved by negotiation rather than conflict, 13 Moorgate (Aston Webb and Ingress Bell 1893). The same attitude informed the GLC's action in defending the National Westminster Bank, Threadneedle Street (Mewes and Davis, 1922–31) together with a number of neighbouring listed and unlisted buildings as an important street group. The opposition on this occasion included the City Corporation.
39. Ministry of Housing and Local Government Circular 61/68, *Historic Buildings and Conservation* (1968).
40. Propaganda but in this case truthful. Leaflet, *Keep the GLC Historic Buildings Division Working for London* (London: GLC, 1984).

Chapter 5

1. Resignation letter from Giles Scott to the Provost of Coventry Cathedral, 2 Jan. 1947 [RIBA].
2. 'The RIBA Annual Dinner', *Journal of the RIBA*, 25 March 1933, p. 467.
3. See John Cornforth, *The Search for a Style: Country Life and Architecture 1897–1935* (London: Deutsch, 1988).
4. Robert Byron, *How We Celebrate the Coronation* (London: Architectural Press, 1937), p. 12.
5. See S. John Teague, 'An Intelligent Interest and a Public Spirit', *Journal of the London Society*, 412 (1986), 3–7, and Hermione Hobhouse, '"P. W. L. at the Helm": the Work of Percy Lovell as Secretary of the London Society, 1912–1940, Part 1', *Journal of the London Society*, 430 (1995), 9–13.
6. Anon., *London Squares and How to Save Them* (The London Society, n.d. [1927]).
7. In *The Thirties Society Journal*, 2 (1981–82), 20, Ernö Goldfinger recalled that, 'The great contribution of England is Georgian. But hardly had I time to look at it they were pulling it down. There is absolutely no respect for architecture in England. My first office in London was in No.7 Bedford Square, on the east side which belonged to the British Museum. You know, they wanted to pull it down. When I was there we got notices (1937–38). Ignorant vandals – unbelievable! . . .' See also S. E. Rasmussen, *London: The Unique City* (London: Jonathan Cape, 1937).
8. E. Beresford Chancellor, *The Private Palaces of London*, (London: Kegan Paul, 1908), p. xiv.
9. See Gavin Stamp, 'Origins of the Group', *The Architects' Journal*, 31 March 1982, pp. 35–38; also Hermione Hobhouse, *Lost London* (London: Macmillan, 1976), pp. 96–8.
10. Canova quoted in Ben Weinreb and Christopher Hibbert (eds), *The London Encyclopaedia* (London: Macmillan, 1983), p. 932; Harold P. Clunn, *The Face of London* (London: Simkin Marshall, 1932), p. 112. Also see Reginald Blomfield, *Memoirs of an Architect* (London: Macmillan, 1932), pp. 296–303, and John Betjeman, 'The Truth about Waterloo Bridge', *Architectural Review*, April 1932, pp. 125–7.
11. J. M. Richards, *Memoirs of an Unjust Fella* (London: Weidenfeld and Nicolson, 1980), p. 127.
12. Goldring to William Palmer, 30 July 1937 [SPAB archives]; see also Douglas Goldring, *Facing the Odds* (London: Cassell, 1940), pp. 44f., which also indicates the difficulties he had with the snobbish and supercilious members of the

original Georgian Group committee.
13. James Lees-Milne to the author, 10 Feb. 1982, quoted in Gavin Stamp, 'Origins of the Group', *The Architects' Journal*, 31 March 1982, pp. 35–8; also see Charles Hind, 'Sound and Fury – The Early Days of the Georgian Group' in *Georgian Group Report and Journal*, 1986, pp. 45–54.
14. *The Times*, 27 May 1937; the letter was signed by Lord Esher but written by Goldring with amendments by Palmer.
15. Byron, *How We Celebrate* (n. 4), pp. 24, 26.
16. Summerson, Betjeman and Richards were all members. As the latter wrote to the author on 18 April 1982: 'There was no question of the modernists wanting to destroy Georgian buildings; in fact . . . they put an extra high value on them as instances of the effective use of standardisation etc. – and many of them chose to occupy Georgian houses. Moreover it was the modernists who led the fight to save Carlton House Terrace from Blomfield and his R.A. allies.'
17. Review in the *Kilburn Times* for September 1937 [?] and letter to Group, n.d. [SPAB archives]; in a letter dated 3 Sept. 1937, Mrs Trotter wrote that, 'Doubtless the pamphlet is a sure seller in cocktail party circles if frequented by the socialite intelligensia and wealthy leisured United-frontites where bishop-baiting is all the rage.' Dorothy Warren Trotter had a dress-shop in Chelsea; an article on her area by Ralph Parker, 'Shutters Up in Portland Town', was published in the *Architectural Review* for June 1938.
18. Margaret Byron to A. E. Richardson 1 Dec. 1941 [Georgian Group archives].
19. Robert Byron, 'Proposed statement of principles to govern relations of Georgian Group and S.P.A.B.', n.d. [*c.* May 1939] [SPAB archives].
20. Copy of typescript of broadcast remarks 'Farewell Brunswick Square' from the late Sir John Summerson; the debate is referred to in the 'Epilogue – Image and Artifact: 1830–1988' in the final edition of Summerson's *Georgian London* (London: Barrie and Jenkins, 1988).
21. Robert Byron to John Summerson, 5 Jan. 1938 [copy from the late Sir John Summerson].
22. Wren's All Hallows', Lombard Street, was demolished after much controversy in 1938, its fittings, together with its re-erected tower, going to the new church of All Hallows at Twickenham designed by Robert Atkinson. See Byron, *How We Celebrate* (n. 4), p. 12.
23. Minutes of Georgian Group committee meeting, 22 Feb. 1939 [Georgian Group archives].
24. The Monkton project is illustrated in *Architectural Review*, Oct. 1938, p. 199.
25. Robert Byron, 'The Secrets of Abingdon Street', *The New Statesman & Nation*, 4 June 1938, p. 949; see also Sir Campbell Stuart, *Memorial to a King* (London: Batchworth Press, 1954).
26. This might not have happened, however, as by November 1938 Scotland Yard and the London traffic authorities were maintaining that the Arch could not be re-erected in front of the new station on the Euston Road 'for technical reasons', although by this time it was evident that the LMS could not afford to proceed with the project.
27. Kenneth Clark, 'A Letter to Michael Sadleir', in *The Gothic Revival*, 2nd edn (London: John Murray, 1949), p. 2.
28. Nikolaus Pevsner, 'Chairman's Page', *Victorian Society Annual Report 1967–8*, p. 4.
29. Mark Girouard, 'The Evolving Taste for Victorian Architecture', *Apollo*, February 1973, pp. 127–35. Girouard sagely observed that 'the Victorian fashion is so much on the increase [that] one can already envisage the completely different situation arising of too many Victorian buildings being preserved with too little discrimination as to their quality'.
30. John Summerson, 'The Evaluation of Victorian Architecture', *The Victorian Society Annual 1968–9*, pp. 45–6, reprinted in Summerson, *Victorian Architecture: Four Studies in Evaluation*, (New York and London: Columbia University Press, 1970). For the present writer, aet. 18, the 1960 Grey Arrow paperback edition of *First and Last Loves*, purchased in 1966, was a revelation and an inspiration.
31. See, for example, Anthony Symondson, 'John Betjeman and the Cult of J. N. Comper', *The Thirties Society*

Journal, 7 (1991), 2–13.
32. H. S. Goodhart-Rendel, 'Victorian Conservanda', in *Journal of the London Society*, February 1959, reprinted as a pamphlet for the Victorian Society, p. 2. Also see Paul Thompson, 'The Victorian Society' in *Victorian Studies*, 7 (1964), 387–92.
33. An account by Pevsner of the foundation of the Victorian Society, together with lists of those present at the two meetings, is given in *The Victorian Society Annual 1968–9*, pp. 4–6.
34. *The Victorian Society Report 1961–2*, p. 3.
35. J. M. Richards, *Memoirs* (n. 11), pp. 216–17.
36. Ibid., p. 216; Alison and Peter Smithson, *The Euston Arch and the Growth of the London Midland & Scottish Railway* (London: Thames and Hudson, 1968).
37. *The Victorian Society Report 1961–2*, p. 1.
38. *The Victorian Society Annual 1972–3*, p. 8.
39. Betjeman to John Summerson, 14 June 1966, in Candida Lycett Green (ed.), *John Betjeman Letters, vol. 2, 1951 to 1984* (London: Methuen, 1995), p. 319.
40. Sam Lambert, 'Historic Pioneers', *Architects' Journal*, 11 March 1970, pp. 594–7.
41. John Summerson, 'Introduction', in Trevor Dannatt, *Modern Architecture in Britain* (London: Batsford, 1959), p. 11.
42. Gavin Stamp (ed.), 'Britain in the Thirties', *Architectural Design*, 49, nos. 10–11 (Oct.–Nov. 1979).
43. Reyner Banham, 'King Lut's Navy', *New Society*, 12 Nov. 1981, p. 284.
44. Alan Powers, 'Corinthian Epics – The Architecture of Sir Edwin Cooper', *The Thirties Society Journal*, 2 (1982), 15–16.
45. See further Chapter 8. The two public inquiries, 1984 and 1988, provoked by Palumbo ought to have been written up as a book, as the battle was between almost every conservation body and a dogmatically modernist establishment.
46. The history of the foundation of the Thirties Society has yet to be written; this account is based on the recollections of Bevis Hillier, Simon Jenkins and Marcus Binney.
47. Bevis Hillier to the author, 1 Nov. 1995.
48. Marcus Binney to the author, n.d. [Nov. 1995].
49. See, for example, *Building Design*, 8 July 1983.
50. Simon Jenkins, 'The Anger of Firestone', *The Thirties Society Journal*, 1 (1981), 1.
51. Alan Powers (ed.), *End of the Line? The Future of London Underground's Past* (Victorian Society and Thirties Society report, 1987); Gavin Stamp and Clive Aslet, *Monkton: A Vanishing Surrealist Dream* (SAVE Britain's Heritage and Thirties Society report, 1986); for the kiosk saga, see Gavin Stamp, *Telephone Boxes* (London: Chatto and Windus, 1989).
52. The history of the foundation of SAVE has yet to be written, but see Marcus Binney, *Our Vanishing Heritage* (London: Arlington Books, 1984) and twentieth anniversary articles in *Perspectives on Architecture*, May 1995.
53. 'The SAVE Report', special number of the *Architects' Journal*, Dec. 1975.
54. L.M. Angus-Butterworth, 'The Early History of the Ancient Monuments Society', *Transactions of the Ancient Monuments Society*, 20 (1976), 49–84; and also see Mathew Saunders, 'Progress in Conservation of Historic Buildings in Britain since the Second World War' in a festschrift for Sir Bernard Fielden, edited by Stephen Marks, to be published in 1996.
55. *Bulletin of the Scottish Georgian Society*, 1 (1972), 61.
56. For the Cockburn Association see George Bruce, *Some Practical Good* (Edinburgh: Cockburn Association, 1975). Lord Cockburn (1774–1859), the celebrated judge, had written *A Letter to the Lord Provost on the Best Ways of Spoiling the Beauty of Edinburgh* in 1849.
57. See Gavin Stamp, 'The City's Best Modern Building', the *Spectator*, 15 Aug. 1987, p. 14; also see Andrew Saint, *A Change of Heart: English Architecture Since the War, a Policy for Protection* (London: RCHME and English Heritage, 1992).
58. Auberon Waugh, 'Way of the World', the *Daily Telegraph*, 27 Nov. 1995, p. 23.

Chapter 6

1. This chapter presents arguments and evidence that are unfolded more completely in the author's forthcoming book, *'The Stately Homes of England': The English Country House and the National Heritage since the Eighteenth Century* (New Haven and London: Yale University Press, in press). A full list of acknowledgements is also provided there, but for present purposes I must thank Michael Hunter for his unfailing helpfulness and encouragement.

2. Cf. the modest (but statistical) estimate of Heather Clemenson, *English Country Houses and Landed Estates* (London: Croom Helm, 1982), pp. 135–6, and the higher estimates by Mark Girouard, *Architectural Review*, Oct. 1974, pp. 243–4, and Marcus Binney and J. M. Robinson, *Country Life*, 21 Nov. 1974, pp. 1598–9, 16 Jan. 1975, p. 156.

3. This linkage, asserted by Patrick Wright, *On Living in an Old Country* (London: Verso, 1985) and Robert Hewison, *The Heritage Industry* (London: Methuen, 1987), has been contested by Raphael Samuel, *Theatres of Memory* (London: Verso, 1994), especially pp. 219–21, 227–35, 242, 259–71, 288–308. See also Patrick Wright's riposte in the *Guardian*, 4 Feb. 1995, p. 29.

4. Duke of Rutland, 'The Preservation of Ancient Monuments', *The Times*, 12 Nov. 1911, p. 3.

5. *Report of the Ancient Monuments Advisory Committee, 1921* (London: HMSO, 1921), pp. 3–4, 14, 19–20, 27–9.

6. *The Times*, 25 Jan. 1932, p. 8.

7. For these contrasts, see Mandler, *Stately Homes* (n. 1), chs. 5, 6.

8. Sir Henry Miers, *A Report on the Public Museums of the British Isles* (Edinburgh: T. and A. Constable, 1928), pp. 23, 25.

9. On the neo-Georgian as a country house style, see Clive Aslet, *The Last Country Houses* (New Haven and London: Yale University Press, 1982). I am here ignoring urban Georgianism.

10. Lees-Milne's diaries for 1946–7 are published as *Caves of Ice* (London: Chatto and Windus, 1983); they are preceded by *Ancestral Voices* (London: Chatto and Windus, 1975) and followed by *Prophesying Peace* (London: Chatto and Windus, 1977), *Midway on the Waves* (London: Faber and Faber, 1985), and the more fragmentary *A Mingled Measure* (London: John Murray, 1994).

11. Reyner Banham, 'Revenge of the Picturesque: English Architectural Polemics, 1945–1965', in John Summerson (ed.), *Concerning Architecture* (London: Allen Lane, 1968), pp. 265–73.

12. These are specific suggestions from the general public in National Trust MSS, 36, in response to Lees-Milne's article, 'We Must Stop This Ruin', *Sunday Pictorial*, 16 Sept. 1945, p. 6. Such was Lees-Milne's despair at this point that he found himself agreeing with many of the suggestions.

13. See correspondence in National Trust MSS, 36, L. E. Morris to D. M. Matheson, 1 Nov. 1943 and Matheson's subsequent responses; Lees-Milne, *Caves of Ice* (n. 10), p. 67.

14. Dalton's Budget Broadcast, 9 Apr. 1946, in Dalton MSS, British Library of Political and Economic Science, 9/2/4–12.

15. The members of the committee were Gowers, Lady Anderson (wife of the wartime minister Sir John Anderson), the archaeologist Sir Cyril Fox, the architect W. H. Ansell, the art historian Anthony Blunt, the jurist J. D. Imrie and the trade unionist J. C. Little.

16. HM Treasury, *Report of the Committee on Houses of Outstanding Historic or Architectural Interest* (London: HMSO, 1950).

17. *Country Life*, 30 June 1950, p. 1954, surveys the limited press reaction.

18. *Parliamentary Debates, Commons, 1952–3*, vol. 510, 6 Feb. 1953, cols. 2208–9.

19. See the analysis of HBCE expenditure in John Cornforth, *Country Houses in Britain: Can They Survive?* (London: Country Life, 1974), pp. 24–5.

20. From the preface to the 1959 edition, retained in subsequent reprints.

21. See above, n. 2.

22. See, for instance, the submissions of the Central Landowners Association and the Land Union, Public Record Office, Kew, T 219/179, 30 Apr. 1949, T 219/183,

19 May 1949.
23. Ibid., 28 July 1949.
24. Calculated from the *Country Life* annual, *Country Houses Open to the Public*, augmented by Index Publishers' annual *Historic Houses, Castles and Gardens*. The HBC for England came up with similar figures in its annual reports.
25. Cornforth's estimate in 1974 was that of 950 important houses in England, Wales and Scotland, 430 were privately owned and not open to the public, 152 privately owned and open, 95 belonged to the National Trusts, 40 to government bodies, and 225 were in alternative use. Cornforth, *Country Houses* (n. 19), p. 4.
26. Andrew Cox, *Adversary Politics and Land* (Cambridge University Press, 1984), pp. 103–14.
27. 'The Open House', *New Statesman*, 18 June 1955, p. 847.
28. Lord Montagu of Beaulieu, *The Gilt and the Gingerbread, or How to Live in a Stately Home and Make Money* (London: Michael Joseph, 1967), pp. 203–5.
29. John Gaze, *Figures in a Landscape: A History of the National Trust* (London: Barrie and Jenkins, 1988), p. 193.
30. See the correspondence between Smith and Lord Crawford, the outgoing NT chairman, 1963–5, in Crawford MSS, National Library of Scotland, Acc 9679/101/27.
31. The official histories are factual but defensive: see Gaze, *Figures in a Landscape* (n. 29), chs. 15–16, and Jennifer Jenkins and Patrick James, *From Acorn to Oak Tree: The Growth of the National Trust 1895–1994* (London: Macmillan, 1994), chs. 10–11. A good antidote is provided by Paula Weideger, *Gilding the Acorn: Behind the Facade of the National Trust* (London: Simon & Schuster, 1994), especially chs. 4–5, breezily critical but not unfair.
32. For books, see for example Douglas Sutherland, *The Landowners* (London: Anthony Blond, 1968); Roy Perrott, *The Aristocrats* (London: Macmillan, 1968); Robert Harling, *Historic Houses* (London: Condé Nast, 1969). Films include *Nudist Paradise*, shot at Woburn in 1958 at the Duke's behest; the Tommy Steele film *Half-a-Sixpence*, shot at Blenheim; *Lady L* with Sophia Loren (which provided most people's vision of Castle Howard before the TV *Brideshead*); and *Trial by Combat*, the best known of several films shot at Knebworth.
33. *Country Life*, 8 Nov. 1973, pp. 1426–8.
34. The Mentmore fracas and the making of the National Heritage Memorial Fund have been narrated by one of the participants, the Conservative MP Arthur Jones, in *Britain's Heritage: The Creation of the National Heritage Memorial Fund* (London: Weidenfeld and Nicolson, 1985).
35. Sophie Andreae and Marcus Binney, *Tomorrow's Ruins?* (London: David Pearce, 1978), pp. 1–2.
36. Samuel, *Theatres of Memory* (n. 3), while right to cast doubt on the prevalence of the country house obsession before the 1970s, is, I think, wrong to minimise its more recent significance: see, for example, pp. 242–6, 302, 307.
37. Michael Sayer, *The Disintegration of a Heritage* (Wilby: Michael Russell, 1993).
38. In 1986, there were over 350 privately owned châteaux (and just over 100 publicly or charitably maintained châteaux) open to the public in France; this compares with approximately 200 privately owned country houses (and another 150 publicly or charitably maintained houses) open in England. French figures calculated from the Ministry of Culture's *Historic Houses, Castles and Gardens of France* (Twickenham: Newnes Books, 1986).

Chapter 7

I am grateful to Neil Burton, Stephen Croad, John Earl, Michael Hunter and, particularly, Peter Mandler for help and advice over this chapter.

1. Official numbers of listed buildings in England quoted in *English Heritage Annual Report* (London: English Heritage, 1994); revised projections of real numbers from an unpublished study by Richard Griffith.
2. G. Baldwin Brown, *The Care of Ancient Monuments* (Cambridge University Press, 1905), pp. 164–5.
3. G. Baldwin Brown, 'Urban Legislation in the Interests of Amenity at Home and

Abroad', *RIBA Journal*, 12 (1905), 70–8.
4. See Chapter 3.
5. See Chapter 2.
6. John Sheail, *Rural Conservation in Inter-War Britain* (Oxford University Press, 1981).
7. Ibid, pp. 48–62.
8. Ibid, pp. 63–79, especially pp. 71–5.
9. This assessment of the genesis of Clause 17 incorporates information and views kindly received from Peter Mandler, who writes that 'the "Bath clause" in the Bath Corporation Act of 1925 was also seen as something of a model'.
10. *Parliamentary Debates, Commons, 1931–2*, vol. 266, 3 June 1932, cols. 1555–61 and 7 June 1932, cols. 1814ff.; *Parliamentary Debates, Lords, 1931–2*, vol. 85, 30 June 1932, cols. 355–69.
11. *Parliamentary Debates, Commons, 1936–7*, vol. 320, 10 Feb. 1937, cols. 419–481.
12. Ibid., col. 426.
13. Ibid., col. 433.
14. This account of the wartime ministries is based chiefly on C. M. Kohan, *Works and Buildings* (London: HMSO, 1952); J. B. Cullingworth, *Reconstruction and Land Use Planning*, vol. 1 of *Environmental Planning 1939–1969*, (London: HMSO, 1975); and Gordon E. Cherry and Leith Penny, *Holford* (London: Mansell, 1986).
15. Public Record Office (henceforward PRO), HLG 103/32, memo. by Mr Raby, 1945.
16. Kohan, *Works and Buildings* (n. 14), pp. 386–90.
17. PRO, HLG 103/1, memo. from S. L. G. Beaufoy, 5 Sept. 1942.
18. For the LCC contribution to inventorisation and listing, see Chapter 4.
19. E. Wamsley Lewis, 'Buildings for Preservation', *Proceedings of the Dorset Natural History and Archaeological Society*, 64 (1943), 112–17.
20. PRO, HLG 103/1, note of July 1943.
21. John H. Harvey, 'The Origin of Listed Buildings', *Transactions of the Ancient Monuments Society*, 37 (1993), 1–8.
22. *Fifty Years of the National Buildings Record* (Beckenham: Trigon Press in conjunction with RCHM, 1991), notably the introduction by Sir John Summerson, pp. 2–10; Stephen Croad, 'The National Buildings Record, The Early Years', *Transactions of the Ancient Monuments Society*, 36 (1992), 79–98.
23. W. H. Godfrey, 'National Buildings Record', *RIBA Journal*, 48 (1941), 115–17, on p. 115.
24. F. S. M. Donnison, *Civil Affairs and Military Government: Central Organisation and Planning*, History of World War II, UK Military Series (London: HMSO, 1966), pp. 211–36; see also now Lynn H. Nicholas, *The Rape of Europa* (London: Macmillan, 1994).
25. For the Methuen debate see PRO, HLG 103/32, and *Parliamentary Debates, Lords*, 1945–6, vol. 137, 21 Nov. 1945, cols. 1061–87.
26. Lewis, 'Buildings for Preservation' (n. 19), p. 114.
27. For the early history of the Georgian Group see Chapter 5, and Gavin Stamp and John Robinson in *Architects' Journal*, 31 March 1982, pp. 35–41.
28. Georgian Group archives: Minute Books, 1939–44; Policy Sub-Committee papers, 1944; Annual Report, 1944; misc. papers.
29. Georgian Group archives, Angus Acworth to Albert Richardson, 18 Feb. 1944.
30. Georgian Group archives, 5th Report of Policy Sub-Committee, 16 June 1944.
31. *The Times*, 12 July 1944, p. 8.
32. Georgian Group Archives: Minutes, 19 July, 27 Sept. and 21 Oct. 1944; Annual Report, 1944, p. 8.
33. John H. Harvey, 'Listing as I Knew it in 1949', *Transactions of the Ancient Monuments Society*, 38 (1994), 97–104, on p. 99.
34. *Parliamentary Debates, Commons, 1943–4*, vol. 403, 5 Oct.1944, cols. 1179–88; 9 Oct. 1944, cols. 1511–18; 18 Oct. 1944, cols. 2403–10, 2444–8 and 2467–73; *Parliamentary Debates, Lords, 1943–4*, vol. 133, 8 Nov. 1944, cols. 930–70.
35. *Parliamentary Debates, Commons, 1943–4*, vol. 403, 5 Oct. 1944, col. 1185.
36. Ibid., 5 Oct. 1944, col. 1187.
37. Ibid., 9 Oct. 1944, col. 1513.
38. Georgian Group archives, report of AGM, 16 Oct. 1944. In 1946 the Minister of Town and Country Planning, Lewis Silkin, told the Georgian Group's AGM

that its work was 'of special value to my Department'.
39. PRO, HLG 103/46 (meeting of 21 Dec. 1944 referred to).
40. For Wagner see *The Times*, 11 May 1995, and interview by John Robinson in Georgian Group archives.
41. For the Maclagan Committee, see PRO, HLG 103/46.
42. Harvey, 'Listing' (n. 33), pp. 98–9. Peter Mandler, however, tells me that Lord Methuen's papers contain 'much debate . . . between Methuen and his friends about whether Garton was or was not a Good Thing'.
43. PRO, HLG 29/303, memo. from Mr Valentine.
44. PRO, HLG 103/22, 'Estimate of Completion of Listing', papers of 1946–7.
45. PRO, HLG 103/22, memo. from Sir Philip Magnus, 19 March 1947.
46. PRO, HLG 29/303, memo. from T. D. Wickenden.
47. Harvey, 'Listing' (n. 33), pp. 98, 103–4.
48. PRO, HLG 29/303, memo. from T. D. Wickenden.
49. Martin Robertson, 'Listed Buildings: The National Resurvey of England', *Transactions of the Ancient Monuments Society*, 37 (1993), 22–4.
50. PRO, HLG 29/303, exchange between George Tomlinson and Lewis Silkin, Dec. 1946.
51. The *Instructions to Investigators* of 1946 were kindly communicated by John Earl, and are reprinted in his *Building Conservation Philosophy* (Reading: the College of Estate Management, 1996), Appendix 6, 'The Philosophical Background to Listing in Britain', pp. 115–21. See also PRO, HLG 103/42.
52. Earl, *Building Conservation Philosophy* (n. 51), pp. 119–20.
53. Ibid., p. 117.
54. PRO, HLG 103/6, S. R. Garton to Mr Jack, 9 April 1947.
55. Harvey, 'Listing' (n. 33), pp. 102–3. Note: Those shown in the photograph on p. 131 are as follows (left to right):
Front row: Mrs Kelly, Miss E.M. Gardner (Ottery St Mary), Miss M. Ward (Petersfield), Miss M. Francis (London), Mrs M. Tomlinson (Seaton, Devon), Miss M. Blomfield (Colchester), Mrs Garton, Mrs V. M. P. Webster (Grantham), Miss A.M. Brockbank (York).
Second row: W. O. Collier (London), P. S. Spokes (Oxford), A. Dale (Brighton), S. J. Garton (Headquarters), T. D. Wickenden (Headquarters, Principal), E. Wiltshire (Headquarters, Assistant Secretary), G. S. Orpwood (Headquarters, Higher Executive Officer), D. Manning-Sanders (Penzance), E. G. Holt (Bristol)
Third row: A. W. Bickersteth (Kirkby Lonsdale), D. Verey (Bibury, Gloucs.), M. C. Gibb (Sevenoaks), A. Wagner (Member of Advisory Committee), J. H. Harvey (Leatherhead), T. E. Legg (Beccles)
Back row: G. B. Martindale (Carlisle), E. T. Long (Norwich), H. Honeyman (Newcastle-upon-Tyne), J. C. Shepherd (Henley-on-Thames), F. J. Kelly (Towcester, Northants.), C. Harrington (Settle, Yorks), E. C. Francis (Taunton), T. Edwards (Sutton Coldfield, Warwicks.), A. B. Chatwin (Birmingham), D. Sherborn (Headquarters), E. Roberts (Yeadon, Yorks.).

Chapter 8

I am grateful to Saskia Hallam, librarian of the Civic Trust, and to Emma Phillips and Jessica Pocock at SAVE Britain's Heritage, for assistance in preparing this article, and to Michael Hunter for his help and support.
1. Quoted in 'Creative Preservation', *Civic Trust Bulletin*, Autumn 1962, p. 7.
2. *English Heritage Monitor* (London: English Tourist Board and English Heritage, 1995).
3. See the report by SAVE Britain's Heritage, *Mind over Matter* (London: SAVE, 1995).
4. See *Deserted Bastions: Historic Naval and Military Architecture* (London: SAVE, 1993).
5. See *Beauty or the Bulldozer* (London: SAVE, 1994).
6. Michael Middleton, 'Civic Trust, 1957–77: the First Score', *Civic Trust News*, 62 (July–Aug. 1977), 1.
7. On this aspect of the Trust's work, see Lionel Esher, *The Continuing Heritage* (London: Franey, 1982). Other details have been taken from leaflets and other material

in the Civic Trust library.

8. 'Local Amenity Societies', *Civic Trust News*, 62 (July–Aug. 1977), 7.

9. Details of this and of the other episodes referred to here are to be found in 'History of Civic Trust Achievements', in preparation by the Civic Trust.

10. See the obituary of Lord Duncan Sandys, *Heritage Outlook*, 8, no. 1 (1988), 2.

11. From notes accompanying a survey of Conservation Area designation compiled by the Civic Trust in 1973 and 1976, preserved in the Civic Trust library.

12. For an account of these developments by their chief architect, Lord Kennet, see his *Preservation* (London: Temple Smith, 1972), especially ch. 2.

13. The reports, respectively by Colin Buchanan & Associates on Bath, Donald W. Insall & Associates on Chester, by G. S. Burrows on Chichester and by Viscount Esher on York, were jointly published under the title *A Study in Conservation* by the Ministry of Housing and Local Government (London: HMSO, 1968).

14. *Civic Trust Newsletter*, 20 (Oct. 1969), 4.

15. 'Creative Preservation', *Civic Trust Bulletin*, Autumn 1962, p. 7.

16. A. Fergusson, *The Sack of Bath* (Salisbury: Compton Russell, 1973), p. 72.

17. C. Amery and D. Cruickshank, *The Rape of Britain* (London: Paul Elek, 1975), p. 192.

18. SAVE, 'Heritage Year Toll', *Architects' Journal*, 17/24 Dec. 1975.

19. *Financing the Preservation of Old Buildings* (London: Civic Trust, 1971), p. 28.

20. *Architectural Heritage Fund Annual Report*, 1994–5, p. 7.

21. See Mark Girourard, Dan Cruikshank *et al.*, *The Saving of Spitalfields* (London: Spitalfields Historic Building Trust, 1989).

22. *Architectural Heritage Fund Annual Report*, 1980–1, p. 12.

23. *Historic Buildings Council Report*, 1975–6 (London: HMSO, 1976).

24. Marcus Binney and Kit Martin, *The Country House: To Be or Not To Be?* (London: SAVE, 1982), pp. 56–66.

25. Marcus Binney, *Our Vanishing Heritage* (London: Arlington Books, 1984), p. 140 and pp. 139–48 *passim*.

26. *Buildings at Risk: a Sample Survey* (London: English Heritage, 1992).

27. For a brief summary of the whole affair, see Marcus Binney and Marianne Watson-Smyth, *The SAVE Britain's Heritage Action Guide* (London: Collins and Brown, 1991), pp. 104–5.

28. *Townscape in Trouble: Conservation Areas – the Case for Change* (London: Butterworth, 1992).

Chapter 9

1. I am grateful to Richard Harris, George Muirhead, Barrie Trinder, Ian Walden and Christopher Zeuner for information and advice in researching this chapter.

2. R. Harris, 'The Shallow Screen', *Aspect*, 3 (1993–4), 11–15, 41, on p.12.

3. Quoted in R. Allan and P. Lewis, *Beamish: the Making of a Museum* (Beamish: the North of England Open Air Museum, 1991), p. 40.

4. Henry Ford Museum and Greenfield Village, *A Pictorial Souvenir* (Dearborn: Henry Ford Museum, 1994), p. 3.

5. R. Harris, 'The Shallow Screen' (n. 2), p. 12.

6. J. G. Gillette, 'Pilgrim's Progress', *Historic Preservation*, 46, no. 3 (1994), 22–5.

7. P. Robinson, 'The Removal and Re-Erection of Buildings in an Open Air Museum Context' (Diploma dissertation, Institute of Advanced Architectural Studies, University of York, 1976), pp. 6–7.

8. See F. W. B. Charles, *Conservation of Timber Buildings* (London: Donhead, 1984 reprinted, 1995).

9. L. T. C. Rolt, *Landscape with Canals* (London: Allen Lane, 1977); L. T. C. Rolt, *Railway Adventure* (London: Constable, 1953).

10. J. Piper and J. Betjeman, *Shropshire: A Shell Guide* (London: Faber and Faber, 1951), p. 26.

11. B. S. Trinder, 'A Philosophy for the Industrial Open-air Museum', in C. Ahrens (ed.), *Report of the Conference of the Association of European Open Air Museums, Hagen-Detmold 1984* (Hagen: Westfälische Freilicht Museum, 1985), pp. 87–105, on pp. 88–9.

12. J. H. D. Madin & Partners, *Dawley, Wellington, Oakengates: Consultant's Proposals for Development* (London: HMSO, 1966), p. 1.
13. These developments and shifts are carefully documented in A. D. Robinson, 'Forging an Industrial Past: Conservation and the Representation of Britain's Industrial Past' (MA Dissertation, Institute of Advanced Architectural Studies, University of York, 1992), pp. 94–6.
14. S. Linsley and S. B. Smith, 'On-site Preservation of Industrial Monuments', *Transactions of the First International Congress on the Conservation of Industrial Monuments, 1973* (Telford: Ironbridge Gorge Museum, 1975), pp. 55–61.
15. B. S. Trinder, 'A Philosophy for the Industrial Open-Air Museum' (n. 11), p. 90.
16. A. D. Robinson, 'Forging an Industrial Past' (n. 13), pp. 30–2.
17. Quoted in D. Lowenthal, *The Past is a Foreign Country* (Cambridge University Press, 1985) p. 287.
18. Robinson, 'Removal and Re-erection of Buildings' (n. 7), p. 114.
19. *Parliamentary Debates, Commons, 1960–1*, vol. 638, 13 April 1961, col. 644.
20. Robinson, 'Removal and Re-Erection of Buildings' (n. 7), p. 37.
21. F. Atkinson and M. Holton, 'Open-Air and Folk Museums', *Museums Journal*, 72 (1973), 140–2.
22. On the subtleties of industrial landscapes see B. S. Trinder, *The Making of the Industrial Landscape* (London: Dent, 1982).
23. R. Hewison, *The Heritage Industry* (London: Methuen, 1987).
24. D. Lowenthal, 'Showing off the Past: Forging History for Museums', paper from a short course, 'Interpreting the Industrial Past' (Ironbridge Institute, 1986).
25. P. Boylan 'Presidential Address to the Museums Association', *Guardian*, 27 December 1989.
26. Michael Wright of IDEAS Yorkshire presented this theme at seminars held at the Ironbridge Institute, 1993–4.
27. Penny Ritchie Calder, 'A Blazing Success', *Museums Journal*, 90 (1990), 9.
28. Royal Armouries, *Royal Armouries on the Waterfront in Leeds* (Leeds: Royal Armouries, 1994), pp. 2–4.
29. N. Cossons, 'Science Museums in the Age of Enterprise Culture' (Ironbridge Institute Seminar, 7 November 1988).
30. F. Greenwood, P. W. Phillips and I. D. Wallace, 'The Natural History Centre at Liverpool Museum', *The International Journal of Museum Management and Curatorship*, 8 (1989), 215–25.
31. B. West, 'The Making of the English Working Past: A Critical View of the Ironbridge Gorge Museum', in R. Lumley (ed.), *The Museum Time Machine* (London: Routledge, 1988), pp. 36–62.
32. K. Hudson, 'High Technology and Mass Consumerism', paper given at a short course, 'Interpreting the Industrial Past' (Ironbridge Institute, 1986).
33. R. Harris, 'The Shallow Screen' (n. 2), p. 41.
34. M. Wright, 'Dockyard 500: the Sequel', *Heritage Development*, 1 (1995), 26–9.
35. Robert Ronsheim quoted in R. Harris 'The Shallow Screen' (n. 2), p. 15.
36. Trinder, 'A Philosophy for the Open-Air Industrial Museum' (n. 11), pp. 93, 95.
37. P. M. McManus, 'Do You Get My Meaning?', *ILDS Review*, 1 (1988), 62–75.

INDEX

Page numbers in bold type denote illustrations.